A Genealogist's Guide to Discovering Your Germanic Ancestors

A Genealogist's Guide to

DISCOVERING YOUR

Germanic

ANCESTORS

How to find and record your unique heritage

S. Chris Anderson & Ernest Thode

BETTERWAY BOOKS
CINCINNATI, OHIO
www.familytreemagazine.com

About the Authors

Chris Anderson is a nationally Certified Genealogist, a retired university professor, the author of ten books and two manuals, a reviewer for the *National Genealogical Society Quarterly*, and an archival consultant.

Ernie Thode is the manager of the local history and genealogy department of the Washington County Public Library in Marietta, Ohio. He is the author of nine books including *German-English Genealogical Dictionary*, *Address Book for Germanic Genealogy*, and *Genealogical Gazetteer of Alsace-Lorraine*. He is an officer in his local genealogical society.

Both Chris and Ernie have conducted workshops and classes in genealogy as well as been invited speakers for numerous genealogical societies.

A Genealogist's Guide to Discovering Your Germanic Ancestors Copyright © 2000 by S. Chris Anderson and Ernest Thode. Manufactured in the United States of America. All rights reserved. No part of this book may be reproduced in any form or by any electronic or mechanical means including information storage and retrieval systems without permission in writing from the publisher, except by a reviewer, who may quote brief passages in a review. Published by Betterway Books, an imprint of F&W Publications, Inc., 1507 Dana Avenue, Cincinnati, Ohio 45207. (800) 289-0963. First edition.

Other fine Betterway Books are available from your local bookstore or on our Web site at www.familytreemagazine.com.

04 03 02 01 00   5 4 3 2 1

Library of Congress Cataloging-in-Publication Data

Anderson, Chris
    A genealogist's guide to discovering your Germanic ancestors / S. Chris Anderson and Ernest Thode.
        p.   cm.
    Includes bibliographical references and index.
    ISBN 1-55870-520-1
    1. German Americans—Genealogy—Handbooks, manuals, etc. 2. Germany—Genealogy—Handbooks, manuals, etc. I. Thode, Ernest. II. Title.
E184.G3A49   2000
929'.1'08931073—dc21   00-029753
                                                                                CIP

Editor: Sharon DeBartolo Carmack, CG
Production editor: Christine Doyle
Interior designer: Sandy Conopeotis Kent
Cover designer: Wendy Dunning
Cover photo courtesy Nancy Stetler

DEDICATION

*It is our pleasure to dedicate this manuscript to our wives,
Donna Anderson and Barbara Thode, both ladies with some German ancestry.*

Acknowledgments

This book exists due to the foresight and impetus of Bill Brohaugh, an editor with F&W Publications. Thanks, Bill. Special thanks to Sharon DeBartolo Carmack, CG, Tom Clark, and Dr. Richard Dougherty, AG, for reviewing our manuscript.

Icons Used in This Book

 Case Study
Examples of this book's advice at work

 CD Source
Databases and other information available on CD-ROM

\di'fin\ *vb* **Definitions**
Terminology and jargon explained

 For More Info
Where to turn for more in-depth coverage

 Important
Information and tips you can't overlook

 Internet Source
Where on the web to find what you need

 Notes
Thoughts, ideas and related insights

 Printed Source
Directories, books, pamphlets and other paper archives

 Reminder
"Don't-Forget" items to keep in mind

 Research Tip
Ways to make research more efficient

 See Also
Where in this book to find related information

 Sources
Where to go for information, supplies, etc.

 Step By Step
Walkthroughs of important procedures

 Supplies
Advice on day-to-day office tools

 Technique
How to conduct research, solve problems, and get answers

 Timesaver
Shaving minutes and hours off the clock

 Tip
Ways to make research more efficient

 Warning
Stop before you make a mistake

Table of Contents At a Glance

Table of Contents

Foreword

From the late seventeenth century, Germans braved the myriad hardships of migrating to America to become the most numerous immigrant group in America. Recent censuses report that German Americans are the largest ethnic group in the United States, which means vast numbers of Americans have German ancestors. The scope of this book goes beyond the borders of present-day Germany. We will also address the regions of Switzerland, Austria, Alsace-Lorraine (Elsass-Lothringen), and other Germanic areas.

WELCOME

You are about to embark on the adventure of a lifetime—actually of several lifetimes—as you forge deeply into the search for your Germanic ancestors. Can you face adversity and overcome the difficulties? Can you diligently follow a trail, focusing on all the clues to make sure you're on the right track? Do you have what it takes to go the distance? You just might. Let's find out!

In these pages, we will offer you useful hints and illustrations and help you save time and money. Your purchase of this book constitutes a ticket to Germanic adventures of kaleidoscope variety. We cannot guarantee success in searching for your earliest ancestors, but we can offer hope and techniques to improve your chance for success.

It's now time for you to brave the hardships of crossing the Atlantic, just as your ancestors did long ago. It will take planning, preparation, and fortitude. We're delighted to have you join us for these exciting adventures. When you have compiled a reasonable amount of information on your ancestors, you will want to publish a few pages or more about them. Offer copies to everyone who helped, and don't feel bad about charging a moderate fee for your pages, book, or booklet. Share your work with libraries to be certain your efforts aren't wasted and lost.

Introduction

MEET CATHERINE FITZ

Catherine Fitz liked to be called Cassie, and she died in 1947. We met Cassie through her records, never in person. We wanted to find Cassie's German immigrant ancestor (Fitz). We started by following the time-honored trails that we will be sharing with you in the following chapters.

First, we asked relatives. We visited Cassie's son Sterling and he told us what he knew—her maiden name (Catherine Fitz), her husband's name, the number and names of her children, where Cassie lived, where and when she died, and some of her personality traits and other memories he had of her.

Case Study

He knew the names of her parents—John Fitz and Magdalena Falkenstein—and he possessed photographs of Cassie and her father, John Fitz. Sterling didn't know much more, but he told us about his older sister Frances and gave us her address (she lived four states away).

In response to our letter, Frances told us when Cassie was born (8 March 1869) and when and where she died (30 July 1947 in Des Moines, Iowa). Frances reported that Cassie was buried in Dodge Cemetery at Bagley, Iowa. Frances also listed the names and birth dates of Cassie's nine children and told us that Cassie was married in 1893 in Guthrie County, Iowa. Frances said she could give us the names of Cassie's brothers and sisters (which we subsequently requested). She also said that she remembered Cassie talking about "castles on the Rhine," but the details escaped her then.

Frances admitted that she knew very little about her Fitz grandparents (Cassie's parents). She said that Magdalena died when Cassie was fifteen, leaving ten children. John Fitz, a Dunkard preacher and farmer, remarried and died about 1895 and was buried in a Baptist cemetery near Panora, Iowa. These "facts" later were found to be inaccurate, proving again that you must challenge all information you receive and be open to the possibility that later research can revise your information. Magdalena actually died when Cassie was nineteen, not fifteen, and John Fitz died in 1899, not 1895. Frances believed the Fitzes were from Austria or Germany.

Being four states away and holding down 9 to 5's and other family obligations, we didn't pursue much for a month, but Frances had great news and wrote us a letter filled with excitement and discovery. She had written to a Fitz cousin and through this cousin made contact with another cousin, Beulah. She shared a veritable cornucopia of information on the Fitz family.

The six-page letter, which took the seventy-year-old Beulah five days to prepare, included birth and death dates for Catherine Fitz and her nine siblings, for her father John Fitz Jr. (22 March 1843–20 July 1899) and his eight siblings, and for her grandfather John Fitz Sr. (5 March 1817–15 May 1900). It also named John Fitz Sr.'s wife, Marianna Dubs.

The letter further provided a genealogy of John Fitz Sr. (Cassie's grandfather). The family had come to Guthrie County, Iowa, from Fulton County, Illinois, and farther back (before 1860) from York County, Pennsylvania. This was wonderful news. At this point, we had a good basis of information but no documented facts.

As we continued to research the Fitz family, we kept Sterling, Frances, and Beulah aware of our findings too. They had helped us, so we would do no less than share our findings with them. Little did we know how helpful this action would be later as Beulah continued to locate and share vital information with us.

As a result of further inquiry and requests, Frances shared information from John Fitz Jr.'s family Bible, Cassie's teaching certificates, and Cassie's and John's obituaries. We made requests of civil offices in the appropriate locales and received copies of Cassie's death record, her marriage record, and John Fitz Jr.'s death record, estate records, and deeds.

From a library in Guthrie County, we received pages from the county history of 1884, pages from a religious publication giving some biographical data on members of the Fitzes' church, and a number of tombstone inscriptions. We also located census records and a history and an atlas of Fulton County, Illinois. Each record contributed to a more complete picture of the history of this Fitz family.

Most of our research was done long distance and took a large amount of time, but it was necessary to find the records for which we were searching. We also contacted the York County Historical Society, which possessed many sources for an in-depth search of the family, but not before Beulah had pleasantly surprised us again. This time she shared a newly received letter from her cousin Louise. Louise had been independently researching this family too and located the first immigrant of this Fitz family to America. In her research, Louise found another surprise for us: Our John Fitz Sr., as Beulah had called him, was actually John Fitz Jr., son of another John Fitz Sr. So, there were three John Fitzes in succession. We renamed them for clarification purposes—John Fitz I (1775–1845), John Fitz II (1817–1900), and John Fitz III (1843–99), Catherine's father. The York County Historical Society records confirmed this threesome as well as confirming Louise's other discoveries. John Fitz I was the son of Frederick Fitz, who was the son of Johan (the correct spelling is Johann)

Peter Fitz, who immigrated to America in 1750 from Germany.

Wow! We didn't really expect our first step, contacting relatives, to essentially build the entire genealogy back to the German immigrant. We just went along for the ride, picking up documents to confirm the pieces of the puzzle. Don't get us wrong. This wasn't accomplished in a month or two. It took a few years because we had hundreds of other distractions, just as you will.

It was another few years, and many unfruitful searches, before we stumbled onto the connection of Johann Peter Fitz, the immigrant, to his village in Germany. We had made every effort to locate him through the Family History Center databases (see chapter four) with no luck at that time. (This was before the edition of the Ancestral File that includes Johann Peter Fitz. That listing was a result of our locating him and Louise's placing the information in the file.) We did find a general immigration reference in Rupp (see bibliography on page 184). We had investigated numerous periodicals and other sources, all with no luck. We came to a dead end.

In our review of published periodicals, we saw a query that had been placed by a German research student who was working on compiling information about immigrants to America from his home village of Ober-Flörsheim. In his query, he asked for information about Johann Peter Fitz. We quickly responded and were sent copies of baptismal, marriage, and emigration records that were able to confirm that his Johann Peter Fitz was ours.

This information allowed us to utilize the Family History Center Locality Search database to order microfilm from Ober-Flörsheim, Germany, as well as opened up dozens of other options to us, even including traveling to Germany to visit the village itself. We didn't find a "castle on the Rhine," but if we could stumble onto all the other great stuff, so can you. As for Cassie, we will continue documenting her family in chapter seven.

ONE

Getting Started

Important

Yes, it's a jungle out there, but we can help you cut through the seemingly impenetrable and confusing undergrowth of getting a proper start on your own Germanic ancestral search. **An essential factor in Germanic research is finding the exact origin of your Germanic ancestors. To do so requires work here in America first.**

We'll alert you to many of the customary pitfalls of a trek into the domain of genealogy. We'll even aid you in your attempts to cross the vast and sometimes stormy Atlantic Ocean—all the way to Germany, Austria, Switzerland, and other Germanic areas. Our job is to make your journey as smooth as possible.

Now for your job. You must be ready for rough going once in a while and not take the inevitable setbacks too seriously, not because you will always be successful in overcoming them, but because a "positive, won't quit attitude" yields success far more often than its alternative.

WHAT YOU'LL NEED
(THE GENEALOGIST'S EQUIPMENT)

Supplies

- pencils and pens
- a small journal for your journeys
- a standard-sized wireless notebook
- coins for copy machines
- a working copy of your pedigree chart (see page 6)
- working copies of family group sheets (see page 8)
- an alphabetical list of surnames (see page 7)
- magnifying glass (optional)
- audio or video recorder (optional)

Journal

Whenever you embark on a genealogy trip, you'll always want to ask and record six questions: who, what, when, where, why, and how. Use your journal to record the places you visited (where), the dates you visited them (when), what you looked for and how (why and how), the things you found and didn't find (what), and the names, addresses, and phone numbers of those people with whom you talked or corresponded (who). If you ask all of these important questions at each of your stops, you will have the most complete information possible. Find documents (evidence) to confirm what you are told during those interviews. Log unsuccessful searches too—trails that led nowhere—otherwise, you might forget and repeat your search.

Notebook

Generally, you'll want to photocopy important pages of information. If copying is not possible, record the details of your finding in your notebook. Along with the information, record the source. If you are writing in your notebook, note the source information on the page where you begin writing the details of what you found. For a photocopy, record the source on the back of the first page.

Source information should include the complete name of the book (or other source), author, year of publication, publisher's name, page number(s) of the information you collected, and where you found the source. Do this for each item you find. When you remove a sheet from your notebook, all the information you need should be in one place.

Be sure to place information relating to each surname on a separate page of your notebook. Then, you can file each page in separate folders and keep information together on that surname. Mixing surnames on the same page can become a real nightmare later when you are trying to remember what family was on what page. A small investment of time early on to organize your materials can save you tons of time later.

Pedigree Charts and Family Group Sheets

For their fact-finding pilgrimages, family historians keep their materials organized in two simple forms: pedigree charts and family group sheets. These are often available at libraries, or **you can download them on the Internet at sites such as <http://www.familytreemagazine.com>**. While these are indeed simple tools, they are absolutely essential for organizing your research trip (see illustration on pages 6 and 8).

Internet Source

Alphabetical List of Surnames

An extremely important item to take on your genealogical research trips is a list of your family's surnames (see chart on page 7). This can save you a great deal of time searching through files and notebooks. Take each surname you are searching and list the earliest documented ancestor of that line. Add to the list as your research reveals new names.

PEDIGREE CHART

Name of Compiler _____

Address _____

City, State _____

Date _____

Person No. 1 on this chart is the same person as No. _____ on chart No. _____

Chart No._____

```
                                                            16 _____
                                              8 MÜLLER, Wilhelm      b. _____ (Father of No. 8)
                                                 b.           (Father of No. 4)   m.              Cont. on chart no. ___)
                                                 p.b. Glochiem, GER          17 d. _____
 A —— MUELLER, John                              m.                             b. _____ (Mother of No. 8)
   4                                             d.                             d.              Cont. on chart no. ___)
     b.              (Father of No. 2)           p.d.
     p.b.    B                                                               18 _____
     m.                                        9 _____           b. _____ (Father of No. 9)
     d.                                           b.          (Mother of No. 4)  m.              Cont. on chart no. ___)
     p.d.                                         p.b.                       19 d. _____
                                                  d.                            b. _____ (Mother of No. 9)
 2 MILLER, James Robert                           p.d.                          d.              Cont. on chart no. ___)
   b. 14 Sep 1951       (Father of No. 1)                                    20 SCHMIDT, Johann Heinrich
   p.b. Chicago, IL (Cook Co.)        C                                         b. _____ (Father of No. 10)
   m. 19 Jun 1972, Columbus, OH               10 SCHMIDT, Johann Jacob          m.              Cont. on chart no. ___)
   d.                                             b.          (Father of No. 5)  21 d. _____
   p.d.                                           p.b. Joliet, IL               b. _____ (Mother of No. 10)
                                                  m.                            d.              Cont. on chart no. ___)
     5 SMITH, Margaret Ellen                      d.                         22 _____
       b.            (Mother of No. 2)            p.d.                          b. _____ (Father of No. 11)
       p.b                                                                      m.              Cont. on chart no. ___)
       d.                                      11 _____       23 d. _____
       p.d.                                       b.          (Mother of No. 5)  b. _____ (Mother of No. 11)
                                                  p.b.                          d.              Cont. on chart no. ___)
                                                  d.                         24 _____
 1 MILLER, Jennifer LeAnn                         p.d.                          b. _____ (Father of No. 12)
   b. 15 Jun 1976                                                               m.              Cont. on chart no. ___)
   p.b. Denver, CO (Arapahoe Co.) —— D        12 SCHRÖDER, Mathias          25 d. _____
   m.                                             b.          (Father of No. 6)  b. _____ (Mother of No. 12)
   d.                                             p.b. Huttigsweiler, GER       d.              Cont. on chart no. ___)
   p.d.                                           m.                         26 _____
                                                  d.                            b. _____ (Father of No. 13)
     6 SCHRADER, Frederick                        p.d.                          m.              Cont. on chart no. ___)
       b.            (Father of No. 3)                                       27 d. _____
       p.b.                                    13 _____          b. _____ (Mother of No. 13)
       m.                                         b.          (Mother of No. 6)  d.              Cont. on chart no. ___)
       d.    E                                    p.b.
       p.d.                                       d.                         28 _____
                                                  p.d.                          b. _____ (Father of No. 14)
 3 SHRADER, Catherine Marie                                                     m.              Cont. on chart no. ___)
   b. 7 Apr 1952      (Mother of No. 1)       14 WÄBER, Conrad             29 d. _____
   p.b. Columbus, OH (Franklin Co.)               b.          (Father of No. 7)  b. _____ (Mother of No. 14)
   d.                                             p.b. Birmensdorf, SWZ         d.              Cont. on chart no. ___)
   p.d.                                           m. Eppingen, GER
                                                  d.                         30 _____
     7 WEBER, Anna                                p.d.                          b. _____ (Father of No. 15)
       b.            (Mother of No. 3)                                          m.              Cont. on chart no. ___)
       p.b. Lancaster, PA (Lancaster Co.)     15 _____       31 d. _____
       d.                                         b.          (Mother of No. 7)  b. _____ (Mother of No. 15)
       p.d.  F                                    p.b.                          d.              Cont. on chart no. ___)
                                                  d.
                                                  p.d.
   _____
   b.               (Spouse of No. 1)
   p.b.
   d.
   p.d.
```

A pedigree chart is an outline of your ancestry for several generations. Chart number 1 should list you as person number 1. Create a numbering system for additional charts.

EXPLANATION OF PEDIGREE CHART

A. List the last name first and capitalize it.

B. Abbreviations:
   b. = birth
   p.b. = birthplace
   m. = marriage
   d. = death
   p.d. = death place

C. The international date style is used—day, month, and year, in that order (22 Jun 1755). Months should be abbreviated as follows: Jan Feb Mar Apr May Jun Jul Aug Sep Oct Nov Dec

D. For places, include the town/city; county; state or country.

E. The surname of a wife is written as her maiden name.

F. Use the U.S. Postal Service two-letter abbreviations for states.

Sample List of Surnames

Baumgardner, Jacob	b. 1751 PA
Blosser, Isaac	b. 1776 PA
Brown, William	b. 1770 IRE
Carey, Jenny Ann	b. 1825 OH
Creedon, Dennis	b. 1805 IRE
Davis, Peter B.	b. 1785 PA
Dubs, Oswald	b. 1720 SWZ
Englert, Susannah	b. 1747 ?
Gormley, James	b. 1815 IRE
Hamacher, Susanna	b. 1768 PA
Kühne, Heinrich	b. 1740 EUR
McMullan, Michael	b. 1800 IRE
Myers, Susanna	b. 1796 PA
Price, Nathan	b. 1801 OH
Roth, Johannes	b. 1748 PA
Roth, Samuel	b. 1790 PA
Sprankle, James Benjamin	b. 1808 PA
Spurgeon, Eli	b. 1795 PA
Weiland, Clemens	b. 1735 GER

PREPARING FOR YOUR SEARCH

Before we head out on our first search, we'd like to explain why we're headed where we're headed. It's imperative that we plan each step in order to reach our destination as efficiently as possible. Imagine a car on solid ice, its wheels spinning, going nowhere. Genealogy can be like that at times. Right now, for instance, you have a huge array of choices before you regarding what to do

Name of Compiler _Jennifer LeAnn Miller_   Person No. 1 on this chart is the same   Family Group No._____
Address _27 Providence Lane_   person as No. _____ on chart No. _____
City, State _Denver, CO_
Date _5/99_

FAMILY GROUP SHEET

HUSBAND _MILLER, James Robert_ ——A

	B (DATE)	(TOWN OR TOWNSHIP)	**C**	(COUNTY)	(STATE)
Born	_14 Sep 1951_	at _Chicago_ ——	——	_Cook Co._	_IL_
Died		at			
Married					
(1)	_19 Jun 1972_	at _Columbus, OH_	to _Catherine Schrader_		
(2)		at	to		
(3)		at	to		

Father _John Mueller_
Mother _Margaret Ellen Smith_
References _____

————D

WIFE (1) _SHRADER, Catherine Marie_

Born	_7 Apr 1952_	at _Columbus_	_Franklin Co._	_OH_
Died		at		
Other marriages				
( )		at	to	
( )		at	to	

Father _Frederick Schrader_
Mother _Anna Weber_
E— References _____

F— **CHILDREN** (in order of birth)

i   Name _Robert Jason Miller_

Born	_2 Dec 1974_	at _Denver_	_Arapahoe Co._	_CO_
Died		at		
Married	_7 Jun 1998_	at _Denver, CO_	to _Danielle Marie Stanton_	
Reference				

ii   Name _Jennifer LeAnn Miller_

Born	_15 Jun 1976_	at _Denver_	_Arapahoe Co._	_CO_
Died		at		
Married		at	to	
Reference				

iii   Name _____

Born		at		
Died		at		
Married		at	to	
Reference				

A family group sheet is needed for each ancestral family. Chart number 1 should start with you as a child. Create a numbering system for additional charts.

EXPLANATION OF FAMILY GROUP SHEET

A.   List the last name first and capitalize it.

B.   The international date style is used—day, month, and year, in that order (22 Jun 1755).

C.   For places, include the town/city; county; state or country.

D.   For marriages, include the full name of spouse. For the wife's name, use her maiden, or unmarried, name.

E.   List your basic sources under References.

F.   Children are listed in birth order and should include all children, even ones that did not live into adulthood.

with your family history in terms of time, energy, and money.

Look at the list on page 10. Pretend that you have already interviewed the people resources closest to you genealogically (your own family, near and distant relatives). What next?

If you are a novice in a hurry, you might be tempted to actually travel to Germany to conduct your research on site, a very desirable goal. However, look more carefully at the list. **It is imperative that you choose your steps wisely or you could end up "spinning your wheels," wasting your time, energy, and money.**

As an analogy, you certainly wouldn't show up to play a football game without the proper equipment, nor would you try gathering information from eight thousand miles away when some important information may be only a few miles from you. While some people may have more "dollars than sense," most of us need to be wise and frugal in our research efforts. That's why this book is for you. Start with you and work backward. Compile and document information about you, then your parents, grandparents, and on back. Do not assume that because your last name is Clark that you are automatically related to the person for whom the candy bar is named. That is an unacceptable shortcut, genealogywise. Prove each step of relationship from you, then your parents, and so on one generation at a time.

Be sure to do all the homework necessary to make each future step you take as productive as possible. If, for example, you decide to head to Germany, do you know—before you depart—the names of the villages and the names of a large number of your German ancestors from those villages? Do you know that many German villages have the same name? Is your village the one in Baden-Wuerttemberg, Bavaria, or Saxony?

You don't want to show up at the Frankfurt airport asking flight attendants if they know any Schmidts or Schröders living nearby who might be your cousins. If you do, your trip will be a sight-seeing one at best, a trip that will not be productive genealogically.

Timesaver

Where to Go Next?	
census records	writing to archives in Germany
family genealogies	vital records (birth, death, marriage)
family stories	family bibles
cemeteries	trip to Germany
computer CDs	libraries
newspapers	churches
photos	county histories
heirlooms	diaries
Internet Web sites	Family History Centers
funeral homes	immigration records
estate records	genealogy periodicals
tax records	naturalization papers
emigration records	land records
professional genealogists	military records
German genealogy societies	German microfilm

Build from the basics. Frankly, with more than 125,000 current and defunct villages in Germany alone, your chances of finding your ancestors' villages of origin are slight to moderate. But if you follow the steps we've outlined, you'll be following the most logical and efficient path to the information you seek.

From You to Your Past

Step By Step

The most efficient way to research your past is to start in the present and work backward. We suggest that you follow these steps:

1. Start with yourself by collecting documented evidence about you, your birth, and your life, such as your birth certificate, marriage certificate, and so forth.
2. Collect documented evidence from your parents, siblings, grandparents, cousins, and anybody else in your family who could possibly provide you with historical or genealogical information.
3. Go to local or nearby treasure troves (churches, courthouses, cemeteries).
4. Go to local libraries and Family History Centers (see chapter four).
5. Visit treasure troves and libraries that are a greater distance away.
6. Write to places not easily reached for additional civil, church, and archive records.
7. Don't be an island. Make connections with Germanic genealogical societies and other Germanic-specific sources explained in later chapters.
8. **Consider hiring a professional for difficult or distant genealogical research.** You may wish to contact a member of the Board for Certification of Genealogists (P.O. Box 14291, Washington, DC 20044-4291, <http://www.bcg certification.org/>), or the Association of Professional Genealogists (P.O. Box 40393, Denver, CO 80204-0393, <http://www.apgen.org/~apg>), or Accredited Genealogists (35 NW Temple St., Salt Lake City, UT 84150).
9. After exhausting all of the records you can efficiently get your hands on and you know the exact location in Germany to research, go to Germany, if you wish. But, don't make too many assumptions about your trip. For

For More Info

instance, don't assume you will find the tombstones of your ancestors in the cemetery. Due to the value of land in many Germanic areas, many cemeteries no longer contain their original "inhabitants," but newer "arrivals." Finding original records is also a challenge as the records may be scattered among numerous nearby villages and larger archives. Legitimate expectations include the possibility of locating a significant amount of information if you locate the right record source. You may find a living relative who can add substantially to your store of knowledge about the family. Also, you will see firsthand a number of areas historically significant to your ancestors. Certainly, another bonus is enjoying the "flavor" of the old country your ancestors inhabited.

THE SEARCH BEGINS

Your first search will not be one simple stop. You need to collect extensive data on you and your family in the New World. **You may wish to refer to a basic how-to guide, such as** *The Complete Idiot's Guide to Genealogy* **by Christine Rose and Kay Ingalls,** *First Steps in Genealogy* **by Desmond Walls Allen, or** *Unpuzzling Your Past* **by Emily Croom.** You will need to plan out a large number of trips to visit relatives, libraries, and courthouses. Your first search can take you weeks if you are footloose and fancy-free, or years if you're tied down to a 9 to 5 and other duties. Your personal circumstances are a major factor in dictating how rapidly you make progress.

Printed Source

Another factor is how accessible records on your family are to you. If your ancestors stayed in one community for a significant period of time and you reside near there, all the better for you. Access to those treasure troves will be easier for you than for someone who lives at the other end of the continent. Use as many local resources as you can.

The jewels of information you are looking for on this first set of trips should be those most easily available to you. It is important that you begin with yourself and closely related family members. If they live nearby so that you can call them or visit them inexpensively, then do so as soon as possible. They are a great resource and may be able to answer many of your questions by memory or using actual documents they possess. Or they may direct you to further resources. They also may have photographs of your ancestors, or a family Bible, or even a diary belonging to your great-great-uncle. Who knows until you ask? So, ask!

Other family treasures that relatives might have tucked away include birth, baptismal, and marriage records, family histories, immigration documents, wedding and birth announcements, obituaries, newspaper clippings, memorial cards, military or pension records, or even family traditions and legends. Ask permission to photocopy any documents.

In addition to visiting and writing family members, other travel plans you will want to incorporate as a part of your first search include records from key sources listed on page 12. Because there are already numerous beginning guidebooks on genealogy and family history (see the bibliography), we won't discuss in detail how to find and use common records, such as censuses, vital records, passenger arrival lists, deeds, church and civil records. Instead, we will point out information contained in many of these sources that is important to you as a German-American researcher.

Churches

Church records of interest include baptisms, births, marriages, deaths, confirmations, and membership lists. Some churches keep their historical records locally, others send their records to a central archive, while others simply don't keep older records at all **(see chapters two and three)**.

See Also

Courthouses

County and city records, depending on the state, include the following:

- Probate court has wills and estates, some birth and death records and marriage records. You may also find naturalization papers that indicate the country, state, or district within that applicant's country of origin. These important papers may be found in probate court but can also be found in many different places at county, state, and federal levels.
- Recorder's office has deeds, mortgages, leases, and other land transactions.
- Health department may hold birth and death records. This differs from state to state.
- Treasurer's office has lists of taxpayers and the values of their properties.
- Clerk of courts has most court case records, such as case files and criminal and civil records.

Note that some places restrict public access to their records. Be flexible and kind in your quest.

Libraries

Public and private libraries with family history departments are oftentimes gold mines. Many have census records and indexes (bound copies, Soundex, or Miracode), family histories, surname files, county histories, pedigree charts, cemetery records, partition records, naturalization indexes, and much more. Soundex and Miracode systems are indexes based on the way a surname sounds rather than how it is spelled. Family History Centers are also a useful treasure trove, one we will discuss in greater detail in chapter four.

Cemeteries

You should even plan a chilling adventure to the cemeteries in which your ancestors are at rest. Read tombstones, record data, and make rubbings. Look for clues to relationships since family and friends are often buried near each other.

COATS OF ARMS AND CASTLES

If you think you're going to end up in some Germanic castle on the Rhine or Danube, or that your family's coat of arms is going to be easy to find, we are here to catch you as you fall over in shock. We also have tissues available for criers.

Coats of arms are fairly rare and quite restrictive. Ancestral castle residences are even more unusual. These were clearly signs of royalty and property. Most of us came from the hardy peasant stock who made up about 99 percent of the masses. The nobility, which often was less noble than the peasants, made up about 1 percent of the population.

The reason many people would like to have ancestors from the nobility may be based on greed—visions of an unencumbered estate available for the asking—but genealogists may also like to have ancestors from the nobility because their lives are clearly better documented than the lives of peasants (except some criminals). Most of our ancestors didn't have personal scribes following them around with the sole purpose of recording their historical activities for our pleasure.

But, be not melancholy or dispirited. There are some tremendous resources available to assist you in discovering your Germanic ancestors—sources available right here in America as well as abroad.

And, your ancestors are worth discovering. You should be proud of your ancestors and interested in their history, not just the history of the nobility, criminals, or other famous people. Frankly, until recently, with the advent of schools and books, most families were only familiar with their own families' histories, shared through stories told around the hearth of each home, stories that strengthened and preserved family integrity.

Now, we find the history of 100 percent of the world's people has been condensed and preserved through the stories of less than 1 percent of the world's people—those who make it into the history books shared in our schools. In the past, this was by necessity for written history, but today you can change all that. You can research and publish your history and preserve it for future generations. Don't substitute the history in schoolbooks for your history—stories that are sources of pride, laughter, or sympathy for the children and grandchildren of your lineage. These stories were part of the mysterious fabric that bound a family together. Recapture your past and publish it.

TWO

The Challenges You Will Face

\di'fin\ *vb*

Definitions

Chapter one highlighted the basic knowledge and skills any family historian needs. Now we're going to acquaint you with the specific challenges of Germanic research. We will be reviewing some specific pitfalls of Germanic research and some problems with terminology.

Let's start with why we use the word *Germanic* instead of *German* in this book. First, *Germanic* is a much more inclusive term. "German" ancestors may have come from Germany, yes, but they also may have come from Austria, Switzerland, Alsace (part of France), much of what is now Poland, Luxembourg, southern Denmark, the present Czech Republic, or even a little bit of Russia. *Germany* is not such an exact term either, since modern Germany didn't exist as a separate country until 1871, which is after a lot of our ancestors crossed the ocean. What all these "Germans" had in common was that they were German-*speaking*. Even so, *German-speaking* was not all that homogeneous a term. The number of dialects is much greater than in America, which is all the more amazing considering that the country of Germany today is about the size of Oregon.

RECORDS

The good news is that many German civil and church records exist, commonly as far back as 1650, right after the Thirty Years' War. On this side of the ocean, many records can be found too, such as German newspapers, German-American churches, and Pennsylvania German baptismal certificates.

Unfortunately, the news is not all good. Some records have been damaged or destroyed by wars, bombings, fires, floods, and being thrown out by the authorities. On occasion, you may find that duplicate records of some villages were sent to regional archives. Plan to "look around" for alternate and secondary resources. You may be able to gather information from a baptismal record if a birth record went up in a blaze at the *Rathaus* (city hall).

The next pitfall is that many of the records will be undecipherable from various causes. Damage by water, mold, mildew, animals, smoke, and other natural causes makes reading such records a significant challenge. Unfortunately, there isn't much you can do about these difficulties. Again, you will need to try to "fill in the gaps" with other types of records.

An even greater pitfall to researching Germanic records is the language barrier and the inability of the viewer to read the handwriting or print of a foreign language, whether German, Latin, French, or some other language (see Reading Their Writing in chapter six). Early records are frequently composed in open paragraph form, rather than being nicely laid out in columns of name, birth date, father's name, and so on. Some later records, happily, use this standard post-Napoleonic record format.

Notes

Also, not every set of records is indexed. In the absence of an index, it may be necessary to look through dozens or even hundreds of pages to find a death record, for example.

NAMES

All you need to do Germanic genealogical research is to have the name of your ancestor, the date of an event in the life of your ancestor, and a location for your ancestor. This should be easy, but there are pitfalls. **One of the biggest pitfalls comes in assuming that the name you have is the correct name.** The name may be wrong for several reasons. The surname may have been changed, or even translated by clerks, as a result of your ancestors having contact with English speakers, especially in the early North American colonies. Nicknames may be used instead of the standard given name. What looks like "the" name may not be the right one.

Warning

Anglicizing, Middle Names, and Nicknames

You may know the name of your early Pennsylvania ancestor—John Snyder. Except that is not exactly the way he spelled it when he wrote it himself. He wrote , the German script form of Johann Peter Schneider. John is Johann, a common German name. So his first name is Johann. And Snyder is Schneider. That sounds something like Snyder, which is an anglicized form of Schneider. You might not be able to find him in the census index under Snyder. If you look under Snider too, you might not find him there either. You also need to look under the original German spelling, Schneider.

Even if you know enough to look for him under the name Schneider, another pitfall lurks. What if you drop his middle name and look for him under the name Johann Schneider? To a North American, Peter is just a middle name. We typically go by our first names. But in Germany, what we call a middle name was really usually the name people were called by; everybody called him Peter Schneider. You need to look for him that way in all the records too.

And his wife Maria Baker? Well, by now you know enough to search for her by her middle name, Maria Magdalena Baker. In fact, it is likely that she went by Magdalena, because Anna and Maria were commonly used saints' names that were used with most people (like Johann was for males), and the names they were called by were the second of the two given names. Her name Magdalena is a long one, and it lends itself to a shortened form or nickname, such as Lena. If you find a Lena, keep your mind open to Magda*lena*. She may use some other nickname, like the English Maggie.

Even with a seemingly straightforward name such as Baker, there can be the problem of surname changes. Baker is a direct translation for the very common German surname Becker, which is derived from the baker occupation. In other words, Maria Magdalena Becker might be found under Lena Becker or Maggie Baker or Magdalena Becker or Mary Baker. Even a very common name can be confusing and downright misleading, unless you are aware of the pitfalls.

Don't limit your research to a single spelling or name. Keep records of the variations and examine all the possibilities at each step. Some examples are *Hans* for *Johann* or *Johannes*, *Fritz* for *Friedrich*, *Heinz* for *Heinrich*, *Willy* for *Wilhelm*, *Sepp* for *Josef*, *Trina* for *Catharina*, *Lisa* or *Betty* for *Elisabeth(a)*, *Greta* or *Gretl* for *Margaretha*, *Dora* for *Dorothea*, *Lina* for *Carolina*, *Lena* for *Magdalena* or *Helena*, *Klaus* for *Nicolaus*, and *Hanna* for *Johanna*.

Reminder

Regional and Religious Naming Patterns

Some names are typical of a certain region or a certain religion. Just because it's a saint's name doesn't mean a name is Catholic (Protestants have saints too), but individuals with names such as Franz Xaver or Anton or Josef or Johann Baptist or Maria Theresia or Franziska or Maximiliane are very likely Catholic. Males named Carsten or Jens probably came from Schleswig-Holstein. Females named Frauke or Antje probably came from the north, around the North Sea or the Netherlands. Males named Benedicht or females named Verena or Rosine may be of Swiss origin. Harm and Cord are Hanoverian versions of Hermann and Conrad. Gesche, Mette, and Wiebke are Hanoverian female names. You can find many such examples throughout the different regions.

\di'fin\ *vb*

Definitions

If you have ancestors from northern Germany, around Ostfriesland, you may have a confusing pattern of changing last names. **Last names there were patronymics from the given name of the father.** For example, Peter Hansen's offspring would have the last name of Petersen, as they were the children of Peter, or Peter's sons. You will know you have found this pitfall if your ancestors seem to change their surname every generation (Thomsen, then Petersen, then Hansen, depending on the father's given name).

If your ancestors are from around Westphalia, their surnames may be based on the ownership of a farm. You will know you have found this pitfall if your ancestors' male surnames change when they marry. This was because the woman was the heiress to a farm. Note that patronymics and the use of farm names as surnames are both regional customs, not universal practices throughout the German-speaking lands.

Baptisms of the three official religions (Catholic, Lutheran, Reformed) took place within a few days of birth and involved "christenings," the bestowing of Christian names upon the children. Anabaptists (such as Mennonites) practiced adult baptism at an age of understanding, roughly corresponding to the age of confirmation in the state churches. Anabaptists also bestowed Christian names on their newborn children.

In most areas, there is no general surname index to the inhabitants. This is why the International Genealogical Index (IGI), discussed in chapter four, is so useful. The exception is Switzerland, where citizenship depends on locality. A person can be born in one place, live in another place, work in another place, but the place of citizenship is the official *Heimatort* (hometown), which may be yet a fourth place. This hometown is where the person has voting rights and where all vital records for that family are kept. All Swiss surnames are listed in a Switzerland-wide guide to family names, the *Familiennamenbuch der Schweiz*, which has been printed with a helpful English introduction.

See Also

While we are talking about naming patterns, please note that given names do not always fall into neat patterns. In a few regions, there may be a pattern of the oldest son being given the father's father's name; the oldest daughter being given the mother's mother's name; the second son being given the mother's father's name; and the second daughter being given the father's mother's name. In other areas, the first baptismal sponsor (godfather) provides the first given name; the second one, the second given name. Baptismal sponsors were generally, but not necessarily, related to one of the parents. Be aware that possible regional and religious idiosyncrasies may occur.

In cases of illegitimacy, the mother's surname was generally given to the child, although the pastor or civil official tried to get the name of the father so he could be held liable for support. This is important because only legitimate children could inherit property, become members of a guild, and become full citizens.

Official Name Changes

Did the surname of my ancestor get changed at Ellis Island? Yes and no. Officially, no, but accidentally, it may have been changed. **Despite stories to the contrary, there were no official name changes at Ellis Island.** There were no officials there (or at its predecessor, Castle Garden) with authority to change immigrants' names. Officials had only a few minutes per person to do a physical exam and some paperwork. The basis for the processing that was done at Ellis Island was the ship's manifest or passenger list that already had the names of the immigrants. This manifest was prepared in Europe by Europeans at the port of departure, whether that was a Dutch, French, English, or German port. Anyway, how would the relatives of Johann Dünschmann locate him at Ellis Island or find him later if somebody purposefully changed his name to John Dunn?

Important

If a name happened to change after arrival to America, it was likely done at some other point, although their Ellis Island experience may have affected people's thinking about a name change. For example, if twenty-year-old Johannes Friedrich Schmidt was incorrectly addressed by a clerk as Fred Smith, there may have been a tendency by Johannes Friedrich Schmidt to see this possible name change as a symbol of his breaking away from the old world and identifying with the new. He may have been concerned about anti-Germanic sentiments. For whatever reason, he identified with the new name and adopted it, later accepting it as his correct name and signing further documents as Fred Smith. There are numerous accounts of name changes prior to and after Ellis Island, but their names were not changed at Ellis Island.

Philadelphia arrivals in the 1700s experienced name changes in America more as a result of encountering English-speaking neighbors and clerks than any kind of official decision. In colonial America, Bentz evolved to Pentz and eventually Pence; Zimmermann to Zimmerman or translated to Carpenter; and Schwarzwälder to Blackwelder. We also find as many as a hundred names from a single surname, such as Herchheimer and Zirkel. The list could go on and on.

Another common belief about name changes is demonstrated in the following example: Could there be three brothers of whom one stayed east and kept the name Schwarz, another went west and changed it to Schwartz, and another went south and changed it to Swartz? Such cases are possible, of course, but it is more likely that these are three independent families with similar surnames. This "three brothers" story would only be believable if the brothers all can be traced back with their given names, birth records, and the same parents. As you trace your own line, proving each generation, the resulting relationships you find will answer the questions you have. You can then feel confident about when and where the names changed.

Beware of using census records to decide that an ancestor changed the spelling of his or her name. People did not write their own names on censuses. They (or another family member, or maybe even a neighbor) stated their names and the census enumerator wrote them. One census enumerator may write Müller, another Mueller, and another Miller, depending on various factors. And even within the same document, such as a will, it is not uncommon to find the same name spelled several different ways, even signed with different spellings by the same person. Still, a person's signature is the best way of determining how a person spelled his or her name. Do take into account the possibility that the person may not be very literate. Don't limit your research to just the most common spelling. Be alert to other possibilities, keep records of name variations, and examine all the possibilities at each step.

PLACES

European places of origin are hard to find, hard to identify, and hard to pinpoint geographically. To find any mention of the place of origin, you need to look in the obvious places—censuses, death records, marriage records, obituaries, family Bibles, papers brought from overseas, and family histories. **Don't forget that neighbors in America may have come from the same place as you ancestor, so you may be able to follow the same process with them.** Look for their ancestors in the same sources you did for yours.

Tip

Suppose you find your ancestor's birthplace listed on the 1880 U.S. census as Preisen. You might think your next logical step would be to try to locate a village named Preisen. Before you try too hard, though, you need a reality check. American birthplaces listed in that census aren't specific villages but states. Foreign origins are listed by country. Therefore, we should not expect Preisen to be an exact village but rather a country or state within a country. If it's unlikely that you will find listings such as Cincinnati, Winchester, Stuttgart, Savannah, Nottingham, or Copenhagen, you can't expect Preisen to pinpoint a more precise area than a region or a state.

The only state that resembles Preisen is the largest German state, namely Preußen/Preussen, which translates into Prussia. Just as surnames are often misinterpreted, place-names can be misunderstood too. For instance, our Preisen example is a dialectal pronunciation of Preussen.

In fact, misspelling of place-names is extremely common and we will deal with this subject in chapter three, which is dedicated to helping you locate your ancestors' homeland.

See Also

TIME

As we are discovering, it is not unusual for German words or concepts to be different from their North American counterparts. So it is with dates. Europeans use the international date style of day, month, and year, so 7/4/1776, a significant date to Americans (the fourth of July, 1776), will be interpreted as the seventh of April, 1776, by a German, who will probably write it as 7.4.1776 (the seventh day of the fourth month of the year 1776). Europeans commonly use periods between the numbers rather than slashes.

Suppose you have a birth date for Johann Peter Schneider. He was born on 2/11/22. You mean February 11, 1722. If you write to a European church or civil registration office using that notation, they will search on 2 November 1922 (or 1822 or 1722, guessing which century you mean). Good genealogical notation will prevent this pitfall. If you use 11 Feb 1722, the international date style, there will be no problem. In fact, for correspondence purposes, this is better than putting periods between the dates (11.2.1722) since many Europeans may try to second-guess what you mean anyway.

Germans have historically used numerical abbreviations for months ending in *-ber*, such as *7ber*, *8ber*, *9ber*, and *10ber*. But the seventh and eighth months are, of course, July and August, which do not end in *-ber*. Actually, the origin of this counting goes back to the time when the year began on 25 March, which made March the first month, April the second month, and so on. When you find *7ber*, *8ber*, *9ber*, and *10ber*, the abbreviations refer to September, October, November, and December. Only those four months use the *-ber* suffix. You will never see a *3ber* or a *6ber*. If you see the variations of *7bris*, *8bris*, *9bris*, and *10bris* used, these mean "of September," "of October," "of November," and "of December." Seven is *septem* in Latin, and September was the seventh month in early times, even though it is the ninth month in our current system. Eight is *octo*, but October is the tenth month. Nine is *novem*, but November is the eleventh month. And ten is *decem*, but December is the twelfth month. Even after the calendar was modernized to begin on January 1, *7ber* through *10ber* were used, so don't think that *7ber* is July, for instance.

The names of the months are found in Appendix A. Sometimes Roman numerals are used for the months, but this can be confusing too. For example, if the Roman numeral is written as *Xber*, *Xbr*, or *Xbris*, this is again the Old Style and refers to December. Again, you will only find these suffixes used for September through December (*VIIbr*, *VIIIber*, *IXbris*, *Xber*, for instance). If the Roman numerals are not followed by *-ber*, *-br*, or *-bris*, they conform to the New Style, X for October and XII for December. A record might read as follows: *geboren den 15. V. 1833* (born on 15 May 1833) or *getauft den 3. IV. 1759* (baptized on 3 April 1759).

Another way to distinguish time in Germanic records is their occasional reference to special days. Familiar holidays have specific names—Easter is *Ostern*, Pentecost (Whitsunday) is *Pfingsten*, Christmas is *Weihnachten*, and New Year's Eve is *Silvester*. Saints' days play a bigger role in German lands than in America. Not just St. Nicholas and St. Valentine are celebrated, but many more. Saints' days play a role in name giving (a child born on February 14 may be called Valentin), especially in Catholic areas, but not exclusively so. There are some differences between the Catholic and Protestant catalogs of saints. For other special days often referred to in vital records, see Appendix A.

NOVEL GROUPS

Various Germanic cultural groups had unique roles in the "colonizing" of North America, each having its own special set of circumstances. You may be familiar with such groups as Hessians, Palatines, Pennsylvania Dutch, Amish, and Huguenots, just to name a few.

Perhaps your ancestor was a member of the military in Germany. Actually, there is a very good chance one of your ancestors was. Someone who fought in the so-called German army against Napoleon, was actually a member of the Bavarian army or Saxon army or Hessian army.

\di'fin\ *vb*

Definitions

The Hessians were mercenaries who fought against the colonists in the American Revolution. They were not soldiers of fortune; they were the soldiers that King George paid various European princes for to fight against the colonists. Not all Hessians were from Hesse, either; many were from Waldeck, Brunswick, Anhalt-Zerbst, or Ansbach-Bayreuth, or were recruited across borders into the Hessian or other armies. Sometimes the very colonists the Hessians were fighting against had emigrated a generation before from those very same German-speaking lands. When a Hessian soldier was captured as a prisoner of war (and it was hard enough feeding the colony's troops, let alone keeping up a prisoner-of-war camp), it was entirely possible that he was "farmed out" from a POW camp in Winchester, Virginia, or York, Pennsylvania, to work for a Virginia or Pennsylvania farmer he could understand, who talked his language—German. Is it any wonder, then, that so many Americans can claim to be descended from a Hessian soldier?

This leads us to the Palatines. Palatines are not to be confused with Palestinians. Palatines came from the Palatinate. In the 1700s, the Palatinate was a disjointed, fragmented area on the east and west sides of the Rhine and was ruled from Heidelberg or Mannheim by the prince-elector of the Palatinate. After 1815, the Palatinate was a contiguous area on the west side of the Rhine with its capital at Speyer and ruled by the King of Bavaria. The largest number of Germans in colonial America came from the Palatinate and so people like Benjamin Franklin and others called all Germans Palatines.

The Germans in William Penn's colony were called Pennsylvania Dutch. Though there may have been a handful of Hollanders or Netherlanders, whom we normally refer to as Dutch, the Pennsylvania Dutch were from Germany and were a German-speaking people. Because the German word for the German language is 𝔇𝔢𝔲𝔱𝔰𝔠𝔥, or *Deutsch*, which sounds much like *Dutch*, colonial Americans proceeded to lump *Deutsch* and *Dutch* together indiscriminately.

Another misunderstood name is Anabaptist. This includes a number of religious groups (Mennonites, Brethren, Amish, Hutterites, Baptists, Dunkards, and Schwenkfelders). These are "plain people" who have as little to do with civil government or the military as possible. They dress more or less simply and believe in personal faith. The term *Anabaptist* does not mean "anti-Baptist." Quite the contrary, the word *Anabaptism* means "rebaptism." In other words, those who were baptized as infants did not understand the importance of the rite, so they would need to be rebaptized by choice and from personal conviction, not through the proxy of parents and godparents.

Moravians, just like Palatines or Hessians, do not necessarily originate from the place from which their name is derived. Their religion was founded in Moravia by Jan Hus (John Huss), but their European headquarters at the time of their emigrations to America was located in Herrnhut, Saxony, far to the northwest of Moravia.

Huguenots are the French Protestants. After King Louis XIV's revocation in 1685 of the Edict of Nantes, which had guaranteed them the freedom to practice their religion, the Huguenots dispersed. Many Huguenots remained in France "underground" while hundreds of thousands of their compatriots emigrated from France to Switzerland, Germany, and other European countries. Sometimes they kept their French language and culture within German-speaking areas, and sometimes they adopted the language and customs of those around them. Some Huguenots eventually immigrated to America.

Waldensians are a group who split from the Catholic church very early. They were followers of Peter Waldo, who lived from 1140 to 1217.

We've shown you the challenges—records, names, places, time, novel groups. Don't let the challenges stop you for a minute. There is a good likelihood that you will overcome them, just as thousands of other Germanic researchers have. Always remember, when one road to discovery looks blocked, you will most likely find a detour to the information you seek. Never give up!

THREE

Locating Your Ancestor's Homeland

Supplies

A s we travel deep into Germanic territory, we will cover some information that you will need in order to identify and locate the actual villages of your Germanic ancestors, no matter whether they are Swiss, Austrian, German, or from another German-speaking country. Consider that modern-day Germany's borders encompass more than 125,000 villages. This number does not include defunct villages nor any villages (past or present) outside Germany's current boundaries, such as in Austria, Switzerland, or Alsace-Lorraine. Oftentimes, it is a challenge to find the correct name of the village of your ancestor's origin. This chapter can help you solve the riddle.

RESEARCH TOOLS

First, assemble the necessary tools:
- access to a historical Germanic atlas and gazetteer (see Map Sources)
- pencils, pens
- a small journal
- a wireless notebook
- coins for copy machines
- a working copy of your pedigree chart
- working copies of family group sheets
- an alphabetical list of surnames
- magnifying glass (optional)

Your goal is to locate records that list your ancestor's place of origin, which is the necessary first step to any kind of successful research in German-speaking areas. The place of origin may be found in church records, censuses, passenger lists, naturalization records, death records, obituaries, newspapers, city directories, county histories, family records, and many other sources. Especially important for locating Germanic ancestors are German-language church records in

America, which may give you a village of origin. The majority of Germanic ancestors were Lutheran or Catholic, but keep in mind that spouses did not always attend the same church or belong to the same denomination. **If you locate a marriage or obituary record for your ancestor, try to determine the religious denomination,** if not already known, from contemporary city directories or county histories. Then try to determine what church parish the clergyman served, and if it still exists. If the church parish no longer exists, check with the archives of that denomination (see Appendix B). In some cases, denominations split or merged, so be sure to follow up with reading about the history of that parish.

Somewhere in your research, you will hopefully run into a document that lists a birthplace more specific than Germany. If so, you need only grab a historical atlas that shows a map of German-speaking lands during that period of time and see just what area that encompassed.

Then again, maybe you will have to scrounge to locate the name of your ancestral home. A variety of documents can hold clues to your family's original German home. Following these clues will require additional research, but they may lead you to that all-important name.

For instance, if you found a marriage record in America, you might ask

- Who were the witnesses? Could they be people the couple knew back in the old country? Where did they come from?
- Who performed the ceremony? Was it a clergyman? What congregation was it? Might there be records there? Might there be a published history of the congregation? Maybe even one in German?

If you found an American death record, you might ask yourself the following questions:

- Who was the informant?

Research Tip

Printed Source

For information on a parish, see J. Gordon Melton's *National Directory of Churches, Synagogues, and Other Houses of Worship.*

Sources

MAP SOURCES

http://www.ancestry.com

http://www.expediamaps.com

http://www.falk-online.de

http://feefhs.org

http://www.jewishgen.org/ShtetlSeeker

http://www.mapquest.com

Meyers Orts- und Verkehrslexikon gazetteer available on microfilm at Family History Centers

Müllers Grosses Deutsches Ortsbuch and its partner *Müllers Verzeichnis der Jenseits der Oder-Neiße gelegenen, unter fremder Verwaltung stehenden Ortschaften*

- Was there an obituary published in the English-language paper? Was there a more detailed obituary published in the local German-language paper or the regional religious newspaper?
- Where was the person buried? What do the cemetery sexton's records say? What does the inscription on the tombstone say?
- Who were the survivors?
- What was the deceased's occupation? A railroad worker, government worker, or corporation worker might be found in governmental or business records.
- Were any lodge or organization memberships mentioned in the obituary? There might be lodge records, such as Sons of Hermann or *Schlaraffia*, or society memberships, such as the local *Männerchor* or *Turnverein* (Turners).
- Was the deceased a veteran? Do military pension records or draft records show a place of origin? Those who had to register for the World War I or World War II drafts included men between eighteen and forty-five, whether they eventually went to war or not.
- Were your German-American ancestors aliens during World War I? Aliens had to register too. Some of these records survive.

Sources

Passenger arrival lists may have your ancestor's homeland. **For the early arrivals to New York (about 1710), check Henry Z Jones Jr.'s** *The Palatine Families of New York: 1710.* **Check Ralph Strassburger and William Hinke's** *Pennsylvania German Pioneers* **for immigrants to Philadelphia from 1727 to 1808. Check the National Archives indexes to arrivals in all U.S. ports after 1820. For 1850 to 1893, check the** *Germans to America* **series.** For 1847 to 1871, there are published lists of some arrivals from Bremen in New York. For all years, check William Filby's *Passenger and Immigration Lists Index* volumes and FTM CD-ROMs.

However, there are some disappointing gaps in the availability of passenger lists. There are no indexes to the Port of New York between 1847 and 1896. And, as Murpheimer's Law states (we can't call it Murphy's Law in a book about Germanic ancestry, can we?), the list for the ship your ancestor came on is not indexed.

Many early Philadelphia arrivals gave only a few listed places of origin, and then only in very general terms, such as "a shipload of Palatines and Switzers." **The** *Germans to America* **series is notorious for its errors and omissions, so you always should check the original passenger lists, and use the books primarily as an index to the lists.** If your ancestor is not in *Germans to America,* that means that you need to crank through the microfilm of all the passenger lists.

Research Tip

To help narrow down dates of arrival, you can search city directories to see when the immigrant first shows up. Immigrants tend to appear in city directories a few years after arrival. You can also check naturalization records and twentieth-century censuses to determine the approximate year the immigrant arrived. If an immigrant ancestor was living in 1900, for example, the 1900 federal census states the year of arrival, which allows a follow-up search of passenger lists. Be aware, however, that this date may be off by a couple of years, since we do not know who supplied the information for the census taker—the immigrant or someone else. Note that for ancestors who immigrated much earlier (say 1750), this method won't work, and you will need to check other sources listed earlier. Narrowing down the likely date of arrival can shorten the search considerably.

If your ancestors arrived between 1850 and 1934, you will want to look at the Hamburg passenger lists, which are indexed and available on microfilm through Family History Centers. Millions of emigrants left through the port of Hamburg, Germany. These lists are especially helpful because they note the immigrant's last village of residence in Europe.

Hamburg passenger lists are of two types: direct and indirect. Because your ancestor could have either sailed "nonstop" or gone to Hull and overland to Liverpool, England, both lists need to be checked. There are indexes to each. The first few years are in rough alphabetical order; that is, all the *As* are together under *A*, all the *Bs* under *B*, but they were entered chronologically as they emigrated. There is also an index by the late Hans Werner Klueber (Family History Library Catalog microfilm number 1,961,710; enter this number in the Family Number Search option).

Once you find a ship name and date, you search the Family History Library Catalog under the Film Number Search option for the pertinent passenger list. Order and view that film and photocopy the headings and the entry for your ancestor. (As always, don't ignore the other people on the same ship, since some of them could be relatives.) You will see much information in the headings, but most important is the *letzter Wohnort*, or last place of residence in Europe. This is not necessarily the birthplace, but it can lead to other records, and your research will actually have made it "across the pond."

The best documented region for emigrants, at least in an English-language publication, is Wuerttemberg. **If your ancestors came between 1750 and 1900, you can search** *The Wuerttemberg Emigration Index,* **compiled by Trudy Schenk, Ruth Froelke, and Inge Bork.** There are seven volumes at this writing, and it is also available online at <http://www.ancestry.com>. These lists name thousands of people who applied to emigrate from Wuerttemberg, Germany.

Printed Source

You will need to search all volumes, but especially the one that concentrates on the *Oberamt* (county) of origin. Each volume is in the form of an alphabetical listing, with name, birth date, birthplace, an abbreviated *Oberamt* name, the application date, and the destination.

The first emigrant in volume 7, for example, is Abel, Auguste J.W.—wife. She is the wife of another emigrant. Compare the emigration dates and film numbers to see who else emigrated together. Auguste was born 22 October 1845 in Horrheim. The exact birth date and place are usually given, but sometimes only an age. Her emigration took place from Oberamt Vaihingen, and the date of her application was September 1867. The destination was "N.-Amer." (North America). The destination is usually North America, but sometimes other places are mentioned, such as Russia or a state in North America. The Family History Library film number for Auguste's application is 856,398. On that film, you would then find a copy of her application to emigrate. From here, you would also look for Horrheim in the Family History Library Catalog, Locality Search, to see if there are any microfilmed church records. Then you can carry on your research in baptismal, marriage, or burial records, or in the *Familienregister*, which are also so common in Wuerttemberg after 1808.

WILDGANSJAGD (WILD-GOOSE CHASE)

Let's pretend you have a place of origin handed down in the family. But wait: Rube Goldberg's corollary to Murpheimer's Law states that when you first find the place of origin, it absolutely must have been misspelled by a barely literate German priest, writing in an unintelligible scrawl in faded and blotted ink on a torn page, in tiny, idiosyncratic German script that was ultimately microfilmed by natural light on an overcast day at dusk in the local castle dungeon. It was then reproduced out of focus on a machine with a toner shortage onto a photocopy, which was destroyed in a flood, which occurred after a fire had burnt up the microfilm, and the clouded backup security copy was used. The family historian read the document onto magnetic tape, pronouncing the place name in her best German accent. The historian's grandson told his cousin over a bad phone connection what he thought he had heard. The cousin wrote it down on a slip of paper, then mispronounced it to his wife, who then mistyped it onto a family group sheet, which was used as the basis of the family history book passed around at the reunion. You can see there might have been the possibility of "mispeling" here, but fortunately there were so many errors that they all cancel each other out, and the place-name Xbyzolwxiqr is actually the correct spelling of the place of origin. Yep, Xbyzolwxiqr!

SOME MISINTERPRETED PLACES

Warning

On the other hand, in very rare cases, this canceling out may not occur, so you may have misinterpretations left. **The misspelling of place-names is extremely common.** Misspellings can result from legitimate spelling variations (*Coblenz* or *Koblenz*), misreading old German script (*Livikum* for *Brockum*) or Gothic carving on tombstones (*Meingartd* for *Weingarts*), transcribing errors (*Oldenberg* for *Oldenburg*), typing mistakes (*Burgelmintz* for *Burglemnitz*), misprints, transposing letters (*Sulwackey* for *Suwalky*), phonetic attempts at writing a name from oral tradition (*Wallnau* for *Wahlenau*), and interference from other languages, such as English (*Bingham* for *Bingen*), Scottish (*Lamebaugh* for *Lembach*), French (*Erbershausen* for *Herbertshausen*), and German dialects (*Neinkirken* for *Neuenkirchen*).

We have seen many examples of misspellings: *Birnbernbaum* for *Burgbernheim*, *Copenhagen* for *Rockenhausen*, *Drothbruck* for *Krottelbach*, *Gachinang* for *Backnang*, *Jankersenßadt* for *Dankersen*, *Kornaberg* for *Quarnebeck*, *Lulla* for *Talle*, *Outwaelen* for *Alsweiler*, *Steindersspher* for *Niederasphe*. Or perhaps somebody had trouble writing a place-name from oral tradition: *Hattenfeltz* for *Hartenfels*, *Amlikime* for *Emlichheim*. Or somebody had trouble transcribing *Helerfeld* for *Herlefeld*, *Tulkinberg* for *Tecklenburg*, or even *Wein* for *Wien*.

Unusual symbols used in the German language can result in misspellings (see also chapter six):

- *Alte Haften* for *Altenhaßlau* (misreading handwritten *ß* as *ft*)
- *Brenzow* for *Bünzow* (misreading handwritten *ü* as *re*)
- *Schonaii* for *Schönau* (the two dots [umlaut] weren't directly over the *o*).

Germanic Territories—and Their Misspellings

We've listed the most commonly encountered territories below, along with real examples of some misspellings:

Notes

Alsace/Elsass/Elsaß

Baden

Bavaria/Bayern/Baiern
    with misspellings such as *Bayran, Beiren, Biern, Bine, Bryon,* and *Byron*

Darmstadt/Hessen-Darmstadt
    with misspellings such as *Hessin Darm, Armstad, Darmstatd,* and *Kesse Darmsdorf*

Electoral Hesse/Kurhessen/Churhessen
    with misspellings such as *Churchessia, Coeur Hessen, Essex, Kor Hessen,* and *Kurkessen*

Hanover/Hannover

Hesse/Hessen
    with misspellings such as *Hashen, Hefse, Hessie,* and *Hesson*

Hessen-Kassel
    with misspellings such as *Hedenkassel, Hepen Bapel,* and *Hessen-Kessel*

Lippe-Detmold

Mecklenburg

Nassau
    with misspellings such as *Napan, Nashua,* and *Nausau*

Oldenburg

Palatinate/Pfalz
    with misspellings such as *Falls, Palfz, Pflaz, Phals,* and *Phetz*

Pomerania/Pommern
    with misspellings such as *Pammen, Pömer, Pommer,* and *Pummer*

Prussia/Preußen
    with misspellings such as *Briesen, Ponissia, Prenpen, Preussem, Pruessen,* and *Prupia*

Rhine Bavaria/Rheinbayern/Rheinbaiern
    with misspellings such as *Rein Biern, Reinbier, Rheinbirn, Rhembayern, Rhine Baran,* and *Rhinebier*

Rhine Palatinate/Rheinpfalz
    with misspellings such as *Rheinfalls, Rheinfals, Reinwalz, Rheinplaz,* and *Rinefall*

Saxony/Sachsen

Silesia/Schlesien

Thuringia/Thüringen

Waldeck

Westphalia/Westfalen
Wuerttemberg/Württemberg
   with misspellings such as *Guttenberg, Wertenburg, Wirtemburg, Wittenberg, Wortenburg, Woodenburg,* and *Wurtenburg.*

Again, these are all real instances of misspellings, some quite common.

Alternate Place-Names

Once in a while, you might run across a place that has changed its name (*Veyl* or *Feil* to *Feilbingert*), an abbreviated form of a longer place-name (*Bbronn* for *Büchenbronn*), a village that no longer exists (*Ronnenberg* is now in the *Baumholder* military firing range), a translation of the place-name (*Newton* for *Neustadt*), the Latin name of the place (*Treverorum,* from *Trier*), or an alternate form of the name (*Gostyn* and *Gostingen*). If you don't find a place-name you think you should find, review older gazetteers and lists of Latin forms of place-names. You can find these through your local library or Family History Center.

Prefixes

Frequently a prefix or an additional word is added or dropped on place-names. Some common examples are *Alt-, Alten-, Bad, Dorf, Gau-, Groß (Gross), Hinter-, Hoch-, Hohen-, Klein, Markt, Mittel-, Nieder-, Ober-, Kirch-, Kirchen-, Neu-, Neuen-, Nord-, Norder-, Old-, Olden-, Ost-, Oster-, Stadt, Süd/ Sued-, Süden/Sueder-, Unter-, Vorder-, West-,* and *Wester-.* If you have trouble locating a place-name that may have one of these prefixes, look under the other basic form. For example, if you can't find *Ostercappeln,* look under *Cappeln* or vice versa.

Warning

Different gazetteers or indexes use different alphabetical rules for compound place-names, such as dropping the prefix *Bad*, which is used for certain officially approved spas. If you don't find *Bad Kissingen,* look also under *Kissingen.* Spacing sometimes counts. Some indexes list places alphabetically *Neu A, Neu B, Neu Z,* then *Neua, Neub, Neuz*; others list them *Neua, Neu A, Neub, Neu B, Neuz, Neu Z.* In general, *ä* can be listed as if it were simply *a,* but may be considered *ae,* between *ad* and *af*; *ö* can be listed like an *o,* but may be considered *oe,* between *od* and *of*; and *ü* like a *u,* but it may be considered *ue,* between *ud* and *uf.*

Duplicate Place-Names

Sometimes there are several places with the same name. For instance, there are numerous places called *Neustadt.* Pay careful attention to any additional identifiers: *Neustadt an der Saale*; *Neustadt bei Chemnitz*; *Neustadt, Baden.* The large city of *Frankfurt am Main* is in central Germany on the Main River; the city of *Frankfurt an der Oder* is in eastern Germany on the Oder River. To ensure that you have correctly identified which place you have and that there are not any other places by that name, check the state or province to which the place belonged.

JURISDICTIONAL MISINTERPRETATIONS

Some confusion about homelands arises when researchers misattribute whether a given place is a village or the next higher jurisdiction, such as a county or district. In English, if someone comes from County Cork, Ireland, we know that county is not the name of a village in Cork because *county* is an English word. But, because you don't know all the possible German words for county or district, you might incorrectly assume that, for instance, *Kreis* is the name of a village. Just because it's written in German, don't think that *Amt* or *Regierungsbezirk* or *Kreis* or *Oberamt* are names of villages rather than names for districts. *Oberamt Balingen* means the District of Balingen, *Regierungsbezirk Trier* means the District of Trier, and *Kreis Wittmund* means the District of Wittmund. The same thing occurs with mother churches and branch churches. *Kirchspiel* and *Kirchensprengel* both mean "church parish." If you find *Kirchspiel Lienen*, it refers to the church parish of Lienen, not a village named Kirchspiel.

A similar problem occurs in the names of larger jurisdictions. *Königreich* means "kingdom," *Herzogtum* means "duchy," and *Grafschaft* means "county" or "earldom." One additional complication in this last example is that there actually *are* at least three villages in Germany named *Grafschaft*; however, in the vast majority of cases, the reference would be to a district or county rather than a particular village. There are exceptions to nearly every rule you can imagine. For a list of German words referring to jurisdictions, see Appendix A.

LOOKING FOR YOUR ANCESTOR'S VILLAGE

Locating your ancestral village may not be as simple as opening a map. Most of the places our ancestors left behind were not large places. A farmer's hometown, for instance, was probably no more than a little crossroads hamlet. Such a wide spot in the road isn't likely to appear on a modern European map, even one that shows a few hundred of the largest places in Germany. Even smaller towns, where masters of crafts or trades practiced their occupations, may not be found on general maps of a country. **You don't need an atlas or map so much as a gazetteer (a place-name dictionary without maps) to find the place.** Gazetteers of modern Germany show as many as 125,000 places (*Müllers Grosses Deutsches Ortsbuch*). Another good one is *Meyers Orts- und Verkehrslexikon* (reprinted 2000 by Genealogical Publishing Company), which is often available at LDS Family History Centers (see chapter four).

If you can narrow down the area to a province, you can use *The Atlantic Bridge to Germany*, a multivolume series by Charles M. Hall. This source is in English and pinpoints each community in map form, which you won't get in a gazetteer. You can also select a more specific gazetteer for Hannover or Wuerttemberg or Bavaria.

\di'fin\ *vb*

Definitions

Technique

Troublesome Letter Combinations

If you still cannot locate a place-name, there are certain letter combinations to check:

- If you have a place starting with *Sh-* it surely must be an error for *Sch-*. German does not spell that sound as *Sh-*.
- If you have a consonant in the *c/ch/ck/g/k* group, check for variations of that spelling. If you can't find *Cusel* in the gazetteer, look for *Chusel*, *Gusel*, or *Kusel* for example. There is a *Kusel*.
- Another such group is *f/pf/ph*. If your place is *Phorzheim*, check for *Forzheim* or *Pforzheim*. There is a *Pforzheim*.
- A third group is *c/ts/tz/z*. Cell may be *Tsell*, *Tzell*, or *Zell*, and the last one is the most likely.
- Places in eastern German-speaking areas can have the combinations *cz/tsch/tzsch/zsch* (*Czarnikow, Tscharnikow, Tzscharnikow, Zscharnikow*).
- The *b/p* pair is often transposed, as in the case of *Bolle* or *Polle*.
- The group *f/v/w* is another that is easily confused, for example *Ferden*, *Verden*, and *Werden*.
- Some sounds can be represented in several ways. For instance, the letters *chs/cks/ks/x* can be found in *Luchsemburg, Lucksemburg, Luksemburg,* or *Luxemburg*.
- The dental sounds *d/t/th* are somewhat interchangeable, as in *Dierbach*, *Tierbach*, and *Thierbach*.
- Also try doubling vowels or adding the sign of a long vowel, which is an *h* (*Lor, Loor, Lohr*).

Equivalent Place-Names

Finally, some larger places have equivalent names in English. *Cologne* is actually *Köln* to the people who live there; *Prussia* was *Preußen/Preussen*; *Bavaria* is *Bayern*; the *Palatinate* is called *die Pfalz*; *Austria* is *Österreich*; *Switzerland* is called *die Schweiz*; *Berne* is *Bern*; *Munich* is *München*; *Vienna* is *Wien*; *Nuremberg* is *Nürnberg*; *Silesia* is *Schlesien*; *Poznan* is *Posen*; *Westphalia* is *Westfalen*. What is sometimes called *Aix-la-Chappelle* is *Aachen*; *Ratisbon* is *Regensburg*; *Treves* is *Trier*; *Spire* is *Speyer*; *Coblence* or *Coblentz* is *Koblenz*.

Name That Village

See Also

If you now couple your deciphering skills with the help of our terminology guide in chapter two and our handwriting guide in chapter six, you may be able to untangle the spelling of the German place-name as you have found it written. If you can't find the place-name in a good gazetteer, you need to be alert. At this point, according to Murpheimer's Law, you can rest assured that the correct spelling will fall into one of the following categories.

Tip

It is really a word meaning kingdom, province, county, church parish, or the like.

Some examples are *Königreich* (kingdom), *Bezirk* (district), *Gebiet* (region), *Oberamt* (county), *Amt* (county), *Kirchspiel* (church parish), *Gemeinde* (community, parish), *Grafschaft* (count's territory), *Fürstentum* (principality), *Herrschaft* (lordship), *Kurfürstentum* (electorate), *Herzogtum* (duchy), *Bistum* (bishopric).

It is really the name of a specific kingdom, province, county, church, parish, or the like, not a particular village.

These include *Bayern* (Bavaria), *Rheinbayern* (Rhine Bavaria), *Preußen* (Prussia), *Sachsen* (Saxony), *Württemberg* (Wuerttemberg), *Hessen* (Hesse), *Pfalz* (Palatinate), *Rheinpfalz* (Rhine Palatinate).

There are several places with the same name.

Altenkirchen (old church), *Neuhaus* (new house), *Grünberg* (green mountain), and *Steinbach* (stone creek) fall into this category.

There is interference from English or other languages, such as French.

Bingen could have been written by a native of Great Britain as *Bingham*. The Pennsylvania county clerk could have written *Lembach* as *Lamebaugh*. The Scottish-born minister could have written *Glayburgh* for *Kleeburg*. The French-speaking priest could have put *Erbershausen* for *Herbertshausen*, *Grumbretshoffe* for *Gumbrechtshoffen*, and *Pelican* for *Billigheim*.

There is interference from German dialects.

Your ancestor may have called it *Neinkirken* in his north German dialect, and that is the way the court clerk wrote it on his naturalization papers, but the place is shown on the maps as *Neuenkirchen*. Your ancestor from the Palatinate may have called it *Taschemoschel*, and the German-speaking minister from Saxony wrote it just as your ancestor said it, but it is shown on the maps as *Teschenmoschel*.

It is actually a translation of the place-name.

Newton was actually *Neustadt*. *Bruin's Rest* was actually *Bärenhütte*. *Borussia* is Latin for *Prussia*. *Treverorum* is Latin, referring to *Trier*. *Waslia* is Latin for *Wesel*. *Strasbourg* is the French name for *Straßburg*.

It is actually a legitimate variation of another place-name.

Gostyn is the same as *Gostingen*. *Litzmannstadt* is the same as *Lodz*. *Zuzemperk* is the same as *Seisenberg*. *Cröv* is the same as *Kröv*. *Coblentz* is the same as *Koblenz*.

There is a prefix or suffix that is generally used with it.

Allendorf is now *Stadtallendorf*. *Indersdorf* is now *Markt Indersdorf*. *Gütingen* is called *Dorfgütingen*. *Wimpfen* is now *Bad Wimpfen*. *Grehweiler* may be

Waldgrehweiler or *Gaugrehweiler*. On the other hand, *Preußisch Minden* is now just plain *Minden*. *Hannoversch Münden* is *Hann Münden* or *Münden*. *Ostercappeln* is called *Cappeln* for short. And lots of pairs of villages use *Groß* (big) and *Klein* (little), *Neu* (new) and *Alt* (old), *Ober* (upper) and *Nieder* or *Unter* (lower), or even *Mittel* (middle).

The entire village no longer exists.
Sespenroth was a village of button makers whose trade was lost when button factories came into being, so they went kit and caboodle to Wisconsin. *Ronnenberg* became part of the military training grounds at *Baumholder*. *Pappenberg* was lost to the military proving grounds near *Grafenwöhr*.

The name has changed.
Chemnitz became *Karl-Marx-Stadt* for the Communist period and is now back to *Chemnitz*. *Barmen* and *Elberfeld* merged to form *Wuppertal*. *Kirchheim* and *Bolanden* formed *Kirchheimbolanden*. *Idar* and *Oberstein* formed *Idar-Oberstein*.

FOUR

Visiting the Family History Library or a Family History Center

T his chapter prepares you for a trip to the world's largest genealogical repository, or to one of its many branches. We are headed to the Family History Library (FHL) in Salt Lake City or a Family History Center (FHC). Also known as LDS Family History Centers, these centers are located in many cities throughout the world. To find the center nearest you, contact your closest Church of Jesus Christ of Latter-day Saints and ask for the location and hours of operation of the closest center, or check the Web site at <**http:// www.familysearch.org**>. See the Online Searching section in this chapter for more details on this option.

Internet Source

These centers provide access to the world's largest genealogical collection through the FamilySearch databases. These databases make up the most complete and diverse genealogical data researching opportunities you will find on earth, and you will want to take full advantage of them. There are a number of different databases, but we will review four specific ones:

- IGI (International Genealogical Index)
- Ancestral File
- Locality Search (and films)
- Surname Search (and films)

At a Family History Center, sign up for one of its computers (the fastest searching method) or leisurely browse through its microfiche collections. The workers there are volunteers, but they are among the most patient and attentive volunteers you'll ever meet.

There is no charge to browse either the computer databases or the microfiche. There are minimal charges for film rental and other services if you need them. The volunteers can help you with a general explanation of services, as well as familiarize you with the databases, computers, microfiche reading machines, microfilm reading machines (both machines are called readers), and a number of genealogical forms and charts (from ten cents to a couple dollars). We really like the centers' fifteen-generation pedigree charts.

RESEARCH TOOLS

Supplies

Once again you'll need to assemble some tools to aid you in your research:

- this book (*A Genealogist's Guide to Discovering Your Germanic Ancestors*)
- pencils, pens
- a small journal or notebook
- a standard wireless notebook
- coins for copy machines
- cash for film rental and other fees (about three dollars per film; if you visit the main library in Salt Lake City, Utah, there is no rental fee)
- a working copy of your pedigree chart
- working copies of family group sheets
- your alphabetical list of surnames
- a magnifying glass (optional)

Why take this book with you? The step-by-step guide that follows will help make your visit more comfortable and will allow you to be more self-sufficient.

SCOPING OUT THE TERRITORY

Let's begin our introduction to the Family History Center with a review of the International Genealogical Index (IGI), which contains millions of birth, baptismal, marriage, will, and other records. It is the world's largest single genealogical database.

As huge as it is, it is unlikely that you will find a high percentage of your ancestors in the IGI; however, this and the other databases are added to and updated every few years. It is also important to note that this index generally covers only pre-1900 materials. That is one of the reasons we don't suggest starting your family search here. You've got to have the basics first.

You can travel through the databases at light speed or hiking speed, by either computer or microfiche reader. Which one for you on this first trip? If you want quickness, the computer is the way to go, but the computers are popular and often have time limits. If you don't like computer prompts, making screen decisions, or hit-this-button-to-get-the-cookie-type pressure, the microfiche are for you. See page 42 for an example. But microfiche require that you fish around the storage cabinets for the fiche for each locale, state by state. The computer lumps all fifty U.S. states together, so it's much more convenient.

Computer searches are more comprehensive and efficient than those using the microfiche. If you choose to search by computer, we can help you with our step-by-step methods. Still, choose the method that suits you.

If you are uncomfortable around computers, please remember that they have no teeth, no claws, no thorns! We have found the computer programs at the Family

History Centers to be user-friendly, and our step-by-step guide makes them even easier to use. If you give them a chance, you may be rewarded sevenfold.

When you first sit down at your computer, there are a series of introductory screens. Simply compare the screens with those that follow and you're on your way.

SEARCHING THE INTERNATIONAL GENEALOGICAL INDEX

Searching the IGI

(International Genealogical Index®)

    A. FamilySearch®
    B. Personal Ancestral File
    C. Word Perfect 5.1
    D. Extraction
    E. Microfilm Ordering Program

Screen 1. Menu
To open the FamilySearch program from this menu, press the A key.

Step By Step

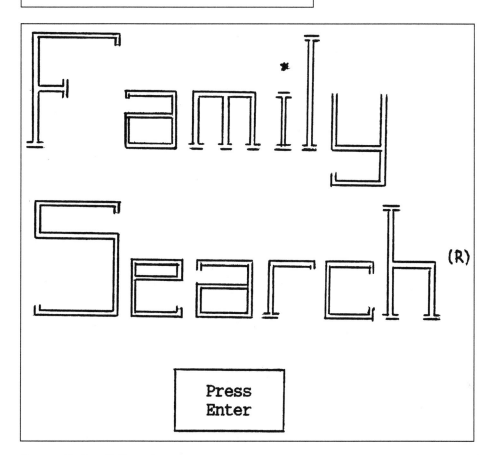

Press Enter

Screen 2. FamilySearch
Press the Enter key to see the FamilySearch Main Menu.

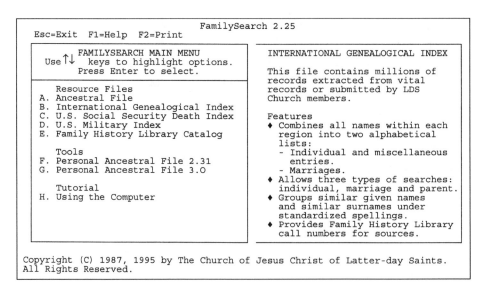

Screen 3. FamilySearch Main Menu

In the left box are the various databases in FamilySearch. Information in the right box is determined by what line is highlighted on the left. Since we want to examine the International Genealogical Index (IGI), move the cursor to item B. After reviewing the description of the IGI in the right box, press Enter or B.

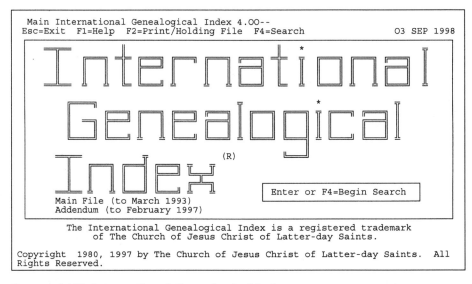

Screen 4-IGI. International Genealogical Index

Press Enter or the F4 key on the top row of your keyboard.

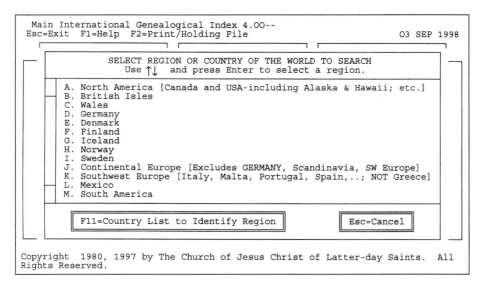

```
Main International Genealogical Index 4.00--
Esc=Exit  F1=Help  F2=Print/Holding File                03 SEP 1998

          SELECT REGION OR COUNTRY OF THE WORLD TO SEARCH
              Use ↑↓   and press Enter to select a region.

      A. North America [Canada and USA-including Alaska & Hawaii; etc.]
      B. British Isles
      C. Wales
      D. Germany
      E. Denmark
      F. Finland
      G. Iceland
      H. Norway
      I. Sweden
      J. Continental Europe [Excludes GERMANY, Scandinavia, SW Europe]
      K. Southwest Europe [Italy, Malta, Portugal, Spain,..; NOT Greece]
      L. Mexico
      M. South America


       F11=Country List to Identify Region        Esc=Cancel


Copyright  1980, 1997 by The Church of Jesus Christ of Latter-day Saints.  All
Rights Reserved.
```

Screen 5-IGI. Region or Country

Look at your thirteen options. You need to begin your search close to home to confirm information you already have and to find much more information in the states before you are ready to search in other countries. So begin your search in North America (select key A). Once you've thoroughly checked North America, you're ready for Germany (choice D), which is the example we'll use. The formats for Germany and North America are basically the same.

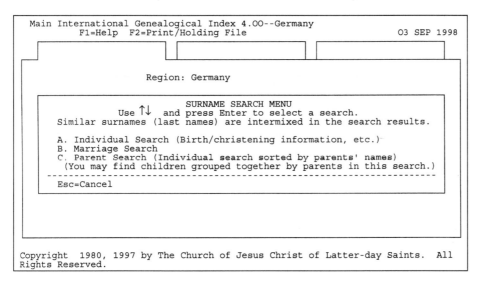

```
Main International Genealogical Index 4.00--Germany
         F1=Help  F2=Print/Holding File              03 SEP 1998




              Region: Germany


                      SURNAME SEARCH MENU
             Use ↑↓  and press Enter to select a search.
       Similar surnames (last names) are intermixed in the search results.

       A. Individual Search (Birth/christening information, etc.)
       B. Marriage Search
       C. Parent Search (Individual search sorted by parents' names)
        (You may find children grouped together by parents in this search.)
       ---------------------------------------------------------------
       Esc=Cancel




Copyright  1980, 1997 by The Church of Jesus Christ of Latter-day Saints.  All
Rights Reserved.
```

Screen 6-IGI. Surname Search Menu

You have three options here: Individual Search, Marriage Search, and Parent Search. You may easily search through any of these three options while using the IGI (you will see the options listed at the top of screens 8-IGI, 10-IGI, and 11-IGI). You will proceed more efficiently as you learn the skill of moving from one option to another in your search. It's a regular treasure hunt. To get started, press A, for Individual Search.

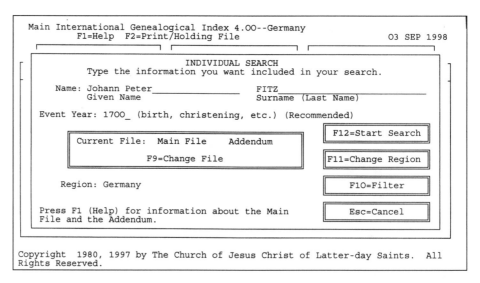

```
Main International Genealogical Index 4.00--Germany
        F1=Help  F2=Print/Holding File                      03 SEP 1998

                        INDIVIDUAL SEARCH
              Type the information you want included in your search.

        Name: Johann Peter_____    FITZ_____
              Given Name                       Surname (Last Name)

        Event Year: 1700_ (birth, christening, etc.) (Recommended)

                                                    ┌──────────────────┐
        ┌─────────────────────────────────────┐    │ F12=Start Search │
        │  Current File:  Main File   Addendum│    └──────────────────┘
        │                                      │    ┌──────────────────┐
        │          F9=Change File              │    │ F11=Change Region│
        └─────────────────────────────────────┘    └──────────────────┘

        Region: Germany                              ┌──────────────────┐
                                                     │    F10=Filter    │
                                                     └──────────────────┘
        Press F1 (Help) for information about the Main    ┌──────────────┐
        File and the Addendum.                            │  Esc=Cancel  │
                                                          └──────────────┘
```

Screen 7-IGI. Individual Search

In Screen 7-IGI, you will enter the name of any individual you want to search. Type in the first (given) name of one of your ancestors who came from Germany, and press the Enter key. It is not necessary to capitalize as the computer handles that for you automatically. Now, type in the ancestor's last name (surname) and press Enter. We will use Johann Peter Fitz for our example. Next, type in the approximate year of that person's birth, 1700. If you are unsure of that information, as is often the case, try to estimate. If you guess incorrectly, don't worry; you can move forward or backward chronologically through the next screen.

Press Enter or the F12 key located on the top row of the keyboard. If the data is not stored in the hard drive, you will be using a CD-ROM system and will be instructed to find a specific compact disc and place it into the disc drive of the computer. In some Family History Centers, this step may not be necessary because the discs are on a hard drive or changer.

From this screen on, the IGI can provide data that has been added since the disc was created. Select the F9 key to access this additional information.

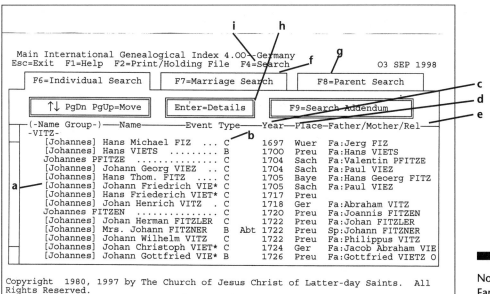

```
                                                    i              h
Main International Genealogical Index 4.00-Germany            g
Esc=Exit  F1=Help  F2=Print/Holding File  F4=Search  f              03 SEP 1998

    F6=Individual Search        F7=Marriage Search        F8=Parent Search            c
                                                                                       d
    ↑↓ PgDn PgUp=Move         Enter=Details        F9=Search Addendum                  e

  (-Name Group-)——Name————Event Type——Year——Place-Father/Mother/Rel—
  -VITZ-                                        b
      [Johannes] Hans Michael FIZ  ... C    1697  Wuer  Fa:Jerg FIZ
      [Johannes] Hans VIETS ......... B    1700  Preu  Fa:Hans VIETS
      Johannes PFITZE .............. C    1704  Sach  Fa:Valentin PFITZE
      [Johannes] Johann Georg VIEZ  .. C    1704  Sach  Fa:Paul VIEZ
      [Johannes] Hans Thom. FITZ  .... C    1705  Baye  Fa:Hans Geoerg FITZ
a     [Johannes] Johann Friedrich VIE* C   1705  Sach  Fa:Paul VIEZ
      [Johannes] Hans Friederich VIET* C   1717  Preu
      [Johannes] Johan Henrich VITZ  . C    1718  Ger   Fa:Abraham VITZ
      Johannes FITZEN .............. C    1720  Preu  Fa:Joannis FITZEN
      [Johannes] Johan Herman FITZLER  C    1722  Preu  Fa:Johan FITZLER
      [Johannes] Mrs. Johann FITZNER   B Abt 1722  Preu  Sp:Johann FITZNER
      [Johannes] Johann Wilhelm VITZ   C    1722  Preu  Fa:Philippus VITZ
      [Johannes] Johan Christoph VIET* C    1724  Ger   Fa:Jacob Abraham VIE
      [Johannes] Johann Gottfried VIE* B    1726  Preu  Fa:Gottfried VIETZ O

Copyright  1980, 1997 by The Church of Jesus Christ of Latter-day Saints.  All
Rights Reserved.
```

Warning

Screen 8-IGI. Name Index

This screen shows an infinitesimal section of an alphabetical listing of all the people who have records placed in the IGI. Here's how to decipher the information you're seeing.

a = Name. Similar surnames (Smith, Smyth, Smythe, Smithe) are often listed together, so don't be surprised by the variety of spellings.

b = Event Type. This is the type of record, such as *B* for birth, *C* for christening or baptism, *W* for will.

c = Year. This indicates the year of the record.

d = Place. This tells where the record was recorded. When accessing U.S. records, note that prior to some areas becoming states, their records would have been included in another state. For example, West Virginia did not become its own state until 1863. If you wanted a record for 1850, you would most likely find that record in Virginia. For Germany, this is even more difficult. Review historic Germanic maps so you can better interpret the regions (fifteen states currently) and hopefully avoid getting confused regarding the political areas in Germany. Many of these areas have changed dramatically over the years.

e = Relation. Usually, this will be the father's name (see item h below).

f = Press F7, located on the top row of your keyboard, to find a possible marriage for the person you have highlighted. (See Screen 10-IGI.)

g = Press F8 to find possible siblings of the highlighted person. (See Screen 11-IGI.)

h = Press Enter to find the month and year, town, parish, county, and father and mother of the highlighted person, if that data is known here. (See Screen 9-IGI.)

i = Press F4 when you want to stop looking here and start a search for another ancestor. This will take you to Screen 6-IGI. Follow the directions

Note that the FamilySearch program uses the German geographic divisions of the 1871–1918 German Empire, not the current ones. Be especially wary of using current maps for Bayern (Bavaria) or Preussen (Prussia) because the geographic areas have changed significantly, as pointed out in chapter five.

and enter the next ancestor you are searching for and proceed from Screen 6-IGI again.

Since we don't see our Johann Peter Fitz listed here, we selected F4. That took us back to Screen 6-IGI, where we selected A and entered *Peter Fitz* (on Screen 7-IGI). This exercise was not productive either. For illustration purposes, let's look at [Johannes] Hans VIETS, born in 1700. You may press the arrow keys or PgDn (page down) and PgUp (page up) keys to move around on this screen. Once you find a name you want to investigate, be sure to move the arrow keys until the cursor (a shaded, colored, or highlighted horizontal strip) covers the name of the person you are researching. This step is important for ensuring that future screens relate to the individual you want to investigate. Once you highlight a name, you have many options, including Enter for details, F7 for marriage search, and F8 for parent search. See screens 9-IGI, 10-IGI, and 11-IGI.

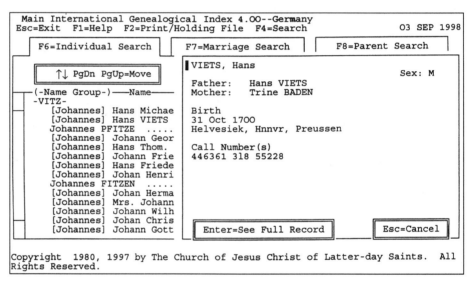

```
Main International Genealogical Index 4.00--Germany
Esc=Exit  F1=Help  F2=Print/Holding File  F4=Search        03 SEP 1998

   F6=Individual Search      F7=Marriage Search      F8=Parent Search

                                  VIETS, Hans
         ↑↓ PgDn PgUp=Move                                    Sex: M

   (-Name Group-)———Name———     Father:    Hans VIETS
   -VITZ-                       Mother:    Trine BADEN
     [Johannes] Hans Michae
     [Johannes] Hans VIETS      Birth
     Johannes PFITZE  .....     31 Oct 1700
     [Johannes] Johann Geor     Helvesiek, Hnnvr, Preussen
     [Johannes] Hans Thom.
     [Johannes] Johann Frie     Call Number(s)
     [Johannes] Hans Friede     446361 318 55228
     [Johannes] Johan Henri
     Johannes FITZEN  .....
     [Johannes] Johan Herma
     [Johannes] Mrs. Johann
     [Johannes] Johann Wilh
     [Johannes] Johan Chris      Enter=See Full Record      Esc=Cancel
     [Johannes] Johann Gott

Copyright  1980, 1997 by The Church of Jesus Christ of Latter-day Saints.  All
Rights Reserved.
```

Screen 9-IGI. Details
Press Enter for more details of this record.

Press Esc when you want to return to Screen 8-IGI. You may select F7 for a marriage search (see Screen 10-IGI), or F8 for a parent search (see Screen 11-IGI).

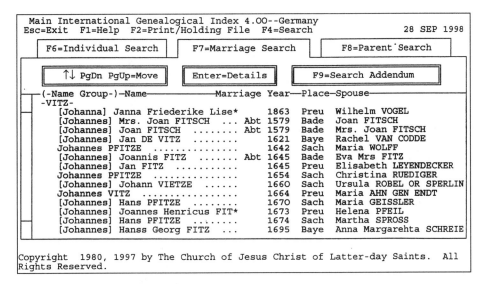

```
Main International Genealogical Index 4.00--Germany
Esc=Exit  F1=Help  F2=Print/Holding File  F4=Search        28 SEP 1998
   ┌─────────────────────┐ ┌───────────────────┐ ┌─────────────────────┐
   │ F6=Individual Search│ │ F7=Marriage Search│ │ F8=Parent Search    │
   └─────────────────────┘ └───────────────────┘ └─────────────────────┘
   ┌─────────────────────┐ ┌───────────────────┐ ┌─────────────────────┐
   │ ↑↓ PgDn PgUp=Move   │ │  Enter=Details    │ │  F9=Search Addendum │
   └─────────────────────┘ └───────────────────┘ └─────────────────────┘
   (-Name Group-)-Name───────────Marriage Year──Place─Spouse──────
   -VITZ-
      [Johanna] Janna Friederike Lise*     1863   Preu  Wilhelm VOGEL
      [Johannes] Mrs. Joan FITSCH ... Abt 1579   Bade  Joan FITSCH
      [Johannes] Joan FITSCH ........ Abt 1579   Bade  Mrs. Joan FITSCH
      [Johannes] Jan DE VITZ ........     1621   Baye  Rachel VAN CODDE
      Johannes PFITZE .............     1642   Sach  Maria WOLFF
      [Johannes] Joannis FITZ ....... Abt 1645   Bade  Eva Mrs FITZ
      [Johannes] Jan FITZ ..........     1645   Preu  Elisabeth LEYENDECKER
      Johannes PFITZE .............     1654   Sach  Christina RUEDIGER
      [Johannes] Johann VIETZE ......     1660   Sach  Ursula ROBEL OR SPERLIN
      Johannes VITZ ...............     1664   Preu  Maria AHN GEN ENDT
      [Johannes] Hans PFITZE ........     1670   Sach  Maria GEISSLER
      [Johannes] Joannes Henricus FIT*     1673   Preu  Helena PFEIL
      [Johannes] Hans PFITZE .......     1674   Sach  Martha SPROSS
      [Johannes] Hanss Georg FITZ ...     1695   Baye  Anna Margarehta SCHREIE

Copyright  1980, 1997 by The Church of Jesus Christ of Latter-day Saints.  All
Rights Reserved.
```

Screen 10-IGI. Marriage Record

This is what appears when you select F7 at Screen 8-IGI. From left to right, we see the individual's name, the year of the marriage, the place (usually the German state) of the marriage, and the spouse's name.

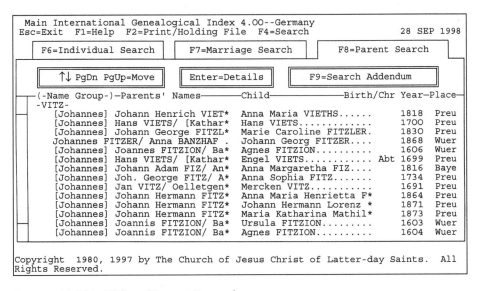

```
Main International Genealogical Index 4.00--Germany
Esc=Exit  F1=Help  F2=Print/Holding File  F4=Search        28 SEP 1998
   ┌─────────────────────┐ ┌───────────────────┐ ┌─────────────────────┐
   │ F6=Individual Search│ │ F7=Marriage Search│ │ F8=Parent Search    │
   └─────────────────────┘ └───────────────────┘ └─────────────────────┘
   ┌─────────────────────┐ ┌───────────────────┐ ┌─────────────────────┐
   │ ↑↓ PgDn PgUp=Move   │ │  Enter=Details    │ │  F9=Search Addendum │
   └─────────────────────┘ └───────────────────┘ └─────────────────────┘
   (-Name Group-)─Parents' Names────────Child──────────Birth/Chr Year─Place─
   -VITZ-
      [Johannes] Johann Henrich VIET*  Anna Maria VIETHS......     1818  Preu
      [Johannes] Hans VIETS/ [Kathar*  Hans VIETS............     1700  Preu
      [Johannes] Johann George FITZL*  Marie Caroline FITZLER.     1830  Preu
      Johannes FITZER/ Anna BANZHAF .  Johann Georg FITZER....     1868  Wuer
      [Johannes] Joannes FITZION/ Ba*  Agnes FITZION.........     1606  Wuer
      [Johannes] Hans VIETS/ [Kathar*  Engel VIETS........... Abt 1699  Preu
      [Johannes] Johann Adam FIZ/ An*  Anna Margaretha FIZ....     1816  Baye
      [Johannes] Joh. George FITZ/ A*  Anna Sophia FITZ.......     1734  Preu
      [Johannes] Jan VITZ/ Oelletgen*  Mercken VITZ..........     1691  Preu
      [Johannes] Johann Hermann FITZ*  Anna Maria Henrietta F*     1864  Preu
      [Johannes] Johann Hermann FITZ*  Johann Hermann Lorenz *     1871  Preu
      [Johannes] Johann Hermann FITZ*  Maria Katharina Mathil*     1873  Preu
      [Johannes] Joannis FITZION/ Ba*  Ursula FITZION........     1603  Wuer
      [Johannes] Joannis FITZION/ Ba*  Agnes FITZION.........     1604  Wuer

Copyright  1980, 1997 by The Church of Jesus Christ of Latter-day Saints.  All
Rights Reserved.
```

Screen 11-IGI. Sibling/Parent Record

This is what appears when you select F8 at Screen 8-IGI. From left to right, we see the name of the parents (usually cut off, so use the Enter key to see both parents' names, then the Esc key to return here), the child's name, the year of the child's birth or christening, and the place of the event. (To see the information as it appears on microfiche, see page 42.)

To go from one regional database to another (such as North America to Germany), press Esc (the escape key). You will be asked if you want to return to the beginning of this program (Screen 4-IGI) or to the main menu (Screen 3). Choose "back to the beginning of this program." Once there, press Enter to access Screen 5-IGI. Then select the appropriate region.

a = name

b = sex/relation

c = type of event

d = event date

e = place of event

f = B, E, S (LDS church data)

g = source (important information for film orders)

Tip

Microfiche sample

The Holding File and Copying Materials

As you travel through the IGI database, you may find information that you want to keep. Rather than writing the data in your notebook, you have the option of getting a printout of the record. **When you find an item you want to save, you can place it into a "holding file."** After you have placed all the items you want in your file, you can print the records. Note that if you change databases from the IGI to any other database (see Screen 3), such as the Ancestral File, your holding file will be lost, so be sure to print your holding file before moving to the next database. Only the IGI has a holding file. No other FHC database has one. See Screen 12-IGI below for an example, and then we'll show you how to place items into your own holding file.

```
International Genealogical Index (R) - Version 4.00

03 SEP 1998                        HOLDING FILE ENTRIES                        Page 1
==================================================================================================

                                                              Batch and Source
Names (Sex)                    Event Date/Place               Information
--------------------------------------------------------------------------------------------------
Hans VIETS (M)...................... B: 31 Oct 1700                F#: 446361         @
   Father: Hans VIETS               Helvesiek, Hnnvr, Preussen    P#: 318
   Mother: Trine BADEN                                            O#: 55228

Johannes PFITZE (M)................. C: 28 Dec 1704                Ba: 7816420 33
   Father: Valentin PFITZE          Kiebitz, Leipzig, Sachsen     So: 1126328
   Mother: Maria GRAUPNITZ

Johann Georg VIEZ (M)............... C: 1 Jan 1704                 Ba: 1390079 92
   Father: Paul VIEZ                Brambach, Zwickau, Sachsen     So: 1395924

Hans Thom. FITZ (M)................. C: 20 Jan 1705                Ba: C989581
   Father: Hans Geoerg FITZ         Evangelisch, Kapellen-drusweiler,  So: 193930
   Mother: Margar.                  Pfalz, Bayern

Johann Friedrich VIEZ (M)........... C: 14 Aug 1705               Ba: 1390079 46
   Father: Paul VIEZ                Brambach, Zwickau, Sachsen     So: 1395924

Hans Friederich VIETS (M)........... C: 30 Nov 1717               F#: 1761056        *
   (no parents listed)              Evangelisch, Holzhausen Minden,
                                    Westfalen, Preussen

Johan Henrich VITZ (M).............. C: 20 Mar 1718               Ba: J990321
   Father: Abraham VITZ             Evangelisch, Barntrup, Lippe,  So: 809896
                                    Germany

Johannes FITZEN (M)................. C: 18 Apr 1720               Ba: C987891
   Father: Joannis FITZEN           Sankt Viktor Katholisch, Birten,  So: 893090
   Mother: Elisabethae PAGLANDTS    Rheinland, Preussen

==================================================================================================
     Events:   A=Adult Chr  B=Birth  C=Chr  D=Death  M=Marr  S=Misc  N=Census  W=Will
  Batch/Source: Ba=Batch  So=Source  Pr=Printout  F#=Film Number  P#=Page Number  O#=Ordinance Number
Special Symbols: * Film contains no additional information.   ^ Some information was estimated or altered.
                @ Names and relationships of others stated in source.   & Parents listed may not be birth parents.
                > Additional information from Special Services, Temple Dept.   # Additional relatives listed in source.
                + Additional sources for batch.
==================================================================================================
Copyright © 1980, 1997 by The Church of Jesus Christ of Latter-day Saints.  All rights reserved.
```

Screen 12-IGI. Holding File Printout

This screen lists the contents of a holding file. In the first column is the name of the individual, under which is the name of the person's father and mother (if known) for birth and baptismal records, or the name of the spouse for marriage records. The second column shares the date and place of the event, normally giving the day, month, and year, and the village, county/parish/district, and state. The third column includes the batch and serial number, which are necessary to order a copy of the record from the librarian.

```
                    PRINT/HOLDING FILE


        Use ↑↓ and press Enter to select an option.



        A. Print Individual Record (highlighted person)
        B. Print screen only
        C. Advance paper in printer
        D. Cancel current print job

        HOLDING FILE
        Select a group of records to print or copy.


        E. Create or add entries to the Holding File
        F. View Holding File and delete entries
        G. Erase Holding File
        H. Print Holding File
        I. Copy Holding File to diskette


        Esc = Cancel
```

Screen HF-1. Print/Holding File

To place an item into your holding file, highlight that item with your cursor as before. Then press F2, which is the Print/Holding File function, to see Screen HF-1. This screen shows you some options regarding your file. Press E to create your holding file. A box containing holding file information will appear in the right lower section of your screen. This box gives you directions for putting records in your file and keeps count of them too.

Line up the highlight bar on the record that you want entered into your holding file and press Enter. We'll put eight consecutive entries into our example file, from Hans Viets to Johannes Fitzen.

Press F12 to stop making entries and you're back at Screen HF-1 above. Press F (View Holding File) to view what you have entered.

```
┌─────────────────────────────────────────────────────────────┐
│                                                               │
│                  VIEW HOLDING FILE                            │
│                                                               │
│                                                               │
│   VIETS, Hans              B. 1700 Preu     Fa.               │
│   PFITZE, Johannes         C. 1704 Sach     Fa.               │
│   VIEZ, Johann Georg       C. 1704 Sach     Fa.               │
│   FITZ, Hans Thom.         C. 1705 Baye     Fa.               │
│   VIEZ, Johann Friedrich   C. 1705 Sach     Fa.               │
│   VIETS, Hans Friederich   C. 1717 Preu     Fa.               │
│   VITZ, Johan Henrich      C. 1718 Ger      Fa.               │
│   FITZEN, Johannes         C. 1720 Preu     Fa.               │
│                                                               │
└─────────────────────────────────────────────────────────────┘
```

Screen HF-2. View Holding File

After verifying your entries, press F12 to return to Screen HF-1. You are now ready to print your holding file, which, in our example, contains eight items. You can place hundreds of entries into your holding file, and you can place entries in your holding file from multiple regions as long as you stay within the IGI. But remember our earlier tip: Confine your printout to one surname for ease in filing your information later. The records print one after the other; each record will not print on a separate page. See Screen 12-IGI again for a review of a printout.

Press H to initiate the print process. The next screen asks you to confirm the print process. Press F12 to begin printing. There is a small charge for copies, but the copies (about 25 cents each) are real time-savers.

SEARCHING THE ANCESTRAL FILE

The Ancestral File is a compilation of entries submitted by individuals (not just LDS members) listing their relatives. Living individuals are shown only if they are LDS members and specifically give permission. Your distant relative may have submitted your mutual relatives to this file. To access the Ancestral File, follow the previous IGI search through Screens 1 and 2. At Screen 3, move the cursor to item A (Ancestral File). That will show you Screen 3-AF.

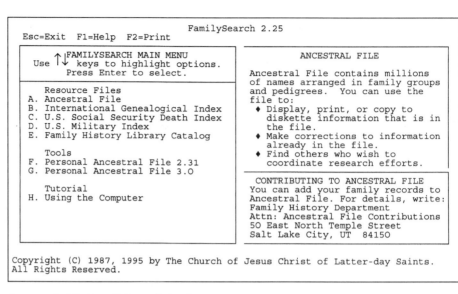

Screen 3-AF. FamilySearch Main Menu

Press A on your keyboard.

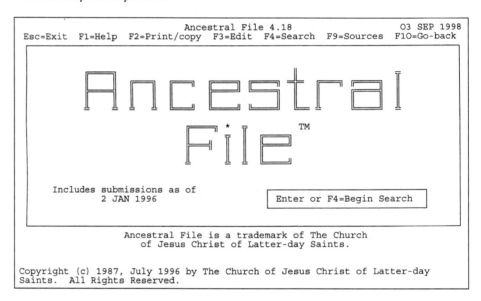

Screen 4-AF. Ancestral File

Press the Enter or F4 key. In the next screen (not shown), select A for Similar Surname. That will take you to Screen 5-AF.

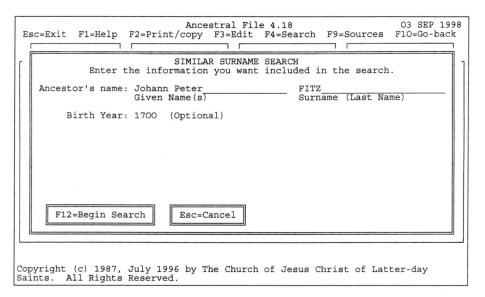

```
                          Ancestral File 4.18                   03 SEP 1998
     Esc=Exit  F1=Help  F2=Print/copy  F3=Edit  F4=Search  F9=Sources  F10=Go-back

                            SIMILAR SURNAME SEARCH
                  Enter the information you want included in the search.

       Ancestor's name: Johann Peter_____        FITZ_____
                        Given Name(s)               Surname (Last Name)

             Birth Year: 1700  (Optional)




            ┌────────────────────┐    ┌──────────────────┐
            │  F12=Begin Search   │    │   Esc=Cancel     │
            └────────────────────┘    └──────────────────┘


     Copyright (c) 1987, July 1996 by The Church of Jesus Christ of Latter-day
     Saints.  All Rights Reserved.
```

Screen 5-AF. Similar Surname Search

Enter the name of the individual you wish to locate. For our example, we will use Johann Peter Fitz, born about 1700. As in the IGI, the computer automatically capitalizes, so just type in the information. Then press F12. Insert the disc into the CD-ROM drive if requested.

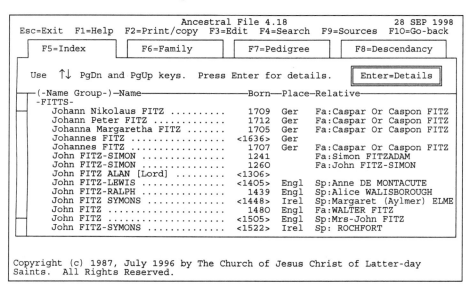

```
                          Ancestral File 4.18                   28 SEP 1998
     Esc=Exit  F1=Help  F2=Print/copy  F3=Edit  F4=Search  F9=Sources  F10=Go-back
     ┌──────────────┐  ┌──────────────┐  ┌──────────────┐  ┌──────────────────┐
     │  F5=Index    │  │  F6=Family   │  │  F7=Pedigree │  │  F8=Descendancy  │

       Use   ↑↓  PgDn and PgUp keys.  Press Enter for details.   ┌──────────────┐
                                                                 │ Enter=Details│
                                                                 └──────────────┘
     ┌(-Name Group-)─Name─────────────────Born──Place─Relative──────────────
      -FITTS-
          Johann Nikolaus FITZ .......... 1709   Ger   Fa:Caspar Or Caspon FITZ
          Johann Peter FITZ ............. 1712   Ger   Fa:Caspar Or Caspon FITZ
          Johanna Margaretha FITZ ....... 1705   Ger   Fa:Caspar Or Caspon FITZ
          Johannes FITZ ................. <1636> Ger
          Johannes FITZ ................. 1707   Ger   Fa:Caspar Or Caspon FITZ
          John FITZ-SIMON ............... 1241         Fa:Simon FITZADAM
          John FITZ-SIMON ............... 1260         Fa:John FITZ-SIMON
          John FITZ ALAN [Lord] ......... <1306>
          John FITZ-LEWIS ............... <1405> Engl  Sp:Anne DE MONTACUTE
          John FITZ-RALPH ............... 1439   Engl  Sp:Alice WALISBOROUGH
          John FITZ SYMONS .............. <1448> Irel  Sp:Margaret (Aylmer) ELME
          John FITZ ..................... 1480   Engl  Fa:WALTER FITZ
          John FITZ ..................... <1505> Engl  Sp:Mrs-John FITZ
          John FITZ-SYMONS .............. <1522> Irel  Sp: ROCHFORT


     Copyright (c) 1987, July 1996 by The Church of Jesus Christ of Latter-day
     Saints.  All Rights Reserved.
```

Screen 6-AF. Ancestral File Index

Here we find a Johann Peter Fitz. He was born in 1712. Highlight his name and press Enter to see more details that confirm that this is indeed the ancestor we have been trying to find. We can gather more information by highlighting his entry and pressing F6 for a Family Group Record (see Screens 7-AF, 8-AF, and 9-AF), F7 for a Pedigree Chart (see Screen 11-AF), or F8 for a Descendancy Chart (see Screen 10-AF).

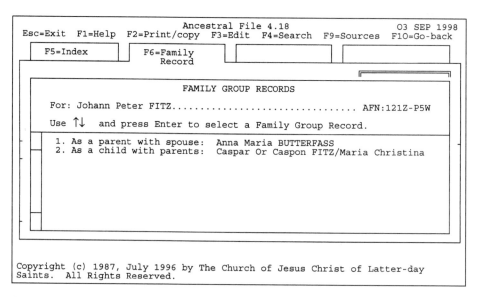

Screen 7-AF. Family Group Records

This is what appears when we select F6 at Screen 6-AF. We are given two choices to search: Johann Peter Fitz as a parent with his spouse, Anna Maria Butterfass, or as a child with his parents, Caspar Fitz and Maria Christina (maiden name unknown). We will highlight option 2 and press Enter.

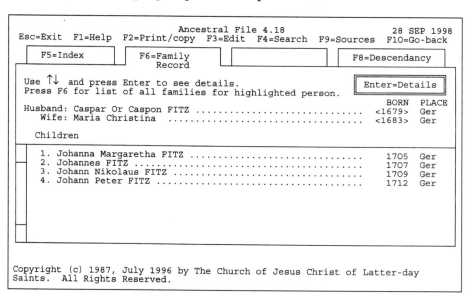

Screen 8-AF. Family Record

From this screen, we see that Johann Peter Fitz is the fourth and youngest child (of those listed) of Caspar Fitz and his wife, Maria Christina. You can get more details by highlighting any name and pressing Enter.

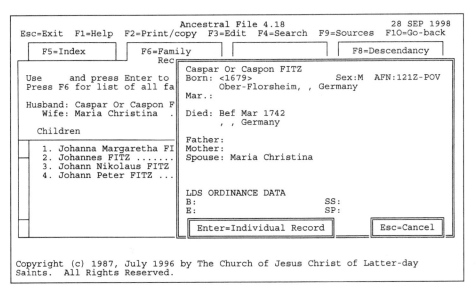

```
                    Ancestral File 4.18                28 SEP 1998
      Esc=Exit  F1=Help  F2=Print/copy  F3=Edit  F4=Search  F9=Sources  F10=Go-back

          F5=Index          F6=Family                          F8=Descendancy
                             Rec┌──────────────────────────────────────────────┐
      Use      and press Enter to │ Caspar Or Caspon FITZ                         │
      Press F6 for list of all fa │ Born: <1679>                  Sex:M  AFN:121Z-POV │
                                  │       Ober-Florsheim, , Germany               │
      Husband: Caspar Or Caspon F │ Mar.:                                         │
         Wife: Maria Christina  . │                                               │
                                  │ Died: Bef Mar 1742                            │
         Children                 │       , , Germany                             │
                                  │                                               │
      ┌──────────────────────────┐│ Father:                                       │
      │  1. Johanna Margaretha FI ││ Mother:                                       │
      │  2. Johannes FITZ ....... ││ Spouse: Maria Christina                       │
      │  3. Johann Nikolaus FITZ  ││                                               │
      │  4. Johann Peter FITZ ... ││                                               │
      │                           ││ LDS ORDINANCE DATA                            │
      │                           ││ B:                        SS:                 │
      │                           ││ E:                        SP:                 │
      │                           ││                                               │
      │                           ││ ┌──────────────────────┐ ┌──────────────┐    │
      └──────────────────────────┘│ │ Enter=Individual Record│ │ Esc=Cancel   │   │
                                  │ └──────────────────────┘ └──────────────┘    │
                                  └──────────────────────────────────────────────┘

      Copyright (c) 1987, July 1996 by The Church of Jesus Christ of Latter-day
      Saints.  All Rights Reserved.
```

Screen 9-AF. Details

These are the details on Johann Peter Fitz's father, Caspar Fitz. After reviewing the details of each person in whom you have interest, press Esc on your keyboard. This returns you to Screen 8-AF. The name Caspar Fitz should still be highlighted. Now press F8 to create a descendancy chart for him.

The next screen (not shown) will confirm the individual, stating, "You have chosen to build a Descendancy Chart for: Caspar Fitz." You will then be asked how many generations you want to view. For our example, we will choose five, the maximum number available per search. Select 5, then press Enter. You may be asked to place discs in the CD-ROM drive. There may be a number of requests as the computer accesses different files in compiling your chart.

```
Ancestral File (TM) - ver 4.18                  DESCENDANCY CHART                    28 SEP 1998      Page 1
==================================================================================================================
Caspar Or Caspon FITZ (121Z-P0V)      Born: <1679> Ober-Florsheim, , Germany
==================================================================================================================
1-- Caspar Or Caspon FITZ (121Z-P0V)      Born: <1679> Ober-Florsheim, , Germany
 sp-Maria Christina  (121Z-P13)      Born: <1683> <Ober-Florsheim, , Germany>
  2-- Johanna Margaretha FITZ (121Z-P29)      Born:  7 Sep 1705 Ober-Florsheim, , Germany
  2-- Johannes FITZ (121Z-P3H)      Born: 21 Oct 1707 Ober-Florsheim, , Germany
  2-- Johann Nikolaus FITZ (121Z-P4P)      Born: 23 Jan 1709 Ober-Florsheim, , Germany
  2-- Johann Peter FITZ (121Z-P5W)      Born: 18 Sep 1712 Ober-Florsheim, , Germany
   sp-Anna Maria BUTTERFASS (121Z-MGF)      Born: <1716> Nieder-Florsheim, , Germany
    3-- Johann Balthasar FITZ (121Z-PT2)      Born: 14 May 1738 Ober-Florsheim, , Germany
     sp-Elizabeth SHULTZ (121Z-PV8)      Born: <1742> <Ober-Florsheim, , Germany>
      4-- Magdalena FITZ (121Z-PWG)      Born: <1744> <Ober-Florsheim, , Germany>
      4-- Anna Magdalena FITZ (121Z-PXN)      Born:  5 Oct 1746 Ober-Florsheim, , Germany
      4-- Mary FITZ (121Z-PZV)      Born: <1748> <Ober-Florsheim, , Germany>
      4-- Christiana FITZ (121Z-Q02)      Born: <1750> <Ober-Florsheim, , Germany>
      4-- Barbara FITZ (121Z-Q18)      Born: <1752> <Ober-Florsheim, , Germany>
      4-- Elizabeth FITZ (121Z-Q2G)      Born: <1754> <Ober-Florsheim, , Germany>
      4-- Susanna FITZ (121Z-Q3N)      Born: <1756> <Ober-Florsheim, , Germany>
      4-- Jacob FITZ (121Z-Q4V)      Born: <1758> <Ober-Florsheim, , Germany>
    3-- Johann Leonhard FITZ (121Z-MJT)      Born: 22 Aug 1739 Ober-Florsheim, , Germany
    3-- Katharina Elisabetha FITZ (121Z-MK2)      Born: 22 May 1742 <Ober-Florsheim, , Germany>
    3-- Johann Friedrich FITZ (121Z-ML8)      Born:  6 Sep 1744 Ober-Florsheim, , Germany
     sp-Elizabeth  (121Z-LZC)      Born: <1748> <Ober-Florsheim, , Germany>
      4-- John FITZ (121Z-M0J)      Born: 11 Apr 1775 <Ober-Florsheim, , Germany>
       sp-Catherine ROTH (121Z-Z2N)      Born: 11 Feb 1779 <, York, PA>
        5-- Susanna FITZ (121Z-7TM)      Born: <1804> <, York, PA>
        5-- Elizabeth FITZ (121Z-7VT)      Born: <1806> <, York, PA>
        5-- Samuel FITZ (XC18-F5)      Born: 16 May 1808 , York, PA
         sp-Sarah E KITZMILLER (XC18-GB)      Born: 13 Mar 1817 , York, PA
         sp-Catherine KITZMILLER (121Z-QXT)      Born: <1812> <, York, PA>
        5-- Barbara FITZ (121Z-7X8)      Born: <1810> <, York, PA>
        5-- Nancy FITZ (121Z-7ZG)      Born: <1812> <, York Co., Pennsylvania>
        5-- John FITZ (121Z-MNN)      Born:  5 Mar 1817 , York Co., Pennsylvania
         sp-Mary Ann DUBS (121Z-MTP)      Born: 14 Jun 1816 , , Pennsylvania
         sp-Mary C. YEAST (121Z-MPV)      Born: 17 Jun 1838 , , Maryland
      4-- Barbara FITZ (121Z-M1Q)      Born: <1777> <, York, PA>
      4-- Maria Or Mary FITZ (121Z-M2X)      Born: <1779> <, York, PA>
      4-- Susanna FITZ (121Z-M35)      Born: <1781> <, York, PA>
      4-- Elizabeth FITZ (121Z-M4C)      Born: <1783> <, York, PA>
      4-- Nancy FITZ (121Z-M5K)      Born: <1785> <, York, PA>
      4-- Peter FITZ (121Z-M70)      Born: Abt 1788 <, York, PA>
       sp-Mary  (121Z-M86)      Born: <1792>
        5-- Jacob FITZ (121Z-M9D)      Born:  4 Apr 1814
        5-- Joseph FITZ (121Z-MBL)      Born: 12 Nov 1816
        5-- Frederick FITZ (121Z-MCS)      Born: 15 Dec 1818
        5-- Mary FITZ (121Z-MD1)      Born: 25 Nov 1821
    3-- Johann Heinrich FITZ (121Z-MMG)      Born: 15 Aug 1748 <Ober-Florsheim, , Germany>
==================================================================================================================
Copyright (c) 1987, July 1996 by The Church of Jesus Christ of Latter-day Saints.  All rights reserved.
```

Screen 10-AF. Descendancy Chart

This is what appears when we select F8 at Screen 6-AF. The descendancy chart first lists the ancestor you highlighted on Screen 8-AF as "1-- Caspar Or Caspon FITZ." Following his name is his ancestral number (assigned to him by the person submitting the data), followed by his birth date and place. His spouse is listed on the next line ("sp-Maria Christina"). His children are denoted by "2--," his grandchildren by "3--," and so forth.

This program works in either direction. We arrived at this database knowing Johann Peter Fitz. We then found a record for his father, Caspar Fitz, and using that name, we created a descendancy chart. Had we only known Johann Peter Fitz's great-grandson, John Fitz (born in 1817), we could have looked backward through the family history by creating a pedigree chart (see Screen 11-AF).

Through the descendancy chart, you may find numerous other relatives. As a part of the descendancy search, you can ask the computer for its sources, who submitted the information, their addresses, the names of other interested researchers, their addresses, and a history of the changes made to the record. **You want to know who else is researching your ancestor so you can contact them regarding their sources of information.** If any changes were made, you want to know which is considered more accurate. To print a copy, press F2.

Important

Next, let's have the computer prepare a pedigree chart. In our example, Caspar Fitz is the earliest known Fitz, so requesting the pedigree chart for Caspar is not going to be productive. We have plenty of information on Caspar's descendants from our descendancy chart (Screen 10-AF). Let's use, for our example, Caspar Fitz's great-great-grandson, John Fitz, who was born in 1817 in York County, Pennsylvania. Find him in the descendancy chart, highlight him, and press F7. You may feed compact discs to the CD-ROM drive again.

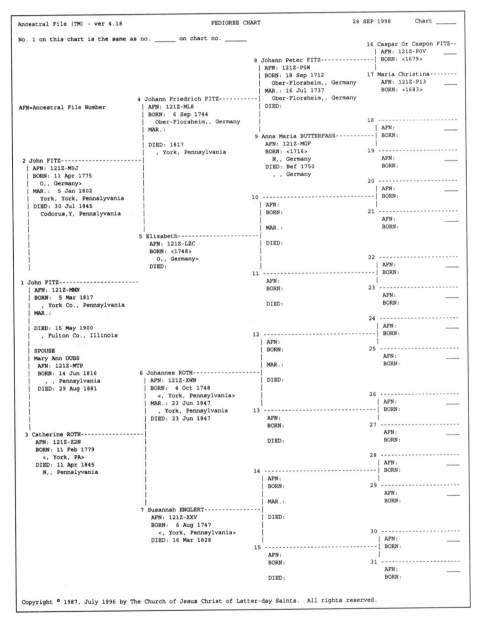

```
Ancestral File (TM) - ver 4.18               PEDIGREE CHART            28 SEP 1998     Chart _____

No. 1 on this chart is the same as no. _____ on chart no. _____
                                                                          16 Caspar Or Caspon FITZ--
                                                                          | AFN: 121Z-P0V      ____
                                                  8 Johann Peter FITZ--------------|
                                                  | AFN: 121Z-P5W                  |
                                                  | BORN: 18 Sep 1712              17 Maria Christina--------
                                                  |   Ober-Florsheim,, Germany     AFN: 121Z-P13      ____
                                                  | MAR.: 16 Jul 1737              BORN: <1683>
                                                  |   Ober-Florsheim,, Germany
                          4 Johann Friedrich FITZ----------|  DIED:
                          | AFN: 121Z-ML8             |
AFN=Ancestral File Number | BORN:  6 Sep 1744         |                            18 ----------------------
                          |   Ober-Florsheim,, Germany|                            | AFN:              ____
                          | MAR.:                     |                            | BORN:
                          |                           9 Anna Maria BUTTERFASS----------|
                          |                           | AFN: 121Z-MGF              19 ----------------------
                          | DIED: 1817                | BORN: <1716>               AFN:               ____
                          |   , York, Pennsylvania    |   N,, Germany              BORN:
         2 John FITZ---------------------|            | DIED: Bef 1750
         | AFN: 121Z-M0J                 |            |   , , Germany              20 ----------------------
         | BORN: 11 Apr 1775             |                                         | AFN:              ____
         |   O,, Germany>                |                                         | BORN:
         | MAR.:  5 Jan 1802             |            10 ----------------------    21 ----------------------
         |   York, York, Pennsylvania   |            | AFN:                        AFN:               ____
         | DIED: 30 Jul 1845             |            | BORN:                       BORN:
         |   Codorus,Y, Pennsylvania     |            |
         |                               |            | MAR.:
         |                               5 Elizabeth----------------|              22 ----------------------
         |                               | AFN: 121Z-LZC            | DIED:        | AFN:              ____
         |                               | BORN: <1748>             |              | BORN:
         |                               |   O,, Germany>           |
         |                               | DIED:                    11 ----------------------              23 ----------------------
1 John FITZ----------------------                    AFN:                          AFN:               ____
| AFN: 121Z-MNN                                      BORN:                         BORN:
| BORN:  5 Mar 1817                                                                24 ----------------------
|   , York Co., Pennsylvania                         DIED:                         | AFN:              ____
| MAR.:                                                                            | BORN:
|                                      12 ----------------------                   25 ----------------------
| DIED: 15 May 1900                    | AFN:                                      AFN:               ____
|   , Fulton Co., Illinois             | BORN:                                     BORN:
|                                      |
| SPOUSE                               | MAR.:
| Mary Ann DUBS                        6 Johannes ROTH------------------|          26 ----------------------
|   AFN: 121Z-MTP                      | AFN: 121Z-XWN         | DIED:             | AFN:              ____
|   BORN: 14 Jun 1816                  | BORN:  4 Oct 1748     |                   | BORN:
|     , , Pennsylvania                 |   <, York, Pennsylvania>|
|   DIED: 29 Aug 1881                  | MAR.: 23 Jun 1847     13 ----------------------              27 ----------------------
|                                      |   , York, Pennsylvania  AFN:                                 AFN:               ____
|                                      | DIED: 23 Jun 1847     BORN:                                  BORN:
|                                      |
3 Catherine ROTH------------------|                            DIED:              28 ----------------------
| AFN: 121Z-Z2N                    |                                               | AFN:              ____
| BORN: 11 Feb 1779                |                                               | BORN:
|   <, York, PA>                   |                           14 ----------------------              29 ----------------------
| DIED: 11 Apr 1845                |                           | AFN:                                 AFN:               ____
|   N,, Pennsylvania               |                           | BORN:                                BORN:
|                                  |                           |
|                                  |                           | MAR.:
|                                  7 Susannah ENGLERT----------------|            30 ----------------------
|                                  | AFN: 121Z-XXV             | DIED:            | AFN:              ____
                                   | BORN:  6 Aug 1747         |                  | BORN:
                                   |   <, York, Pennsylvania>  |
                                   | DIED: 16 Mar 1828         15 ----------------------              31 ----------------------
                                                               AFN:                                   AFN:               ____
                                                               BORN:                                  BORN:

                                                               DIED:

Copyright © 1987, July 1996 by The Church of Jesus Christ of Latter-day Saints.  All rights reserved.
```

Screen 11-AF. Pedigree Chart

This five-generation chart lists the individual's ancestors who are known by the person submitting the information. To print a copy, press F2 and follow the instructions.

CHECKING THE LOCALITY AND SURNAME SEARCHES

Sometimes the most effective way to find records of your ancestors may be to use a surname or locality search. A surname search will help you locate genealogies of your surname, and the locality search will show you what records the Family History Center can access on your village or county of interest. To access the Locality and Surname Searches, follow the previous IGI search through Screens 1 and 2. At Screen 3, move the cursor to item E. That will show you Screen 3-LS/SS below. We will conduct a locality search first, then a surname search.

Step By Step

```
                              FamilySearch 2.25
Esc=Exit  F1=Help  F2=Print

   ┌──────────────────────────────┐   ┌──────────────────────────────┐
   │      FAMILYSEARCH MAIN MENU   │   │ FAMILY HISTORY LIBRARY CATALOG│
   │ Use ↑↓  keys to highlight options.│   │                          │
   │     Press Enter to select.   │   │ The automated catalog describes│
   │                              │   │ all of the materials held by the│
   │   Resource Files             │   │ Family History Library in Salt│
   │ A. Ancestral File            │   │ Lake City.                   │
   │ B. International Genealogical Index│ │                          │
   │ C. U.S. Social Security Death Index│ │ Features                 │
   │ D. U.S. Military Index        │   │ ♦ Describes over 3 million books,│
   │ E. Family History Library Catalog│  │   microfilms, microfiche, maps,│
   │                              │   │   and other materials.       │
   │   Tools                      │   │ ♦ Searches descriptions by film│
   │ F. Personal Ancestral File 2.31│  │   number, locality, or surname.│
   │ G. Personal Ancestral File 3.0│   │ ♦ Gives call numbers used to │
   │                              │   │   locate or order the materials.│
   │   Tutorial                   │   │ ♦ Lists the family history centers│
   │ H. Using the Computer         │   │   where each film is located.│
   │                              │   │ ♦ Prints or downloads information│
   │                              │   │   from the catalog.          │
   └──────────────────────────────┘   └──────────────────────────────┘

Copyright (C) 1987, 1995 by The Church of Jesus Christ of Latter-day Saints.
All Rights Reserved.
```

Screen 3-LS/SS. FamilySearch Main Menu
Press the E key.

```
              Family History Library Catalog 2.03 - Menu
    Esc=Exit  F1=Help  F2=Print/Copy

   ┌──────────────────────────────┐    ┌──────────────────────────────┐
   │  LIBRARY CATALOG MAIN MENU    │    │      LOCALITY SEARCH         │
   │                              │    │                              │
   │ PATRON SEARCHES              │    │ Use this search when:        │
   │                              │    │   You want records for a certain│
   │   A. Locality Search          │    │     place.                   │
   │   B. Locality Browse          │    │                              │
   │   C. Surname Search           │    │                              │
   │   D. Film/Fiche Number Search │    │ F1=More information about search.│
   │   E. Computer Number Search   │    │                              │
   │   F. Introduction             │    │                              │
   │                              │    │                              │
   │                              │    │                              │
   │                              │    ┌──────────────────────────────┐
   │                              │    │ Catalog entries as of:       │
   │   Use ↑↓ and press ENTER.     │    │      Mar 31, 1997            │
   │   Press ESC to cancel menu.   │    └──────────────────────────────┘
   └──────────────────────────────┘

Family History Library Catalog Copyright (c) 1987, Mar 1997 by
The Church of Jesus Christ of Latter-day Saints.  All Rights Reserved.
```

Screen 4-LS. Library Catalog Main Menu
Press the A key.

Locality Search

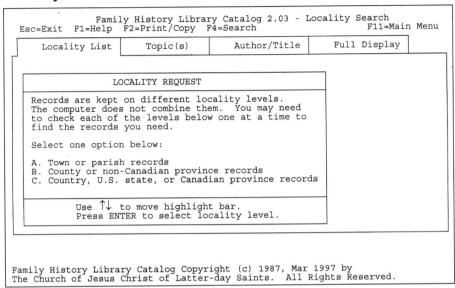

```
              Family History Library Catalog 2.03 - Locality Search
       Esc=Exit  F1=Help  F2=Print/Copy  F4=Search              F11=Main Menu
      ┌──────────────┬──────────────┬──────────────┬──────────────────┐
      │ Locality List│  Topic(s)    │ Author/Title │  Full Display    │
      └──────────────┴──────────────┴──────────────┴──────────────────┘
            ┌─────────────────────────────────────────────┐
            │              LOCALITY REQUEST               │
            ├─────────────────────────────────────────────┤
            │ Records are kept on different locality levels.│
            │ The computer does not combine them.  You may need│
            │ to check each of the levels below one at a time to│
            │ find the records you need.                  │
            │                                             │
            │ Select one option below:                    │
            │                                             │
            │ A. Town or parish records                   │
            │ B. County or non-Canadian province records  │
            │ C. Country, U.S. state, or Canadian province records│
            ├─────────────────────────────────────────────┤
            │      Use ↑↓ to move highlight bar.          │
            │      Press ENTER to select locality level.  │
            └─────────────────────────────────────────────┘

       Family History Library Catalog Copyright (c) 1987, Mar 1997 by
       The Church of Jesus Christ of Latter-day Saints.  All Rights Reserved.
```

Screen 5-LS. Locality Request

Press the A key.

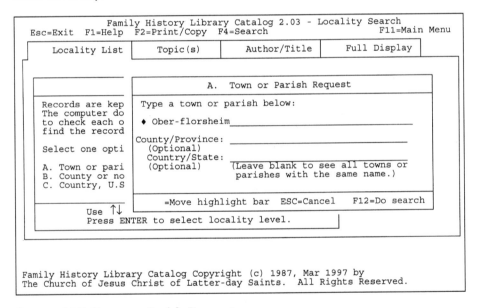

```
              Family History Library Catalog 2.03 - Locality Search
       Esc=Exit  F1=Help  F2=Print/Copy  F4=Search              F11=Main Menu
      ┌──────────────┬──────────────┬──────────────┬──────────────────┐
      │ Locality List│  Topic(s)    │ Author/Title │  Full Display    │
      └──────────────┴──────────────┴──────────────┴──────────────────┘
         ┌──────────┬─────────────────────────────────────────┐
         │          │      A.  Town or Parish Request          │
         │Records are kep│ Type a town or parish below:        │
         │The computer do│                                     │
         │to check each o│ ♦ Ober-florsheim_____ │
         │find the record│                                     │
         │          │County/Province: _____     │
         │Select one opti│  (Optional)                         │
         │          │Country/State: _____       │
         │A. Town or pari│  (Optional)  (Leave blank to see all towns or│
         │B. County or no│              parishes with the same name.)│
         │C. Country, U.S│                                     │
         │          ├─────────────────────────────────────────┤
         │  Use ↑↓  │=Move highlight bar  ESC=Cancel   F12=Do search│
         │Press ENTER to select locality level.               │
         └──────────┴─────────────────────────────────────────┘

       Family History Library Catalog Copyright (c) 1987, Mar 1997 by
       The Church of Jesus Christ of Latter-day Saints.  All Rights Reserved.
```

Screen 6-LS. Town or Parish Request

Enter information for the town or parish of your choice. For our example, enter Ober-florsheim for Ober-Flörsheim, a village in Germany where the Fitzes resided. Press F12. This will give you a list (not shown) of all records for the location you requested. Press F6 to locate the topics, and highlight one topic of interest (we chose "church records"). Press F7 to see titles available.

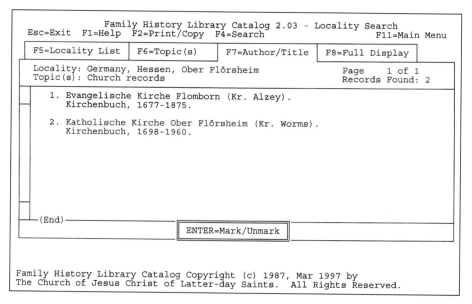

```
              Family History Library Catalog 2.03 - Locality Search
     Esc=Exit  F1=Help  F2=Print/Copy  F4=Search              F11=Main Menu

     F5=Locality List    F6=Topic(s)      F7=Author/Title    F8=Full Display

     Locality: Germany, Hessen, Ober Flörsheim         Page    1 of 1
     Topic(s): Church records                          Records Found: 2

         1. Evangelische Kirche Flomborn (Kr. Alzey).
            Kirchenbuch, 1677-1875.

         2. Katholische Kirche Ober Flörsheim (Kr. Worms).
            Kirchenbuch, 1698-1960.




     (End)
                           ENTER=Mark/Unmark


     Family History Library Catalog Copyright (c) 1987, Mar 1997 by
     The Church of Jesus Christ of Latter-day Saints.  All Rights Reserved.
```

Screen 7-LS. Author/Title

Select the reference you wish to explore. We chose the Evangelische Kirche (Evangelical Church) records for Ober Flörsheim, which are recorded in Flomborn, Alzey, Hessen, Germany, according to the previous search. Highlight item 1 and press F8 for a full display.

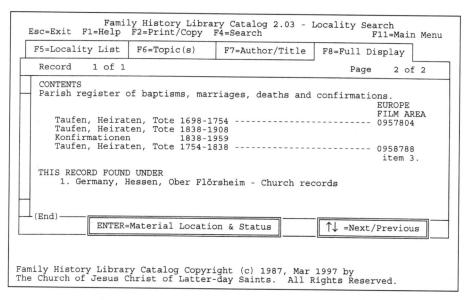

```
              Family History Library Catalog 2.03 - Locality Search
     Esc=Exit  F1=Help  F2=Print/Copy  F4=Search              F11=Main Menu

     F5=Locality List    F6=Topic(s)      F7=Author/Title    F8=Full Display

     Record    1 of 1                                  Page    2 of 2

     CONTENTS
     Parish register of baptisms, marriages, deaths and confirmations.
                                                              EUROPE
                                                              FILM AREA
       Taufen, Heiraten, Tote 1698-1754 ---------------------- 0957804
       Taufen, Heiraten, Tote 1838-1908
       Konfirmationen         1838-1959
       Taufen, Heiraten, Tote 1754-1838 ---------------------- 0958788
                                                              item 3.

     THIS RECORD FOUND UNDER
         1. Germany, Hessen, Ober Flörsheim - Church records


     (End)
                 ENTER=Material Location & Status        ↑↓ =Next/Previous


     Family History Library Catalog Copyright (c) 1987, Mar 1997 by
     The Church of Jesus Christ of Latter-day Saints.  All Rights Reserved.
```

Screen 8-LS. Parish Register

This screen shows a portion of the parish register. Note the film numbers in the right column. These will be used if you decide to rent these records on microfilm. Cost is minimal. Ask the volunteers for information on ordering films and rental times.

Surname Search

To access the Surname Search from the Locality Search, press Esc, then A to return to the beginning of the program. This takes you back to Screen 4-SS.

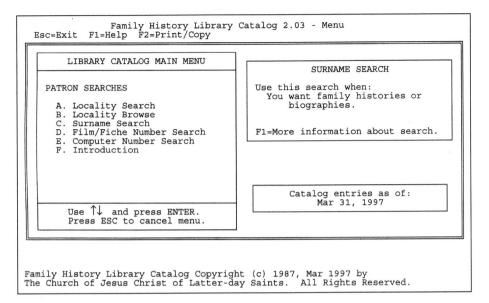

```
            Family History Library Catalog 2.03 - Menu
   Esc=Exit  F1=Help  F2=Print/Copy

  ┌─────────────────────────────────┐ ┌──────────────────────────────────┐
  │   LIBRARY CATALOG MAIN MENU      │ │         SURNAME SEARCH           │
  │                                 │ │                                  │
  │ PATRON SEARCHES                 │ │ Use this search when:            │
  │                                 │ │   You want family histories or   │
  │   A. Locality Search            │ │      biographies.                │
  │   B. Locality Browse            │ │                                  │
  │   C. Surname Search             │ │                                  │
  │   D. Film/Fiche Number Search   │ │ F1=More information about search.│
  │   E. Computer Number Search     │ │                                  │
  │   F. Introduction               │ │                                  │
  │                                 │ └──────────────────────────────────┘
  │                                 │ ┌──────────────────────────────────┐
  │                                 │ │      Catalog entries as of:      │
  │     Use ↑↓  and press ENTER.    │ │          Mar 31, 1997            │
  │     Press ESC to cancel menu.   │ └──────────────────────────────────┘
  └─────────────────────────────────┘

   Family History Library Catalog Copyright (c) 1987, Mar 1997 by
   The Church of Jesus Christ of Latter-day Saints.  All Rights Reserved.
```

Screen 4-SS. Library Catalog Main Menu

Press the C key.

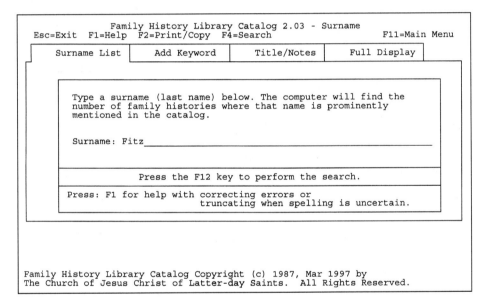

```
            Family History Library Catalog 2.03 - Surname
   Esc=Exit  F1=Help  F2=Print/Copy  F4=Search          F11=Main Menu
  ┌──────────────┬──────────────┬──────────────┬──────────────┐
  │ Surname List │  Add Keyword │  Title/Notes │ Full Display │
  │              └──────────────┴──────────────┴──────────────┴──────────
  │
  │    Type a surname (last name) below. The computer will find the
  │    number of family histories where that name is prominently
  │    mentioned in the catalog.
  │
  │    Surname: Fitz_____
  │
  │    ───────────────────────────────────────────────────────────
  │         Press the F12 key to perform the search.
  │    ───────────────────────────────────────────────────────────
  │    Press: F1 for help with correcting errors or
  │                        truncating when spelling is uncertain.
  │
  └──────────────────────────────────────────────────────────────

   Family History Library Catalog Copyright (c) 1987, Mar 1997 by
   The Church of Jesus Christ of Latter-day Saints.  All Rights Reserved.
```

Screen 5-SS. Surname List

Enter the surname you wish to research. We entered *Fitz*. Press F12.

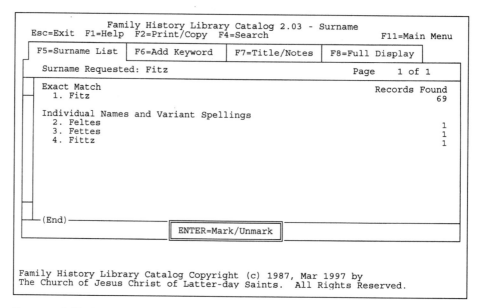

Screen 6-SS. Surname Requested

With sixty-nine records involving the surname Fitz, we are looking at a time-consuming search. To expedite matters, we will add keywords to help us limit the scope of our search. Press F6.

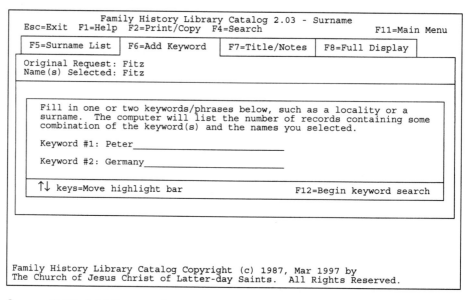

Screen 7-SS. Add Keyword

We will try *Peter* and *Germany*, but you can use any keywords that you think will narrow the search to the names you seek. Press F12 to begin the keyword search. We had no luck with our keyword search, so we were forced to review the abstracts of each of the sixty-nine records to see if any locations and names matched the specific ones we were searching. We found only one that included "our" Fitzes.

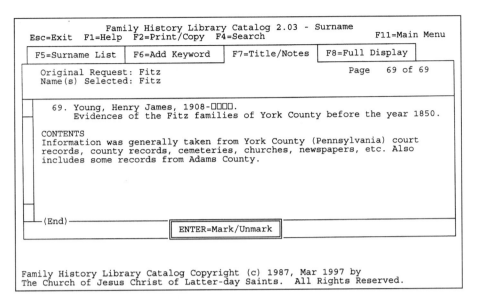

```
                Family History Library Catalog 2.03 - Surname
    Esc=Exit  F1=Help  F2=Print/Copy  F4=Search          F11=Main Menu

    F5=Surname List  | F6=Add Keyword |  F7=Title/Notes  | F8=Full Display

      Original Request: Fitz                     Page    69 of 69
      Name(s) Selected: Fitz

         69. Young, Henry James, 1908-□□□□.
             Evidences of the Fitz families of York County before the year 1850.

         CONTENTS
         Information was generally taken from York County (Pennsylvania) court
         records, county records, cemeteries, churches, newspapers, etc. Also
         includes some records from Adams County.



     (End)
                        | ENTER=Mark/Unmark |


    Family History Library Catalog Copyright (c) 1987, Mar 1997 by
    The Church of Jesus Christ of Latter-day Saints.  All Rights Reserved.
```

Screen 8-SS. Title/Notes

For more details about a particular title, press F8 for a full display (not shown). If you find a genealogy that you would like to read, contact a volunteer regarding microfilm rental/ordering procedures.

OTHER FAMILY SEARCH DATABASES

The Family History Center computer system includes databases other than the four we've examined here. They include the following:

CD Source

- Use the Locality Browse when you want to see lists of localities in the catalog.
- Use the U.S. Social Security Death Index when you want to find information about persons whose deaths were reported to the Social Security Administration from 1937 to 1996. The majority of the death records are from 1962 and later. This index features birth and death dates, the person's last place of residence, the place where death payment was sent, the state where the person lived when issued a social security number, and the person's social security number.
- Use the U.S. Military Index when you want to find any of almost 100,000 U.S. service people who died in the Korean and Vietnam wars. This index features birth and death dates, place of residence, place of death, rank, and service number. For Vietnam casualties only, the index lists religious affiliation, marital status, race, and memorial plaque number.
- Use the Film/Fiche/Computer Number Searches when you want a description of what is on a certain film or fiche or in a certain catalog entry.

Overall, these databases are excellent and helpful. But any of them may contain a few errors. Always attempt to locate documents that verify what you find.

Reminder

Internet Source

ONLINE SEARCHING

Much of what is available at Family History Centers is now available online. The online version offers the obvious convenience of being able to search from a home or anyplace that has Internet access. To access the LDS Web site (the FamilySearch Internet Genealogy Service) from your browser, type in <**http:// www.familysearch.org**> and press Enter. This will bring up a screen called FamilySearch: Search for Ancestors.

LDS Web Site

You will see spaces for you to enter the first name and last name of your ancestor, with a branched pedigree chart to the right showing father (first name and last name) and mother (first name and last name). Below the spaces for your ancestor's name, there are spaces for your ancestor's spouse (first name and last name). Remember, you're not in this set of databases, so select an ancestor.

For most searches, move the cursor to the "First Name" box and click. Once you've typed the first name, you may be tempted to press Enter (as you do with the FHC computers), but don't. To move to the "Last Name" box (and subsequent boxes), use the Tab key or move the cursor and click in the appropriate box. You may continue to fill in all the information you know, but the only required field is the ancestor surname field. So if you want to find all Dinkelheimers in the database, you can just enter *Dinkelheimer* and see what happens.

The resulting screen will tell you how many matches are found in the various areas of the Web site that are available. You will see how many matches are in the Ancestral File, the International Genealogical Index for North America, the International Genealogical Index for the British Isles, or on the many thousands of Web sites available with matches to your person. New information and regions are regularly being added.

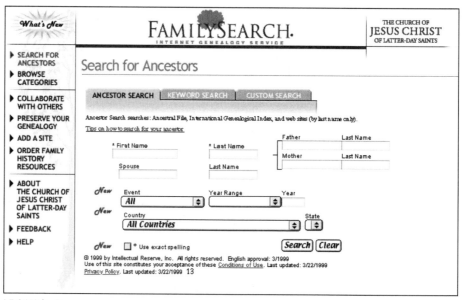

LDS Web site

If you have a common surname such as Schmidt and there are two hundred matches displayed and you have barely gotten past the many Adams and Annas and Antons and Barbaras, you will need to refine your search. Refine Search is a choice displayed on the menu. Click on it and you can choose to view only results from the Ancestral File or from Schmidt Web sites or from some other specified source.

Once you have limited the search to one database, you may be able to see if your ancestor is listed, or at least you may narrow down the field by looking at the date of birth or marriage or the geographic location. Click on the individuals in question to find out more about them. In subsequent screens, feel free to click on items of interest to further explore the data in each.

The amount of information for each listing varies. For example, sometimes on a marriage record you might get the full names of both partners, the day, month, and year of marriage, and the town, county, and state where the marriage took place. Other times, several of the fields may be left blank.

As always, you need to evaluate the quality and accuracy of the information you receive and not take it for gospel. If the record indicates that it was extracted from a marriage register, chances are that it is more accurate than if the record was submitted by an individual who has given only approximate dates, lacks maiden names, and lists only a state or country as the location.

Important

Back on the main screen, there are labels that look like the tabs on file folders. One says Ancestor Search, which we have just visited. A second says Keyword Search, and a third says Custom Search. Click on Keyword Search. A screen appears with a blank for keywords. You can type in one or more keywords that might help refine your search.

The third tab on the imaginary file folder shows Custom Search. Here you can tailor your searching to one database at a time. You can choose the Ancestral File, searching by birth year, christening year, marriage year, death year, or Ancestral File number. You can choose the International Genealogical Index (IGI) and search for a specific year of an event in an individual's life. You can even find the children of a couple by entering the full names of both the mother and the father.

The Family History Library Catalog (FHLC) has over two million catalog entries (mostly microfilms) but also includes hundreds of thousands of many other types of records, such as books and maps. The FHLC is the most neglected search. If there is a book about your ancestor at the Family History Library in Salt Lake City, do not assume that data from any person in that book has been entered into any of the LDS databases. You can search by any term, such as a surname, or a combination of terms, such as a surname and a place. Always try the German-language geographic divisions used in LDS cataloging, such as Preussen for Prussia and Bayern for Bavaria, not just the English term.

Just in case you might have missed any type of search, check out the option on the main screen called Browse Categories. That will serve as a kind of checklist to see if you have omitted any possibilities for finding your ancestor.

FIVE

A Brief History of Germany and German Emigration

Whatever the origin of your Germanic ancestors, it helps to know the social and economic background behind their emigration. The history of German lands helps to explain why people left behind a beloved homeland to go to the New World fraught with uncertainties. To help you put what you've learned into perspective and see the relevance to your own ancestors, let's review the history of Germanic regions at different time periods so that you can see the flux and change going on, especially if you already know a region.

If, for example, your great-great-grandfather said he was from Prussia, that doesn't necessarily mean he was from "modern" Prussia. The region itself has changed and evolved and actually, at times, was split into parts and pieces. If your great-great-grandmother came from Bavaria, you would naturally tend to look within the present borders of Bavaria, but she may have come from the Palatinate (Pfalz), which used to belong to Bavaria.

This can drive you up the wall! Any village may have been absorbed by any number of regional political names. So, not only do you need to know what village your ancestor was from, but you must know which province or region to search under during different time periods to find that village. This capsulated history will help you get started.

The maps we include can help too (see pages 61 and 62), but realize that maps are snapshots in time, just a thin slice of history. If you compare a map from the 1600s to one from the 1700s, things did not change all at once. Boundaries may have shifted yearly in some places, or not for dozens of years or longer in others. To get a real perspective on the transformation of any region during the years you are researching, you need to imagine the map changing yearly, a series of snapshots placed year by year that flows like a movie. There are computer resources that offer this movielike experience, such as Centennia from Clockwork, a program of maps of Europe showing the many, many border changes as they occurred over time.

Historic Germanic Areas

1. This general area was recognized as the Holy Roman Empire at the end of the Thirty Years' War in 1648, as the German Confederation by 1815, and as both the German Empire and a portion of the Austrian Empire by 1871. This area's boundaries, and the political entities it enveloped, were in a constant state of flux and sometimes encompassed hundreds of different, fragmented, virtually sovereign territories.
2. Prussia, **3.** Charolles, and **4.** Savoy, and a few smaller territories, though geographically separate, periodically maintained political connections to area 1.
5. In contrast to the change surrounding it, Switzerland (also known as the Swiss Confederation) remained relatively constant.

6. England	**8.** Denmark	**11.** Poland	**14.** Baltic Sea
7. United Netherlands	**9.** Sweden	**12.** Ottoman Empire	**15.** Adriatic Sea
	10. France	**13.** North Sea	

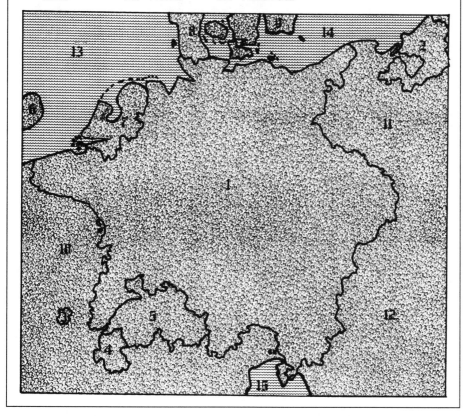

Other helpful resources:

- a German history book, such as *A History of Modern Germany*, by Hajo Holborn; *Germany: 2000 Years*, by Kurt Reinhardt; *A Concise History of Germany*, by Mary Fulbrook; *The Cambridge Illustrated History of Germany*, by Martin Kitchen; or *The Origins of Modern Germany*, by Geoffrey Barraclough
- a historical atlas, such as *The Times Illustrated Atlas of the World*, the *Hammond Historical Atlas*, or Paul Magocsi's *Historical Atlas of East Central Europe* (the latter of which includes all of Germany except the westernmost part)
- a gazetteer (place-name dictionary without maps), such as the German

Printed Source

61

Modern Germany and Environs

This and the previous map allow some comparison between modern Germany and the area historically occupied by the loose political assemblage of the Holy Roman Empire in 1648.

1. Germany	6. England	13. North Sea
2. Austria	7. Netherlands	14. Baltic Sea
3. Luxembourg	8. Denmark	15. Adriatic Sea
4. Belgium	9. Sweden	16. Italy
5. Switzerland (& Liechtenstein located on eastern border)	10. France	17. Slovenia
	11. Poland	18. Russia
	12. Czech Republic	19. Slovakia
		20. Hungary

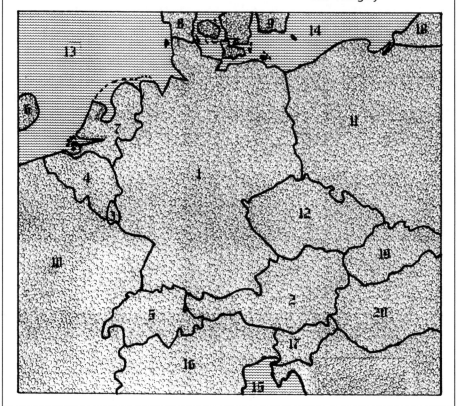

postal code book (*Das Postleitzahlenbuch*), available from the German postal system (Deutsche Bundespost) or *Müllers Grosses Deutsches Orts-buch*, available from German booksellers, such as <http://www.amazon .de>. These books help you identify the places too small to be found on a map.

Since your ancestors probably lived in German-speaking areas for centuries, an understanding of the times will help you understand the wars, famines, plagues, religious and political changes that affected their daily lives and influenced their decisions as much as an influenza epidemic, the Great Depression, or World War II affected twentieth-century Americans.

Any attempt to give you a complete rundown of German history would only leave you completely run-down. Instead, we have chosen to develop a few themes that pertain to our genealogical quest.

GERMANIC TRIBES

In the fourth and fifth centuries A.D., the invasion of wandering tribes of no-madic Asian Huns from the east caused much movement within Europe of the originally Scandinavian Germanic tribes, such as the Goths, the Saxons, the Franks, and the Alemans. These tribes have given their names to everything from territories and countries to architectural movements and writing styles. The Huns pretty much faded out as a force after the death of Attila, but some joined invading forces from the north or the Roman armies.

You can still see the Alemannic presence in Germany in other languages' words for the German language or Germany, such as *Allemagne/Allemand* in French and *Alemania/Aleman* in Spanish. The tribe called the Franks obviously handed down its name to the country France; on a smaller scale, it is seen in Frankfurt am Main in the middle of Germany, Frankfurt an der Oder to the East, and Franken (Franconia) in northern Bavaria. It is even found in the German-style tourist town Frankenmuth, Michigan, whose settlers came from Franconia. The Suebi tribe settled in the region called Schwabenland (Swabia) and spoke the dialect Schwäbisch (Swabian). The Bajuwari became the Bavari-ans in Bayern (Bavaria). The names of two Germanic tribes, Angles and Saxons, remind us of the closeness of the German and English languages (England is actually Angle-Land). English is classified as one of the Germanic languages, as are most of the northwest European languages. From the Slavs, who were once a subjugated people, comes the origin of our word *slave*.

The unifier of the Germanic tribes was the Frankish leader Karl der Grosse (Charles the Great, also known as Charlemagne) because he Christianized the other Germanic tribes, because he left a ton of descendants, and because he founded a European empire (the Holy Roman Empire of the German Nation) that remained more or less together for more than a thousand years (A.D. 800–1806). When his heirs divided up his personal territories, France went to Charles the Bald, Germany to Ludwig (Louis), and the kingdom between the others to Lothar. This middle kingdom still bears Lothar's name. The Germans call Loth-ar's land Lothringen; we and the French call it Lorraine. Even Lorain, Ohio, owes its name to him.

Medieval German lands did not consolidate under a single king or ruler. Rather, the various kingdoms and principalities were members of the Holy Roman Empire of the German Nation, as they called it, loosely under the Holy Roman Emperor. The electors of the emperor were all princes or bishops of German lands. The Empire dissolved about 1806, and the German lands did not become a cohesive modern-style German nation-state until 1871, under Bismarck. In contrast, England, France, and Spain were united under monarch-ies for many centuries. Germany's central position in Europe means that many conflicts were played out in what was a patchwork of hundreds or even thou-sands of secular and religious kingdoms, principalities, duchies, electorates, estates, free cities, and free states, each with its own rulers, laws, and local customs. These countries shrank or expanded, depending on marriage liaisons or military conflicts.

If you have ever traveled in Germany, you no doubt noticed that there is a castle every couple of miles. Each one of those castles was owned by the ruler of a separate country, so to speak, with his own subjects. The operative word is *subjects*, not *citizens*. Only free cities had citizens.

To the genealogist, the feudal system meant that each of these "countries" kept its own records. England has a Public Records Office for the entire country; Germany does not. There are regional archives rather than one national archive. The present German national archive houses records from the post–World War II constitutional government. Prior to that, each territory kept its own records and didn't send them to a national capital. The various German lands each had their own capitals, and the empire had certain major governmental/royal cities, such as Frankfurt and Regensburg and Vienna, and Berlin did not develop into a national capital until sometime after 1871. Even after that, the other German states did not send records on to "headquarters" in Berlin. They kept their own respective archives.

THE HIERARCHY OF FEUDAL LIFE

In German lands, there was a definite hierarchical system until the end of the Holy Roman Empire, when revolutionary ideas of basic human rights took hold after the French Revolution in the Confederation of the Rhine (1806), the freedom movement of the Hambach Festival (1832), the Frankfurt Paulskirche Revolution (1848), and finally the consolidation of German lands into one German Empire in 1871.

Earlier, in the feudal hierarchy of the Holy Roman Empire, average individuals were at the bottom of the food chain. They were subjects of the local lord, who in turn was a vassal of a larger nobleman or bishop, who in turn was a vassal of the empire. Everyone was subject to all the rulers higher up in the chain. Ordinary individuals were subjects, basically slaves, who were considered the property of their lords. They were not citizens (burghers) except in free cities or states (which were still subject to the emperor, but with no intermediary). Over time Burghers gained some privileges, such as markets, guilds, and commerce. In a few places—such as villages in the Swiss cantons, the trading cities of the Hanseatic League, a few rural free states such as Dithmarschen, and some city-states—subjects enjoyed unusual rights. By and large, though, the populace lived in a feudal village social system. Feudal lords received tithes and services from their vassals in return for protecting the vassals, who were their lords' property.

The populace was taxed at every occasion in services and property. If somebody died, the ruler got the best ox. If the ruler needed land plowed, he required ten days of plowing. If the ruler needed grain harvested, he required ten days of harvesting. If the ruler needed grain, he took 10 percent of the grain. If a villager wanted to marry a girl from the next village, he had to wait until the ruler could make a swap of serfs with that village's ruler (a man from the other village marrying a woman from his village). If the ruler decided to throw a party, he took a nice goose. If the ruler needed to raise an army, guess who was called to serve? If someone wanted to receive permission to be released from serfdom in order to emigrate, the ruler took 10 percent in manumission tax, leaving 90 percent. To take the further step of emigration, the ruler took another 10 percent of the person's remaining property (what little there was). These taxes and tithes were not optional. If the king or queen demanded more from his or her dukes and duchesses, counts and countesses, the nobility simply raised taxes on their subjects. Fortunately for genealogists, taxes of all kinds generated records.

For eighteenth-century emigration, which was mainly from southwestern German territories near the Rhine, there are many emigration records available because of manumission or emigration taxes. In earlier times, when the Turks attacked Europe from about 1526 on, there were taxes (*Turkensteuer*, "Turkish taxes") levied on the populace, and lists of these taxpayers (i.e., everybody) exist in many places, if you can trace your families that far back.

REFORMATION

Johannes Gensfleisch (better known as Johann Gutenberg) invented printing in Mainz about 1450, enabling knowledge to be spread to the masses, including religious knowledge, which previously had been reserved for priests and scholars.

In 1517, Martin Luther posted his ninety-five theses at Wittenberg and began a chain of events that he surely did not foresee. Luther wanted to reform the Catholic church, not to found a new one. But his reforms did inspire a new religion, which set a number of events into motion.

One decision became very important for genealogists. In 1545, the (Catholic) religious Council of Trent, partly as a by-product of the Reformation, decided that all marriages and births and deaths were to be recorded by the local parish priest. This is the beginning of church record keeping.

The new Protestant religions—the Lutheran of Martin Luther (1517); the Reformed of Ulrich Zwingli (1518) and John Calvin (1536); the Hussites (1415); the Anabaptists, including Mennonites (1523), Amish (1663), and others—caused consternation in the previously homogeneous Catholic world and the Counter-Reformation ensued.

The development of new competing religions led to a conference that resulted in the principle of the Treaty of Augsburg: *cuius regio, eius religio.* Simply translated from the Latin, this means that "it's my toy, so I get to make up the rules of the game." If you are a king, you get to pick the religion of yourself and all your subjects. People had no choice in their religion, unless they joined a rare dissident group, in which case they were almost always persecuted. It is no coincidence that one of the Amish religious books is called *The Martyr's Mirror,* a listing of the Amish who died because of their religion.

WARS

Next comes the Thirty Years' War, which lasted—that's right—thirty years (1618–48). To get an idea of how long the war lasted, put this book down and pick it back up again after thirty years. That war pitted some Swedes and Danes in the north who were Lutheran, plus their allies the French, versus some Austrians in the south, plus their Spanish allies who were Catholic. They all wanted more territory for their respective religions and political alliances, not to mention personal gain. This war brought pestilence, famine, atrocities, and suspension of travel and trade to German lands. By the time it was over, about a third of the population of German-speaking lands was dead.

At the end of the war, the Peace of Westphalia (1648) left innumerable territories, each with its own rulers. Of course, many records were destroyed in the total devastation brought about by the war, so it is unusual to find church records before 1650. Still, that means records go back 350 years in many parts of Germany, roughly ten generations, which is not too bad as family histories go.

The French must have decided that the Thirty Years' War had not done enough damage to the Palatinate because the French claim was "The Rhine is mine," and French King Louis XIV said "Burn the Palatinate," which his armies did in 1674, 1681, and 1688.

The Palatinate was repopulated, partly with farmers from Switzerland and partly with returnees who finally found it possible to come back to their village. The people of the Palatinate were a hardy group to endure such conditions, but they found it nearly impossible to survive the winter of 1708–9 after the Rhine froze solid: Wine turned into ice and cattle froze to death in their sheds. This became one of the major causes of the Palatine emigration to New York.

CAUSES OF EMIGRATION

Notes

There were many reasons that residents of German-speaking lands chose to leave their homes. Here are some of the most common.

Poverty

Poverty was widespread. It was caused by numerous factors, including the devastation of numerous European wars, disease, floods, bad weather, such as hail and drought, crop failure, food shortages, high prices, and high taxation. Any one of these conditions can trigger a cycle of inflation. Bad weather, for instance, leads to crop failure. Crop failure leads to food shortages, which leads to high prices, which leads to inflation, which results in poverty for the populace, which leads to people moving out.

Illegitimacy

Especially in poorer regions and during times of poverty, there was a relatively high rate of out-of-wedlock births in German lands. Being born out of wedlock meant a person was ineligible for many things—joining a guild, owning property of any kind, or becoming a citizen in a free city. It would not be surprising that someone born out of wedlock might want to emigrate to a place where all "are created equal" and "endowed with unalienable rights." Do not be surprised to find your ancestor among this group.

Inheritance

The Salic law, handed down from the fifth-century Franks, excluded women from inheritance. When King Louis XIV of France attacked the Palatinate in the 1670s and 1680s, it was partially because he wanted to place his cousin Liselotte (Elisabetha Charlotte) on the throne of the Palatinate. (Many European wars have been fought over the right of succession to a throne.)

Rights to an inheritance were not limited to rulers. Even when serfdom was the norm, the right to tenancy of a farm (*Erbpacht*) could be inherited.

The Salic law of the Franks became the basis for Germanic inheritance law, in which property passed strictly through the male line. Inheritance law becomes very important to a genealogist seeking northern German ancestors. Maintaining an intact farm is critical in the north, especially in Westphalia. Further, farm property in that region is indivisible, so the farm name stays with the land and the new owner must adopt the farm name. Women inherit the farm only if there are no sons to carry on the farm. (If a man marries a woman to get her farm, he takes her name.) Sons who are not in line to inherit the farm may have a reason to get a trade or to emigrate, as they will likely never get a chance to own the farm. Some surnames, such as Lenzmeyer, indicate the name of the farm—the *Meyer*, or manager, of the Lenz farm. Sometimes the old surname is given with the new, with terms such as *genannt*, *alias*, *modo*, or *sive*, basically meaning "also known as."

In other parts of Germany, where farms have been divided and subdivided among all heirs since the early nineteenth century, parcels of land keep getting smaller every generation and farmers may own widely scattered parcels. Although there are more landowners, this leads to inefficiency. This is one of the economic factors leading to emigrations from those areas.

Emigration Laws

Emigration laws tightened or relaxed, depending on conditions. One objective was to maintain a populace with enough productive workers and enough soldiers; another was to levy taxes against those who wished to leave. Those who left often took assets, such as gold or their most precious possessions, with them, leaving the ruler's territory poorer.

IMMIGRATION TO AMERICA

Emigration was not always to far-off America. An even more frequent destination in the early eighteenth century was southeastern Europe, such as Hungary. The first major emigration stream to North America began in the late 1720s. Their numbers led the English majority to fear that the Germans might begin to outnumber the English-speaking colonists. That prompted Pennsylvania's colonial governor Patrick Gordon to require a list of all male passengers more than sixteen years of age and to have each sign "a Writing . . . declaring their Allegiance & Subjection to the King of Great Britain." If your ancestor came to America through Philadelphia and was literate, you may even be able to see his signature, which has been reproduced in some of the reprints of Strassburger and Hinke's *Pennsylvania German Pioneers*, namely those by Netti Schreiner-Yantis and Picton Press.

Notes

German Settlement Patterns in America

The 1700s typified emigration from the Palatinate and other southwestern Germanic areas near the Rhine River—down the Rhine to Rotterdam, through Philadelphia. Even before 1700, the first settlement in Germantown near Philadelphia had led to additional immigration to Penn's colony, and Huguenots had settled New Paltz and New Rochelle in New York, and Manakintown near Richmond, Virginia. Other large groups during this period include the 1709 group of Palatines, who arrived in upstate New York (Livingston Manor), and the Germanna, Virginia, settlement of ironworkers from Nassau-Siegen in 1714 and others from Wuerttemberg and Baden. The aptly named German coast of Louisiana (*Les Allemandes*) was settled mostly by Catholics from the Palatinate, Baden, Alsace, and the Augsburg area of Bavaria.

German Baptist Brethren (Tunkers, Dunkards, Schwarzenau Brethren) from Krefeld settled in various parts of Pennsylvania beginning in 1719. Schwenkfelders settled in eastern Pennsylvania in 1734. Other German-speaking people came to North Carolina (New Bern), South Carolina (Charleston, Orangeburg, and Saxe-Gotha), or Georgia (Ebenezer), and Maine (Waldoboro), from Brunswick, Saxony, Wuerttemberg, and the Palatinate.

A group of soldiers known as Hessians did not emigrate voluntarily. They were auxiliary troops sent by the British to fight the colonists in the American Revolution. They came from Hesse-Kassel, Brunswick, Waldeck, Ansbach-Bayreuth, Hesse-Hanau, and Anhalt-Zerbst. Of the 30,000 who were sent to North America, about 6,000 died or were killed, and about 6,000 remained in the newly independent colonies. Typical places of settlement for those who remained in America were in the Winchester, Virginia, or York, Pennsylvania, areas. Some German loyalists went to Canada.

The first half of the 1800s was typified by emigration from southwest Germany via Rotterdam or Le Havre to Philadelphia or New York. Areas of settlement spread as the frontier expanded westward. Some settlements in the early 1800s included the 1816–17 famine emigrants and separatists mostly from Wuerttemberg, Baden, and the Palatinate.

Political emigrés from freedom movements such as the Hambach Festival in 1832 and the Frankfurt Paulskirche Revolution in 1848 moved to the interior of the United States and became advocates of freedom in the gymnastic/free-thinking Turner societies. The greatest numbers came to Pennsylvania, Ohio, Indiana, Michigan, Illinois, Wisconsin, Missouri, Iowa, and Texas.

Around 1839, religious disagreements sent "Old Lutherans" from Pomerania, Silesia, and Saxony to settle in Buffalo and Bergholz, New York, and

Mequon and Freistadt, Wisconsin. That same year "Saxon Lutherans" led by Martin Stephan came to Perry County, Missouri.

A society formed by several members of German nobility to promote emigration to Texas, the Mainzer Adelsverein, led to settlement in several areas of the Republic of Texas beginning in 1842, including New Braunfels, Fredericksburg, and Castell. Another society named Ebenezer (in New York, near Buffalo) was founded by Inspirationists led by Christian Metz in 1843. This group later moved to a colony called Amana, Iowa.

In 1846 and 1847, the potato blight hit German lands as well as Ireland, with similar consequences—hunger, poverty, and emigration. The squelched revolutionary spirit of 1848 and 1849 also forced many to leave hurriedly. The major German emigration port of the nineteenth century was Bremen, but by 1850, Hamburg was offering incentive fares and harbor hotels for immigrants as competition. By this time, we can begin to speak of mass migration. In 1849, there were about 80,000 German immigrants, at that time a record number. But just five years later, German immigrants numbered about 240,000! New York, Baltimore, and now New Orleans became major arrival ports for German settlers in the mid–nineteenth century.

After Prussia's rise to power in the 1860s, emigration from the north and northeast increased greatly. The Prussian ruler, Bismarck, created an anti-Catholic atmosphere, and Prussia had mandatory military service. At the same time, cottage industries, such as weaving, were made obsolete by technology, such as mechanical looms. Many people, especially Catholics, farm laborers, and those in cottage industries, simply chose to leave, culminating in another peak emigration year of 1881.

The rest of the nineteenth century was marked by much "chain migration." One family member would write back and tell others to follow. These people generally joined established German communities instead of founding new settlements, as there was less and less frontier left. The thriving cities of the German heartland filled up with more and more Germans—Cincinnati, St. Louis, Milwaukee, Minneapolis and St. Paul, Chicago, Detroit, Cleveland, Indianapolis, and many more. So did the farms of the Midwest, which were settled by large numbers of farmers from northern and northeastern German lands, plus the Russian Germans who emigrated to the wheat fields of the Great Plains and the northern prairies. (The Germans from Russia had been lured to Russia by Catherine the Great in 1763 with guarantees of free land, low taxes, and freedom from military service in perpetuity, but "perpetuity" turned out to be over in one hundred years when a new regime began treating the Germans like other Russians.)

World War I halted emigration, but it gradually resumed after the war. The greatest numbers of emigrants occurred beginning in 1933, when Jews, intellectuals, scientists, and others fleeing Nazism came to U.S. universities and metropolitan areas. An important colony grew in southern California.

At the end of World War II, many Germans from eastern areas lost their homes when their home provinces were taken over by Communists and became part of Poland or Czechoslovakia. Millions of Germans from these eastern

\di'fin\ *vb*

Definitions

areas, displaced by the war, were shipped to the west and became "displaced persons." Many of these found sponsors and settled in America.

After World War II, American GIs stationed in Germany met local German girls, married them, and brought them to America. These German "war brides" were numerous, and they formed a network that was a significant part of the membership of local German clubs.

Tip

Perhaps you can place your ancestor in one of these groups. If so, each of them has had much written about them, sometimes with documentation on places of origin, reasons for emigration, and the settlements they founded in America. **Check library card catalogs and online catalogs under the name of the group or place of settlement.** Many of these settlements have names taken from German places, or at least were named by Germanic people. Sometimes the place-name reveals the origin of the people or the founder of the place: New Glarus, Wisconsin; New Braunfels, Texas; New Ulm, Minnesota; Oldenburg, Indiana; Frohna, Missouri; or Stuttgart, Arkansas.

Whatever the reason for your emigrant ancestor's departure, such a decision was never taken lightly. That decision changed forever the fate of your ancestor's family, which of course turned out to be *your* family.

CHRONOLOGY OF GERMANIC GROUPS IN AMERICA

A number of Germanic groups migrated to America from very early times.

1607 Germans are among the first settlers at Jamestown. Five unnamed glass-makers and three carpenters made up the first group of Germans.

1683 Germantown, Pennsylvania, now part of Philadelphia, is settled by 13 families of German Mennonites/Quakers from Krefeld and Kriegsheim led by Franz Daniel Pastorius.

1685 Huguenots (French Protestants) settle in Delaware; Maine; Boston and Oxford, Massachusetts; Gravesend, New Amsterdam, New Harlem, New Paltz, New Rochelle, and Woodstock, New York; Pennsylvania; East Greenwich, Kingstown, and Narragansett, Rhode Island; Charleston, South Carolina; Manakintown, Virginia; North and South Carolina. Some of these made stopovers in German lands, for example, Grossvillars, Kleinvillars, Pinache, and in the Palatinate (Deutschhof), where they took on some German customs and perhaps some German-sounding names.

1709+ The Palatines of New York settle in Newburg, Orange County, New York, the Livingston Manor area. They consist of 847 families (or about 3,000 persons) from the Palatinate, Hessen-Darmstadt, Hanau, Isenburg, and Wetterau areas, Franconia; and Catholic areas, such as Alsace, Baden, Nassau, and Zweibrücken.

1710 Mennonites settle in Pennsylvania.

1714 Germanna (now Culpeper), Virginia, is settled by ironworkers from Nassau-Siegen, and by 1717, the colony is expanded by 80 families from Wuerttemberg and Baden.

1719+ The German Coast of Louisiana (Les Allemandes) is settled by about 930 persons from the bishopric of Speyer and the areas of Baden, Alsace, and Augsburg.

1719+ The Pennsylvanian areas of Conestoga, Germantown, the Skippach, Oley, and Muehlbach are settled by German Baptist Brethren (Tunkers, Dunkards, Schwarzenau Brethren) from Krefeld.

1727+ Passenger lists exist for Philadelphia. The Pennsylvanian counties of Berks, Bucks, Lancaster, York, and Adams, and the Shenandoah Valley of Virginia are settled by Pennsylvania Germans (Pennsylvania Dutch), many of them indentured servants.

1732+ Ebenezer, Georgia, is settled by about 300 Salzburger Lutheran religious emigrés who had been expelled by Archbishop Firmian from the Diocese of Salzburg.

1734 About 200 Schwenkfelders settle in the Pennsylvania counties of Lehigh, Montgomery, Bucks, and Berks.

1735+ Swiss and Germans settle in South Carolina at Charleston and Orangeburg, and on the frontier at Amelia, Saxe-Gotha, New Windsor, and Hard Labor Creek.

1740 Immigrants recruited by Samuel Waldo from Brunswick and Saxony, also Wuerttemberg and the Palatinate, settle Waldoboro, Maine.

1804–5 Harmony, Pennsylvania, is settled by 650 members of Rapp's Harmony Society.

1809 Walnut Creek, Ohio, area is settled by Amish led by Bishop Jacob Miller and Jonas Stutzman. It is now the largest Amish settlement in the world.

1832–33 Political emigrés from the Hambach Festival's freedom movement flee to America, for example, Philadelphia, Pennsylvania; Columbus, Ohio; and St. Clair County, Illinois.

1839 Perry County, Missouri, is settled by 700 Saxon Lutherans led by Martin Stephan.

1839+ Buffalo and Bergholz, New York, and Mequon and Freistadt, Wisconsin, are settled by about 1,000 "Old Lutherans" from Pomerania, Silesia, and Saxony.

1842+ New Braunfels, Fredericksburg, and Castell, Texas, become home to 7,380 immigrants of the Mainz Nobility Society, or Adelsverein.

1843+ Ebenezer, New York, is settled by Inspirationists led by Christian Metz.

1848 About 8,000 political refugees, known as Forty-Eighters, fled as a result of the failed Frankfurt constitution. They migrate to Ohio, Pennsylvania, Iowa, Indiana, Michigan, Illinois, Wisconsin, Missouri, and Texas.

1850–WWI German immigration is so heavy that North America is almost one huge German settlement, both in cities and on farms.

1933+ Nazism opponents (Jews, intellectuals, scientists, artists, and others) enrich intellectual and cultural life in U.S. universities, metropolitan areas, and southern California.

1945+ Displaced persons from several eastern German territories find a new life in America.

1945+ German "war brides" are brought to America by returning GIs.

SIX

How to Read Germanic Records

To help you become more familiar with Germanic languages and records, we will share the following:

- German, Latin, and French language basics
- keywords to help you quickly identify what type of record you are reviewing
- transcriptions and translations of marriage, birth, death, baptismal, and emigration records to give you hands-on, practical samples

Studying the language and keywords, and comparing the translations to any Germanic records you possess, will help you unlock the puzzling script or other enigmatic writings. For this chapter, plan to use the charts in this book (for common German genealogical terms, samples of lettering, etc.), a magnifying glass, a German-English dictionary, and any Germanic records you have that you wish to compare to the enclosed records.

READING THEIR WRITING

You do not need to read German fluently to be able to decipher most genealogical records. But our minicourse in German will familiarize you with the most common genealogical scripts and prints so that you will begin recognizing them. This is absolutely essential, since you will not find all German records translated into English by some generous person. In Appendix A, you will find common German genealogical words and translations.

Step By Step

Letters

Look at the Alphabet Chart on page 74. Older German records are prepared in letters similar to the style called Kurrent. We have illustrated two other styles, called Fraktur and Sütterlin, in order to help you see the connection between Kurrent and modern styles.

ALPHABET CHART

1. Modern		2. Fraktur		3. Sütterlin		4. Kurrent		5. Old Handwriting Styles
A	a	𝔄	a	*Cursive*	*cursive*	*Cursive*	*cursive*	*handwriting samples*
B	b	𝔅	b					
C	c	ℭ	c					
D	d	𝔇	d					
E	e	𝔈	e					
F	f	𝔉	f					
G	g	𝔊	g					
H	h	ℌ	h					
I	i	ℑ	i					
J	j	𝔍	j					
K	k	𝔎	k					
L	l	𝔏	l					
M	m	𝔐	m					
N	n	𝔑	n					
O	o	𝔒	o					
P	p	𝔓	p					
Q	q	𝔔	q					
R	r	𝔑	r					
S	s	𝔖	ſs					
T	t	𝔗	t					
U	u	𝔘	u					
V	v	𝔙	v					
W	w	𝔚	w					
X	x	𝔛	x					
Y	y	𝔜	y					
Z	z	ℨ	z					
	ß		ß				ß	
Ä	ä	𝔄̈	ä					
Ö	ö	𝔒̈	ö					
Ü	ü	𝔘̈	ü					

- Column one of the Alphabet Chart includes modern capital and lowercase letters.
- Column two includes the old German typeface called Fraktur, Schwabacher, or Gotisch (see the Gothic Records section on page 79).
- Columns three and four illustrate computer-generated letters of old handwriting styles known as Sütterlin and Kurrent.
- Column five shows variations of handwritten letters copied from real German-language records.

Using the Alphabet Chart, we can see that certain Kurrent letters look very similar. This can make your interpretation of German documents difficult and can lead to a great deal of confusion. Further, the handwriting of individual priests, ministers, and clerks can vary significantly one to another, creating further confusion. We will address the latter problem first.

The idiosyncrasies of each individual's style of forming particular letters can be baffling. One priest's *f* can look exactly like another priest's *s*. To be effective in translating a particular person's handwriting properly, make photocopies of enough samples of one person's writing to be able to decide what the letters are. By becoming familiar with numerous common words written by that person, you will be better able to decipher each word in that person's handwriting.

In the German alphabet, you will find a few surprises, such as the lowercase *s* and other look-alikes (explained below), and the "übiqüitöüs ümläüt" (see page 77).

f h s

Lowercase *f*, *h*, and *s*
Lowercase *f*, *h*, and *s* are easily confused even with the perfectly formed computer-generated letters. If you add a clerk's or priest's individual handwriting to the mix, the possibilities become even more unclear. The long form of the letter *s*, which some people confuse with *f*, never appears at the end of a properly formed word. This is a rule of the German language.

ss
ß

Ess-Tset (Double *s*)
The ess-tset is an unusual German letter. It is transcribed as *ss* and can appear in the middle or at the end of a word. It is *not* a capital *B* and never appears at the beginning of a word. For example, names such as *Groß* and *Heß* are actually *Gross* and *Hess*, not *Grob* and *Heb*. The ess-tset is used only in lowercase. If you're wondering about the strange name ess-tset, this character is sometimes transcribed as *sz*, and the German names for those two letters are

pronounced ess and tset, hence ess-tset. Looking at the shape of the combination, you can actually see the (long) *s* and the *tset* joined together.

e n r u

Lowercase *e*, *n*, *r*, and *u*

The handwritten letter *u* normally has a "smile" over it (like the little u-shaped symbol commonly used for a short vowel); the letter *n* does not. The little u-shaped symbol stands for the letter *u*. However, a double *nn* is often shown as a single *n* with a straight line over it, which is not always neatly made, so it adds to the confusion. The letter *e* is not shaped like the English letter, but more like a thin *n*, and the *r* has a tiny hook on the end. Even though the letter *e* is normally thinner than the *n*, only by becoming familiar with the individual clerk's or minister's letters can you correctly determine a particular letter.

g p q

Lowercase *g*, *p*, and *q*

Letters *g*, *p*, and *q* extend below the line. Usually, the tail of the *q* is not a loop, while the other two normally exhibit the loop. Above the line, the letters *g* and *q* normally have a closed loop, whereas the letter *p* normally does not, oftentimes looking like our English letter *y*. The German letter *y* is rarely used, making it easier for you to identify the German letter *p*.

c i

Lowercase *c* and *i*

The *c* and the *i* are identical except that the *i* is dotted. Occasionally the *c* has a little extra hook on the top heading to the right. It is helpful to remember that the lowercase letter *c* is rarely found alone. It is usually found as *ch* or *ck*.

H h   Y y   Z z

H (h), Y (y), and Z (z)

The upper- and lowercase *H*, *Y*, and *Z* can be distinguished fairly easily. You can almost eliminate *Y* from consideration, as it is almost never used, especially in native German words. There are only two places in Germany that begin with Y, Yburg and Yach. The lowercase *y* is nearly as rare as uppercase Y. Occasionally, the uppercase *H* is a different form, a thicker, more elaborate version of the lowercase *h*. The *Z* and *z* are similar to the English forms.

K R

K R

Uppercase *K* and *R*

The letters *K* and *R* make up one of the hardest pairs to distinguish, especially if they are not well formed. Note that the *K* starts at the top from the upper right, the *R* starts from the upper left.

B C L

B C L

Uppercase *B, C,* and *L*

The *B* and the *L* are identical except for the loop at the bottom of the *B*. The letter *C* is not as elaborate as the *L*, but an individual's handwriting can cause a problem, so make sure you compare your record with other samples of the person's handwriting. For instance, if there is a record for a person named Barbara, that word will tell you what the writer's upper- and lowercase *B*s look like.

O S

O S

Uppercase *O* and *S*

To best distinguish between uppercase *O* and *S*, look at the curl on the top of the *O* and the "ears" on the top of the *S*.

A U

A U

Uppercase *A* and *U*

Note the curlicue on the upper left of uppercase *U*, which is normally absent on uppercase *A*.

I J T

I J T

Uppercase *I, J,* and *T*

The uppercase *J* is a longer form of the *I*. However, in early records, these two are identical. See how far the writer's letter extends below the line and compare to other possible *J*s and *I*s of the writer for a match. The *T* is crossed at the bottom.

Ä ä Ö ö Ü ü

Ä ä Ö ö Ü ü

The Übiqüitöüs Ümläüt

The letters *a, A, o, O, u,* and *U* with two dots over them are called umlauts. The dots, also called umlauts, indicate that the sound of that vowel is changed, with

\di'fin\ *vb*

Definitions

77

the spelling translated into English as *ae*, *oe*, and *ue*. You may rarely find two dots over a *y*, as in the German word *beÿ*, which is an old spelling for *bei*.

Refer to Reading the Old German (Kurrent) Script (below) for a complete review at a glance of all the uppercase and lowercase letters.

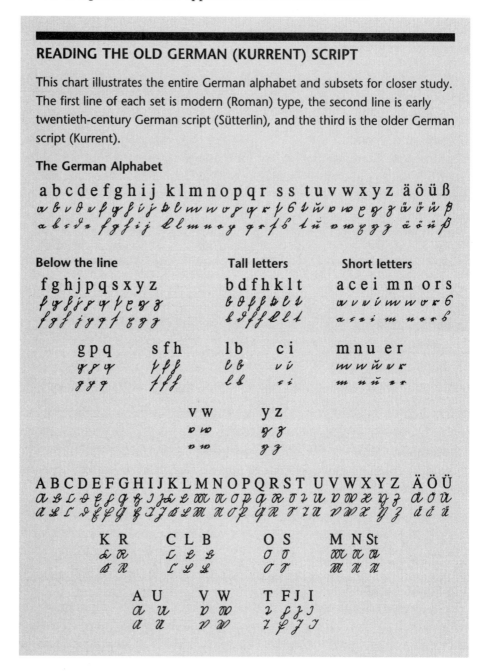

READING THE OLD GERMAN (KURRENT) SCRIPT

This chart illustrates the entire German alphabet and subsets for closer study. The first line of each set is modern (Roman) type, the second line is early twentieth-century German script (Sütterlin), and the third is the older German script (Kurrent).

The German Alphabet

Below the line   **Tall letters**   **Short letters**

Numbers

Numerals are quite similar to English-style numerals, except that the *7* has a European-style line through it to distinguish it from a *1*. Ordinal numerals, such as first, second, and third, have a suffix that is normally shown in smaller letters in superscript, sometimes also underlined.

1 7 1sten 2ten

1 7 *flan 2ten*

1 7 first second

Gothic Records

Reading the old German writing—whether it be the older Kurrent script or the modern Sütterlin script, which was introduced in Prussia in 1915 and all of Germany by 1934, or the older Schwabacher, Fraktur, or Gotisch Old German Gothic typeface styles that were standard until the twentieth century—can be assisted by comparing the writing with the Alphabet Chart on page 74 and transcribing letter by letter.

If you want to become proficient at reading the writing, you should learn by practicing writing. If you have examples of actual genealogical documents, try copying them. Learn how to write the names of your ancestors, their places of

---

READING THE OLD GERMAN (FRAKTUR, SCHWABACHER) TYPEFACE

This chart illustrates the entire German alphabet and subsets for closer study. The first line of each set is modern (Roman) type, the second line is the German Gothic style (Fraktur), and the third is the German Gothic style (Schwabacher).

The German Alphabet

a b c d e f g h i j k l m n o p q r s s t u v w x y z ä ö ü ß

Below the line

f g h j p q s x y z ß

Tall letters

b d f h k l s t ß

Short letters

a c e i m n o r s u v w

A B C D E F G H I J K L M N O P Q R S T U V W X Y Z Ä Ö Ü

Below the line

F H I P Y Z

Wide letters

M W

Crescents

C E G S

"Hats"

F I J

Rounded

D O Q

Two posts ‖

N R U

Riding a wave ~

B L T V

Others

A K X

birth, their dates of birth, and the common genealogy words found in the appendix and other texts you find helpful. You can even begin teaching yourself by using familiar English texts as your first practice pieces, then gradually working your way into German texts.

Please refer to the chart titled Reading the Old German (Fraktur, Schwabacher) Typeface to review the differences and similarities between common Gothic styles. There are different varieties of both the Fraktur and the Schwabacher styles, so we tried to select a popular variety of each for the chart.

Latin Records

Latin was the language of the Catholic church but was also used in early Lutheran records. Latin terms, such as *ditto*, *ejusdem*, *eodem*, *idem*, *item*—all meaning roughly "the same as before"—are sometimes found in the middle of otherwise German documents.

French Records

There are many French-language records in the German areas west of the Rhine because the French, under Napoleon, controlled much of Germany. It is not uncommon to find records describing Pierre Schmidt and Jean Jacques Meyer and discover that they signed the documents as Peter Schmidt and Johann Jakob Meyer. The people were still German-speaking, but the documents were in French.

For help with Latin and/or French genealogical terms, see Ernest Thode's *German-English Genealogical Dictionary* or the *Genealogical Word List: Latin*, published by the Family History Library of the Church of Jesus Christ of Latter-day Saints.

KEYWORDS IN DOCUMENTS

In the following lists, we identify commonly used words found in various types of documents. We show three styles of each keyword for ease in recognition depending on which style you encounter in your own Germanic documents.

Birth and Birth Registers

(symbols used = * ⅄)

English	Roman	Fraktur	Kurrent
Birth	Geburt	Geburt	Geburt
Born	geb., geboren	geb., geboren	geb., geboren
Birth Register	Geburtsregister	Geburtsregister	Geburtsregister
Birth Certificate	Geburtsschein	Geburtsschein	Geburtsschein
Birth Document	Geburtsurkunde	Geburtsurkunde	Geburtsurkunde
Birth Register	Trauschein	Trauschein	Trauschein
Birth Document	Trauurkunde	Trauurkunde	Trauurkunde

Baptism and Baptismal Registers

(symbol used = ~)

English	Roman	Fraktur	Kurrent
Baptism	Taufe	Taufe	
Baptized	get., getauft	get., getauft	
Baptismal Register	Taufregister	Taufregister	
Baptismal Certificate	Taufschein	Taufschein	
Baptismal Document	Taufurkunde	Taufurkunde	

Marriage and Marriage Registers

(symbol used = ∞)

English	Roman	Fraktur	Kurrent
Marriage	Trauung	Trauung	
Marriage Register	Trauregister	Trauregister	
Marriage	Heirat	Heirat	
Marriage Register	Heiratsregister	Heiratsregister	
Marriage Certificate	Heiratsschein	Heiratsschein	
Marriage Document	Heiratsurkunde	Heiratsurkunde	
Marriage	Ehe	Ehe	
Marriage Register	Eheregister	Eheregister	
Marriage	Verehelichung	Verehelichung	
Married	verehelicht	verehelicht	
Got Married	geheiratet	geheiratet	
Married (state)	verheiratet	verheiratet	
Legitimate	ehelich	ehelich	
Out of Wedlock	unehelich	unehelich	

Death and Death Registers

(symbol used = †)

English	Roman	Fraktur	Kurrent
Death	Tod	Tod	
Death Record	Todesakt	Todesakt	
Death Register	Todesregister	Todesregister	
Death Certificate	Todesschein	Todesschein	
Death Document	Todesurkunde	Todesurkunde	
Death	Sterben	Sterben	
Death Register	Sterberegister	Sterberegister	
Died	gestorben	gestorben	
Deceased	verstorben	verstorben	
Passed Away	entschlafen	entschlafen	

Emigration

English	Roman	Fraktur	Kurrent
Emigrant(s)	Auswanderer	Auswanderer	*Auswanderer*
Emigration	Auswanderung	Auswanderung	*Auswanderung*
Emigrate	auswandern	auswandern	*auswandern*
Emigrated	ausgewandert	ausgewandert	*ausgewandert*
Passenger Lists	Passagierlisten	Passagierlisten	*Passagierlisten*
Passport	Reisepaß	Reisepaß	*Reisepaß*
Emigration	Auswanderungs-konsens	Auswanderungs-konsens	*Auswanderungs-konsens*
Emigration List	Auswanderungs-verzeichnis	Auswanderungs-verzeichnis	*Auswanderungs-verzeichnis*
Ship's Lists	Schiffslisten	Schiffslisten	*Schiffslisten*

Confirmation

English	Roman	Fraktur	Kurrent
Confirmation	Firmung	Firmung	*Firmung*
Confirmed	konfirmiert	konfirmiert	*konfirmiert*
Confirmation	Konfirmation	Konfirmation	*Konfirmation*

SOME GERMAN AND OTHER RECORDS

The remainder of this chapter is a collection of copies of original documents and their transcriptions and translations. As we performed the transcriptions, we made efforts to maintain the text as in the original, line by line. We didn't always succeed, but we were largely successful. It wasn't always possible to line up sentences in perfect sequence as we performed the translations because the German and French placement of verbs, nouns, and so forth would not flow correctly in English if we literally translated the documents word by word. However, you'll find the translations easy to follow if you find names (such as Nicolas Fuchs) and places (such as Weylerhoff) to keep you on track.

Some records are in French, some in old-style German handwriting only, some in German handwriting interspersed with printed words, some in Latin, some in Gothic styles, and so on. Please feel free to use the practical lessons for each of these styles by referring to this chapter and becoming familiar with the various German scripts and types.

Our transcriptions and translations may be incorrect due to undecipherable records or for other reasons, but your review of these documents will be an excellent experience for you to gain confidence in reading and understanding early German records.

The following documents will give you a taste of what's to come. The first document is the birth record of Conrad Fuchs, son of Nicolas Fuchs and Margueritte Schorr. The second document is the marriage record of Jean Meyser

---

N. 16 ACTE DE NAISSANCE.

[handwritten original birth record]

Original birth record of Conrad Fuchs.

N. 16 ACTE DE NAISSANCE

L'an *Milhuit Cent Septe* le *Sept* du mois de *Fevrier* ä *Onze* heure du *matin* pardevant nous *Maire* faisant les fonctions d'officier de l'état civil de la Mairie de *Uchtelfangen* Canton de *Ottweiler* Département de la Sarre, est comparu *le Sieur Nicolas Fuchs* âgé de *quarante un* ans, profession de *Cultivateur* domicilié ä *Weylerhoff*, qui nous a présenté un enfant du sexe *Masculin* né ä *Weylerhoff* le *Sept* jour du mois de *Fevrier* ä *un* heure du *matin* de *Nicolas Fuchs* profession de *Cultivateur* domicilié a *Weylerhoff* et de *Margueritte Schorr* son épouse, et auquel enfant il a déclaré vouloir donner les prénoms de *Conrad* les dites déclaration et présentation faites en présence de *Nicolas Berman* âgé de *trente* ans, profession de *Cultivateur* domicilié ä *Weylerhoff* premier témoin et de *François Jochum* âgé de *quarante trois* ans, profession de *Cultivateur* domicilié ä *Uchtelfangen* second témoin, et ont *le pére* et les témoins signé avec nous le présent acte de naissance, aprés qu'il leur en été fait lecture.
Fait ä *Uchtelfangen* les jour, mois et an que dessus. *Le Maire de Uchtelfangen.*
Nicolaus Fuchs   Nicolas Berman   Frantz Jochum   Schneider
Maire

Transcribed birth record of Conrad Fuchs.

Number 16. Record of Birth.

In the year one thousand eight hundred seven on the seventh of the month of February at eleven o'clock in the morning there appeared before ourself, the Mayor, performing the functions of the officer of civil registration of the Mayoralty of Uchtelfangen, Canton of Ottweiler, District of the Saar, Mr. Nicolas Fuchs, aged forty-one years, occupation farmer, resident at Weilerhof, who presented a child of male sex born at Weilerhof on the seventh day of the month of February at one o'clock in the morning, of Nicolas [Nicolaus] Fuchs, occupation farmer, resident at Weilerhof and of Margueritte [Margaretha] Schorr his wife, and to which child he declared that he wished to give the given name of Conrad, said declaration and presentation done in the presence of Nicolas Berman, aged thirty years, occupation farmer, resident at Weilerhof, first witness, and of François [Franz] Jochum, aged forty-three years, occupation farmer, resident at Uchtelfangen, second witness, and the father and the witnesses signed the present birth record together with ourself after it had been read aloud to them. Done at Uchtelfangen on the day, month, and year as above. The Mayor of Uchtelfangen

Nicolaus Fuchs   Nicolas Berman   Frantz Jochum   Schneider

                                                          Mayor

---

Translated birth record of Conrad Fuchs.

and Catherine Woll (see pages 86-88). These records were written in French, in 1807 and 1788 respectively, because these areas were under French control. The format is identical with records written in German under the same Napoleonic laws. The mayors are typically the officers of civil registration; sometimes the vice mayors (adjuncts). They typically sign their names with a flourish. Mayoralty, canton, and district are all French governmental subdivisions. French names are given in the documents, although some persons signed with German names. For example, François signed his name Frantz. If Margueritte had been able to sign, she probably would have signed her name Margaretha. In other cases spellings vary in the documents due to human error.

The marriage record is replete with fill-in-the-blank areas, typical of the fixed format of Napoleonic forms. These standarized forms are a great boon to genealogists because we can tell from one form to another what information goes where and what to expect.

The next three documents are in Latin. The births of Johann Georg Weiland, Anna Dangelmayer, and Agnes Hummel show us two different layouts for a birth record, Anna's and Agnes's being the same layout. The birth record of Johann Georg Weiland is the more typical "open" style, lacking the headings found in Anna's and Agnes's. The open style makes it more difficult to quickly and assuredly locate the important genealogical information. (See pages 89-91.)

Next, we will view the marriage dispensation of Nikolaus Schorr and Margaretha Dreyer, written in Latin on a preprinted form with a seal and a monogram letter (L). This document is not a record of marriage but a document granting permission to allow the couple to be married. Note the reference to the "canonical impediment" amounting to "a fourth degree to a fourth consanguinity," which were hindrances dispensed with henceforth. In other words, they were cousins distant enough relationship-wise to allow their wedding to proceed, but they still needed church approval. (See pages 92-94.)

Then we illustrate two death records, one written in Latin, and another written in German and created in America using an English writing style. Hermann Heinrich Rosebrock is the great-grandfather of Ernest Thode. (See pages 95-96.)

Finally, we have two examples of emigration records. The first record is for Simon Albert, and it was printed in a German newspaper in German Fraktur style. (See page 96.) Such newspaper notices gave warning to creditors that someone intended to leave the country. The second record is for Johann Georg Weiland (Jean Georges Weiland). It is quite extensive and is a copy of the original passport brought to this country and preserved in the family. (See pages 97-112.) Notice that the document is replete with many official stamps, seals, and signatures, largely of customs officials, which allowed his passage through Europe on his way to America. We find a personal description with fifteen characteristics, his signature, the fees he paid, and the path that he traversed on his way to Le Havre, France, where he and his family embarked, leaving a beautiful paper trail. Johann Georg Weiland is a citizen of the Prussian Rhine Province but had to travel through Karlsruhe, Baden, on his way to France. He is the great-great-great-grandfather of Chris Anderson.

Original marriage record of Johann Meiser and Catharina Woll.

No. *18*   ACTE DE MARIAGE.

L'an mil huit cent *Treize* le *Vingt.huit* du mois de *May* à *huit* heure du *matin* pardevant nous *Maire* de la Mairie de *Uchtelfangen* faisant les fonctions d'officier de l'état civil de la Commune de *Gennweiler* ressortissant da ladite Mairie, Canton de *Ottweiler*   Département de la Sarrre, sont comparus le Sieur *Jean Meyser* garçon   âgé de *Vingt quatre*   ans, né à *Gennweiler le seize November 1788*,   profession de *Cultivateur*   domicilie à *Gennweiler* fils *mineur*   du Sieur *Jacques Meyser* profession de *Cultivateur* domicilie à *Gennweiler, y decedé le*

et de la Dame *Catharine Dorr, Ci présente & Consentante*

et la *Demoiselle Catherine Woll*- agée de *dix huit* ans, née à *Quirschied le deux Aout 1795, sans* profession de —domiciliée à *Quirschied* fille *mineur* du Sieur *Andrés Woll*   profession de *Cultivateur* domicilié à *Quirschied, y décédé le*

et de la Dame *Anne Marie Kieffer, Ci présente & Consentante* ,

Meyser Jean marié a Catherine Woll

lesquels futurs époux nous ont requis de procéder à célébration du mariage projetté entre eux, et dont les publications ont été faites devant la principale porte de notre maison commune, savoir: la première le *seize* du mois de *May* de l'an *mil huit Cent Treize* à *Neuf* heure du *matin* et le second le *Vingt-trois* du mois de *May* de l'an *mil huit Cent Treize à Neuf* heure du *matin, les même publications ont en lieu, les mêmes Jours à la Mairie de Heusweiler* .

Aucune opposition audit mariage ne nous ayant été signifiée, et toutes les formalités requises par la loi ayant été remplies, ainsi qu'il résulte des pièces alléguées ci-dessus, nous   *Maire* officier de l'état civil de la Mairie de   *Uchtelfangen*   faisant droit à leur réquisition, après avoir donné lecture de toutes les pièces sus-mentionnees et du chapitre 6 du titre du code civil intitulé *du mariage* , avons demandé au futur époux et à la future épouse s'ils veulent se prendre pour mari et pour femme: chacun d'eux ayant répondu séparément et affirmativement, déclarons au nom de la loi, que le Sieur *Jean Meyser, garçon susdit* et la *Demoiselle Catherine Woll susdite* sont unis par le mariage; de quoi nous avons dressé acte, en présence de *Jean Woll* demeurant à *Quirschied* Département de *la Sarre* profession de *Cultivateur* âgé de *Vingt huit* ans, *frére de le future epouse* de *Jean Schroeder* demeurant à *Gennweiler* Département de *la Sarre* profession de *Cultivateur* âgé de *Trente deux* ans, *Cousin germaine de marié* de *Nicolas Scherschel* demeurant à *Gennweiler* Département de *la Sarre* profession de *Berger* âgé de *Trente un* ans, *Commé témoin* et de *Philippe Nilles* , demeurant à *Illingen* Département de *la Sarre* profession de *Journalier* , âgé de *quarante* ans, *Commé témoin*   ; lesquels après qu'il leur en a été aussi donné lecture, l'ont signé avec nous et les parties contractantes,   *excepté la future epouse, la mére delle & la mére du future epoux, qui ont déclaré ne savoir écrire* .

Fait à *Illingen* les jour, mois et an que dessus. L. *Maire* de *Uchtelfangen*

Johannes Meyser   *Philib Nilles*   *Schneider* .
Johannes Schroeder   *Nickel Scherschel*
Johannes Woll

Transcribed marriage record of Johann Meiser and Catharina Woll.

Number 18.   Marriage Record.

In the year one thousand eight hundred thirteen on the twenty-eighth of the month of May at eight o'clock in the morning there appeared before ourself, Mayor of the Mayoralty of Uchtelfangen, performing the duties of the officer of civil registration of the community of Gennweiler, located within said Mayoralty, Canton of Ottweiler, District of the Saar, the gentleman Jean [= Johannes] Meyser, young man aged twenty-four years, born at Gennweiler on the sixth of November 1788, occupation farmer, resident at Gennweiler, minor son of the gentleman Jacques [= Jacob] Meyser, occupation farmer, resident at Gennweiler, deceased on the ..., and of the lady Catherine [= Catharina] Dorr, present here and consenting, and Miss Catherine Woll, aged eighteen years, born at Quierschied on the second of August 1795, without occupation, resident at Quierschied, minor daughter of the gentleman Andrés [= Andreas] Woll, occupation farmer, resident at Quierschied, deceased on the ..., and of the lady Anne Marie [= Anna Maria] Kieffer, present here and consenting, whereupon the future couple requested ourself to proceed with the conclusion of the marriage intended between them, and since the publications of banns took place before the main door of our town hall, namely the first one on the sixteenth of the month of May of the year one thousand eight hundred thirteen at nine o'clock in the morning and the second one on the twenty-third of the month of May of the year one thousand eight hundred thirteen at nine o'clock in the morning, said publications taking place on the same days at the Mayoralty of Heusweiler.

John Meyser to Catherine Woll

No objection having been made to said marriage, after the banns referred to above, we, the Mayor, officer of civil registration of the Mayoralty of Uchtelfangen, performed their request according to law, after having read all of the aforementioned documents and Chapter 6 entitled "On Marriage" from the Civil Code, having requested the future groom and the future bride if they wish to take one another as husband and as wife, each of them having responded separately and affirmatively, we declare in the name of the law that the gentleman Jean [= Jonannes] Meyser, young man aforementioned, and aforesaid Miss Catherine [= Catharina] Woll are married, whereupon we made out this record in the presence of Jean [= Johannes] Woll, resident at Quierschied, District of the Saar, occupation farmer, aged twenty-eight years, brother of the future bride; of Jean [= Johannes] Schroeder, resident at Gennweiler, District of the Saar, occupation farmer, aged thirty-two years, first cousin of the groom; of Nicolas [= Nicolaus] Scherschel, resident at Gennweiler, District of the Saar, occupation shepherd, aged thirty-one years, as witness; and of Philippe [= Philipp] Nilles, resident at Illingen, District of the Saar, occupation day-laborer, aged forty years, as witness; after which and after it had been read aloud, they signed together with ourself and the contracting parties, excepting the future bride, her mother, and the mother of the future groom, who stated that they are unable to write.

Done at Illingen on the day, month, and year as above. The Mayor of Uchtelfangen.

Schneider.

Johannes Meyser   Philib Nilles
Johannes Schroeder   Nickel Scherschel
Johannes Woll

Translated marriage record of Johann Meiser and Catharina Woll.

Original birth record of Johann Georg Weiland.

1789.
Joes. Georgius
Weyland

Anno Dmô millesimo septuagentesimo octuagesimo nona,
die veso octavâ Decembris circa horam octavam matutinam
natus est, et eodem die baptizatus Joannes Georgius
Weijland filius legitimus Mathiâ Weijland, et Barbarâ Benoit
conjugu ex Genweiler parochiâ de Illingen, levantibus è sancta
fonte joe Georgio Zewé, et Annâ Mariâ Woll utroque ex
Genweiler, Pater et matrina scribendiigsenti subsignant
Patrinus meen subscribens.   *signu*

signu			*ita testator*
Mathiä X Weiland		*An Maria X Woll*	
manuale	*Johan Jerg Zewe*	*manuale*	*J. Marn Pastor*
			in Klingen

Transcribed birth record of Johann Georg Weiland.

1789.
Johann Georg
Weyland

In the year of Our Lord one thousand seven hundred eighty-nine on the feast? day the eighth of December at about the hour of eight o'clock in the morning there was born, and on the same day there was baptized Johann Georg Weyland, legitimate son of Mathias Weyland and Barbara Benoit, a married couple from Gennweiler in the parish of Illingen, with the sponsors at the sacred font Johann Georg Zewe and Anna Maria Woll, both of Gennweiler, the father and godmother, being illiterate, making their marks below, the godfather and I signing below.   Her mark

His mark			Attest thus:
Mathias X Weiland		An Maria X Woll	
signed	Johan Jerg Zewe	signed	J. Marn, Pastor
			in Klingen

Translated birth record of Johann Georg Weiland.

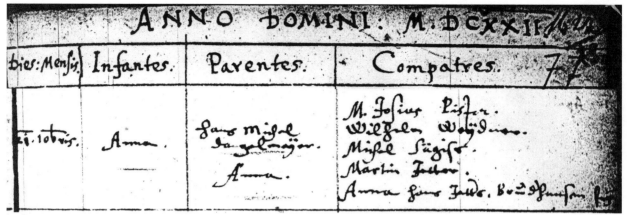

Original birth record of Anna Dangelmayer.

ANNO DOMINI M.DCXXII				
Dies.	Mensis.	Infantes.	Parentes.	Compatres.
21.	10ᵗ bris	Anna.	Hans Michel Dangelmaÿer. Anna	M. Josias Pistor. Wilhelm Weÿdner. Michel Sägist. Martin Fetter. Anna Hans Fetter. Brudhausen P.

Transcribed birth record of Anna Dangelmayer.

In the Year of the Lord 1622				
Day.	Month.	Children.	Parents.	Godparents.
21.	December	Anna.	Hans Michel Dangelmaÿer. Anna	Josias Pistor, master of a trade. Wilhelm Weydner. Michael Saegist. Martin Fetter. Anna, wife of Hans Fetter. Brudhausen, Pastor.

Translated birth record of Anna Dangelmayer.

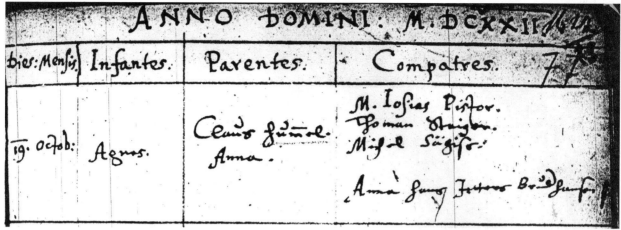

Original birth record of Agnes Hummel.

ANNO DOMINI M.DCXXII				
Dies.	Mensis.	Infantes.	Parentes.	Compatres.
19.	Octob:	Agnes.	Claus Humel.	M. Josias Pistor.
			Anna.	Thomas Steiger.
				Michel Sägist.
				Anna Hans Jochens
				Brudhausen P.

Transcribed birth record of Agnes Hummel.

In the Year of Our Lord 1622				
Day.	Month.	Children.	Parents.	Godparents.
19.	Octob[er]	Agnes.	Claus Hummel.	Josias Pistor, master.
			Anna.	Thomas Steiger.
				Michael Saegist.
				Anna, wife of Hans Jochen.
				Brudhausen, Pastor.

Translated birth record of Agnes Hummel.

 UDOVICUS-JOSEPHUS DE MONTMORENCY-LAVAL, Dei gratiâ & fanctæ Sedis Apoftolicæ auctoritate Epifcopus Metenfis, primus Baro Chriftianus, Sacri Romani Imperii Princeps; dilecto nobis in Chrifto Rectori Parochialis Ecclefiæ *de ottiouillar* ————— Salutem & Benedictionem in Domino. Notum facimus quòd vifâ fupplica-tione nobis oblatâ per *Nicolaum Schorr et margarittam Dreyer, ancbor parachianos tuos*

per quam nobis expofuerunt quòd legitimo Matrimonio conjugi cupientes, impedimentum Canonicum agnoverunt, quia fcilicet *à quarto ad quartam Confanguinitatis gradum fefe invicem attingant* Ideò nos humiliter deprecari fecerunt, ut cum ipfis fuper prædicto impedimento difpenfare dignaremur. Vifâ etiam atque attentiùs perpenfâ inquifitione de contentis in prædictâ fupplicatione, *cu Decreto noftro dé die 31. Januarii currentis anni* Nos certiores facti fupplicum preces veritate niti, petitamque difpenfationem nulli fidelium fcandalo fore, imò iis & fuis plurimùm profuturam, conceffimus ut unâ Matrimonium contrahere valeant, nonobftante dicto impedimento *quarto ad quartum Confanguinitatis gradûs super quo*

————— cum illis (moventibus animum noftrum ad id rationabilibus caufis) difpenfavimus & per præfentes difpenfamus in Domino. Quocircà tibi mandamus quatenùs ad Benedictionem Nuptialem recipias *præfatos Nicolaum et margarittam* ————— nonobftante dicto impedimento, fervatis fervandis, modò nullum aliud obftet impedimentum Canonicum vel Civile. Datum Metis fub Signo *manuali vicarii noftri Generalis*, Sigilloque noftro / ac Secretarii Cameræ noftræ Epifcopalis fubfcriptione, anno Domini millefimo feptingentefimo *feptuagefimo fecundo*, die verò menfis *februarie decimâ quarta*

De *vaxemus Niger*

De Mandato
Machieu

Original marriage dispensation for Nikolaus Schorr and Margaretha Dreyer, in Latin.

udovicus Josephus de Montmorency-Lavae,
Dei gratiâ & sanctae Sedis Apostolicae auctoritate Episcopus Metensis, primus
Baro Christianus, Sacri Romani Imperii Princeps; dilecto nobis in Christo
Rectori Parochialis Ecclesiae *de Ottweiller*
Salutem & Benedictionem in Domino. Notum facimus quòd visa supplica
tione nobis oblatâ per *Nicolaum Schorr et Margarittam*
Dreger, Amberg parochianos Trier

per quam nobis exposuerunt quòd legitimo Matrimonio conjugi cupientes, impedimentum
Canonicum agnoverunt, quia scilicet *a quarto ad quartum Consanguinitatis*
gradium lese? invidineam? attingent.
Ideò nos humiliter deprecari fecerunt, ut com ipsis superpraedicto impedimento dispensare dignaremur.
Visâ etiam atque attentiùs perpensa inquisitione de contentis in praedictâ supplicatione, . . *? decrete nostris*
de die 31. Januarii currenti anni.
Nos certiores facti supplicum preces veritate niti(?), petitamque dispensationem nùlli fidelium scandalo
fore, imòiis & fuis plurimùm profuturam, concessimus ut unà Matrimonium contrahere valeant,
nonobstante dicto impedimento *quarto ad quartum Consanguinitatis*
gradûs, Super, quo

cum illis (moventibus animum nostrum ad id rationabilibus causis) dispensavimus & per
praesentes dispensamús in Domine(?) Quocircà tibi mandamus quatenùs ad Benedictionem Nuptialem
recipias *profates(?) Nicolaum et Margarittam* nonobstante
dicto impedimento, servatis servandis, modò nullum aliud obstet impedimentum Canonicum vel
Civile. Datum Meús sub Signo *manuali vicarie nostri Genèralis*,
Sigilloque nostro ac Secretarii Camerae nostrae Episcopalis subscriptione, anno Domini
millesimo septingentesimo *Septuagesimo Secundo*, die verò mensis *Februarè*
decimae quartae.

Deo vaneines vaperir.(??)
De Mandato.
Maurien. (?)

Transcribed marriage dispensation for Nikolaus Schorr and Margaretha Dreyer.

 udwig Joseph of Montmorency-Lavae,
by the Grace of God the authority of the Holy Apostolic See and the Bishopric of
Mainz, the head Christian Baron and Elector of the Holy Roman Empire; to our
esteemed rector of the church parish of Ottweiler, Greeting & benediction in the Lord. We
take note of your request which we have seen, presented by Nicolaus Schorr and
Margaretha Dreger, Amberg in the parish of Trier

by which we see that you wish this to be a legitimate marriage of a couple, despite the canonical impediment, which
amounts to a fourth degree to a fourth consanguinity.

On that account we humbly make note that we can dispense this aforementioned hindrance.

After seeing the same and weighing attentively the contents of the aforesaid petition, we issued our decree of the 31st
of January of the current year.

We have striven to be certain of the veracity of the facts presented in the preceding petition, and since the petition and
dispensation will cause no scandal in the faith, now and forevermore, we recognize, in order to make a marriage
contract valid, that nothing stands in the way of said marriage of a fourth degree to a fourth consanguinity, we the
above, who are authorized to issue dispensations

(if our spirit is moved on account of the reasonableness of the cause, as in this case) and by this document we issue
this dispensation in the name of the Lord. Wherefore we issue to you this mandate to perform the nuptial ceremony
for Nicolaus and Margaretha, since nothing stands in the way, assuming that nothing else stands in the way as an
impediment in civil or canon law.

Done by me under the hand sign of our vicar general, with our seal and the signature of the secretary of the chamber
of our diocese, in the year of our Lord one thousand seven hundred seventy-two, on the actual fourteenth day of the
month of February.

> By the glory of God.
> According to the mandate.
> Maurien.

Translated marriage dispensation for Nikolaus Schorr and Margaretha Dreyer.

Original death record of Margaretha Hinsberger.

Transcribed death record of Margaretha Hinsberger.

	Exweiler
Death of Margaretha Hinsberger	In the year of the Virgin, (one thousand) seven hundred fifty on the sixth day of January at the age of about seventy-five years, at St. Matthew's Church after being forearmed with the sacred rites there died Margaretha Hinsberger, wife of the deceased Valentin Derenbaecker of Exweiler, and on the eighth day of the same month she was buried in said cemetery at Exweiler according to the Catholic Christian custom at the above according to its mandates, which is attested by
	J.N. Weiler, Vicar of the place Ottweiler.

Translated death record of Margaretha Hinsberger.

Original death record of Hermann Heinrich Rosebrock.

Rosebrock   7. Hermann Heinrich Rosebrock geb. 1 Januar
1841 in Buchholz Hanover starb in Indianapolis
Bluff Road am 17. Juli 1915 und wurde am
20 Juli auf Crown Hill begraben 74. J. 6. M. 17. T.
Foester Text Off. 14.13.

Transcribed death record of Hermann Heinrich Rosebrock.

Rosebrock   7. Hermann Heinrich Rosebrock, born 1 January
1841 in Buchholz, Hanover, died in Indianapolis
on Bluff Road on 17 July 1915 and was buried in
Crown Hill on 20 July, 74 years, 6 months, 17 days.
Foester Text: Revelation 14:13.

Translated death record of Hermann Heinrich Rosebrock.

Detmold. Der Ziegler Simon Albert von Nr. 34 in Diestelbruch will im nächsten Monate nach Amerika auswandern.
Detmold den 30. Mai 1857.
Fürstlich Lippisches Amt. Hasse.

Original emigration record of Simon Albert.

Detmold. Der Ziegler Simon Albert von Nr. 34 in Diestelbruch will
im nächsten Monate nach Amerika auswandern.
Detmold den 30. Mai 1857.
Fürstlich Lippisches Amt. Hase.

Transcribed emigration record of Simon Albert.

Detmold. The brickmaker Simon Albert of No. 34 in Diestelbruch intends to
emigrate to America next month.
Detmold, on 30 May 1857.
Royal Lippe District Office. Hasse.

Translated emigration record of Simon Albert.

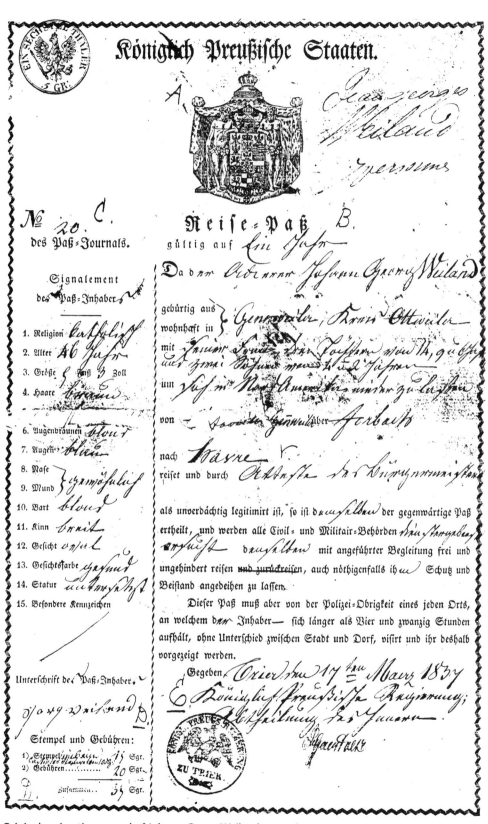

Original emigration record of Johann Georg Weiland, page 1.

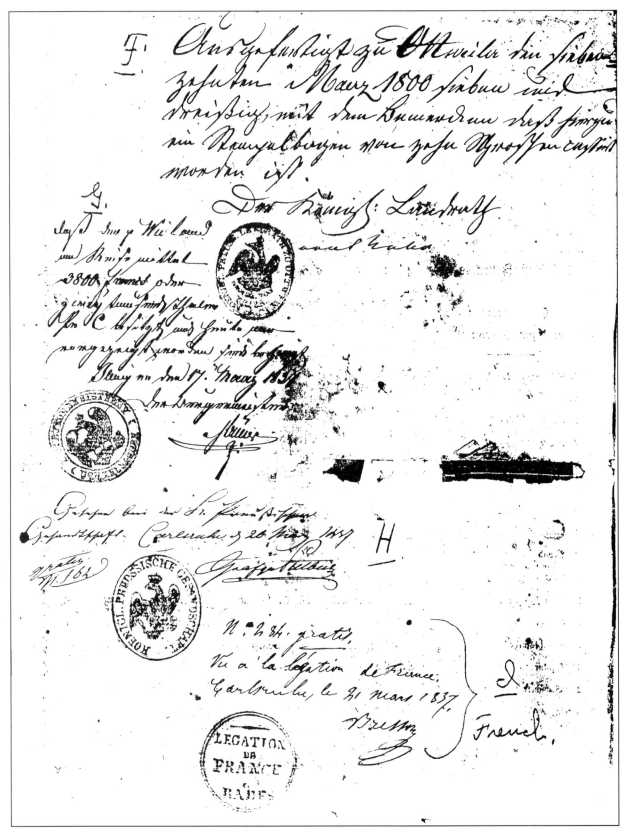

Original emigration record of Johann Georg Weiland, page 2.

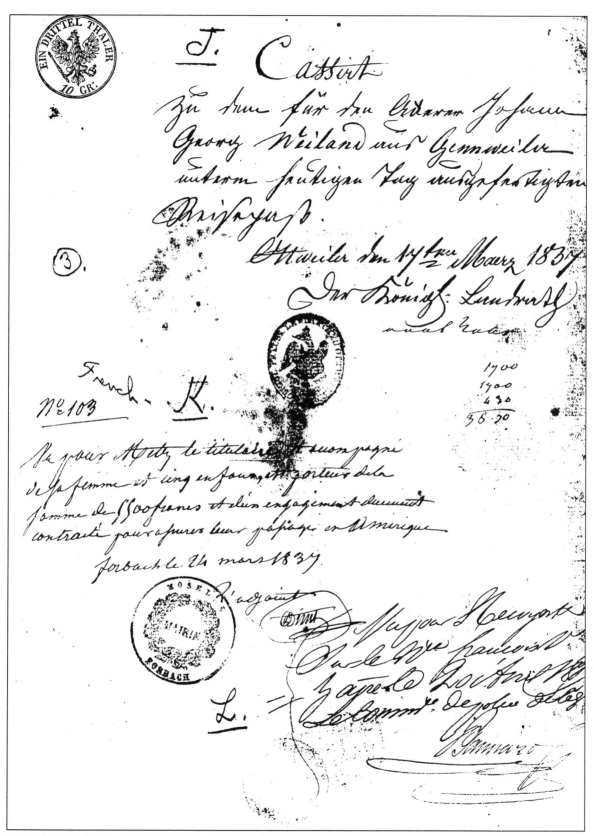

Original emigration record of Johann Georg Weiland, page 3.

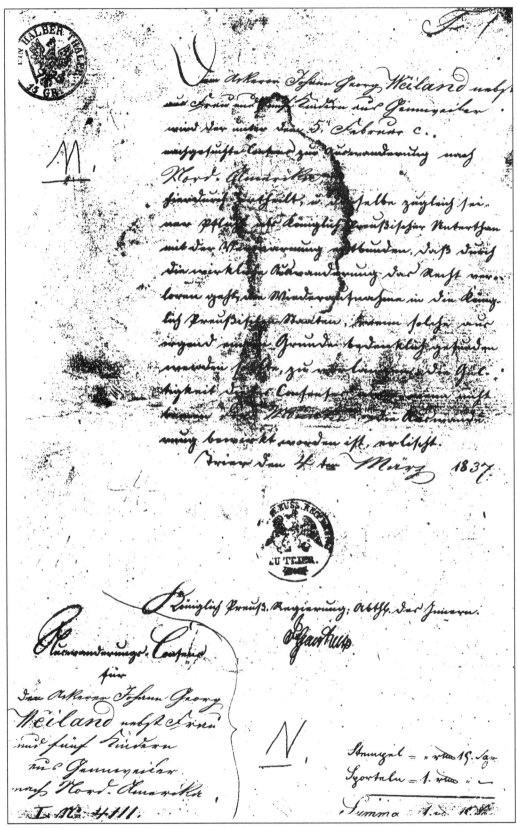

Original emigration record of Johann Georg Weiland, page 4.

Königlich Preußische Staaten.

(Seal) EIN SECHSTEL THALER 5 GR.

Jean Georges
Weiland
7 personen

Nᵒ *20.*
des Paß:Journals.

Reise:Paß
gültig auf *ein Jahr*

Da d *er Ackerer Johann Georg Weiland*

gebürtig aus
Gimmweiler, Kreis Ottweiler
wohnhaft in
mit *seiner Frau, drei Töchtern von 14, 9, 6 Jahren*
und zwei Söhnen von 4 und 2 Jahren
um *sich in NordAmerika nieder zu lassen*

von ~~Gimmweiler~~ *Gimmweiler über Forbach*

nach *Havre*
reiset und durch *Atteste des Bürgermeisters*

als unverdächtig legitimirt ist, so ist *demselben* der gegenwärtige Paß
ertheilt, und werden alle Civil: und Militair: Behörden *dienstergebenst*
ersucht d emselben mit angeführter Begleitung frei und
ungehindert reisen ~~und zurückreisen~~, auch nötigenfalls ih *m* Schutz und
Beistand angedeihen zu lassen.
       Dieser Paß muß aber von der Polizei:Obrigkeit eines jeden Orts,
an welchem d *er* Inhaber --- sich länger als Vier und zwanzig Stunden
aufhält, ohne Unterschied zwischen Stadt und Dorf, visirt und ihr deshalb
vorgezeigt werden.
       Gegeben, *Trier den 17ᵗᵉⁿ März 1837*
Königlich Preußische Regierung;
Abtheilung des Innern.

(illegible signature)

(Seal) KÖNIGL. PREUSS. REGIERUNG ZU TRIER.

Signalement
des Paß:Inhabers

---

1. Religion *katholisch*
2. Alter *46 Jahr*
3. Größe *5 Fuß 3 Zoll*
4. Haare *braun*
5. *???*
6. Augenbrauen *blond*
7. Augen *blau*
8. Nase *gewöhnlich*
9. Mund *gewöhnlich*
10. Bart *blond*
11. Kinn *breit*
12. Gesicht *oval*
13. Gesichtsfarbe *gesund*
14. Statur *untersetzt*
15. Besondere Kennzeichen

Unterschrift des Paß:Inhabers

Georg Weiland

Stempel und Gebühren:

1) Stempel ....15 Sgr.
    (illegible)..............10 Sgr.
2) Gebühren............................. 20 Sgr.

Zusammen   35 Sgr.

Clarified emigration record of Johann Georg Weiland, page 1.

Ausgefertigt zu Ottweiler den siebenzehnten Maerz 1800 sieben und dreißig, mit dem Bemerken daß hierzu ein Stempelbogen von zehn SGroschen caßiert worden ist.

Der Königl: Landrath
Ottweiler

(Seal) KÖNIGL. PREUSS. LANDRATH ZU OTTWEILER REG.BEZ. VON TRIER

Daß der GJ Weiland an Reisemittel 3800 francs oder zwey tausend Thaler Pr L besitzt und heute mir vorgezeigt worden sind bescheinigt

Illingen den 17. Maerz 1837

Der Buergermeister
T. Lauer

(Seal) BUERGERMEISTEREI UCHTELFANGEN

Gesehen bei der C. Preußischen Gesandtschaft. Carlsruhe d. 20 März 1837.

gratis

N. 162

Graf v. Kelbach

(Seal) KÖNIGL. PREUSSISCHE GESANDTSCHAFT

N 284. gratis
vu á la legation de France:
Carlsruhe, le 21 Mars 1837.
Bretton

(Seal) LEGATION DE FRANCE BADE

Clarified emigration record of Johann Georg Weiland, page 2.

(Seal) EIN DRITTEL THALER   10 GR.

Laſſirt

zu dem für den Ackerer Johann
Georg Weiland aus Gennweiler
unterm heutigen Tag ausgefertigten
Reisepaß.

Ottweiler den 17ten Maerz 1837
Der Königl: Landrath
oval Notar

(Seal) KÖNIGL. PREUSS. LANDRAT ZU OTTWEILER

№ 103
Va pour Metz le titulaire et accompagné
de sa femme et enfans, et porteur dela
homme des 5500 francs et .... engagement demeurent?
contracté pour assures leurs passages en Amerique
Forbach le 24 mars 1837.

L'adjoint
(illegible)

(Seal) MAIRIE MOSELLE FORBACH

.... Newyork
...... Havre .....
...... le 20 Avril No.
Le Commd...........
(illegible)

Clarified emigration record of Johann Georg Weiland, page 3.

(Seal) EIN HALBER THALER   15 GR.

*Der Ackerer Johann Georg Weiland nebst ---
Frau und fünf Kindern aus Gemmweiler
wird der unter dem 5. Februar c.
nachgesuchte Consens zur Auswanderung nach
Nord-Amerika;
hierdurch ertheilt, u. derselbe zugleich seiner Pflicht des Königlich preußischen Unterthan
mit der Verwarnung entbunden, daß durch
die wirkliche Auswanderung das Recht ver-
loren geht, die Wiederaufnahme in die Königlich Preußischen Staaten, einem solche aus
irgend einem Grunde bedenklich gefunden
werden wollte, zu verlangen, die Gül-
tigkeit dieses Consenses aber einem nicht
immer drei Monate, die Auswanderung bewirkt worden ist, erlischt.*

Trier den 4ten März 1837.

(Seal) KÖNIGL. PREUSS. REGIERUNG ZU TRIER.

*Königlich Preuß. Regierung, Abthl. des Innern.
J. Gaertner.*

*Auswanderungs-Consens
für
den Ackerer Johann Georg
Weiland nebst Frau
und fünf Kindern
aus Gemmweiler
nach Nord-Amerika.
J. № 4111.*

*Stempel - " rthlr 15. Xgr.
Portaln - 1 rthlr " ====
Summa - 1 rthlr 15 Xgr.*

Clarified emigration record of Johann Georg Weiland, page 4.

Königlich Preußische Staaten.

EIN SECHSTEL THALER 5 GR.

Jean Georges
Weiland
7 personne

No 20.
    des Paß:Journals.

Reise:Paß
gültig auf Ein Jahr

Signalement
des Paß:Inhabers

Da der Ackerer Johann Georg Weiland

gebürtig aus
               Gennweiler, Kreis Ottweiler

1. Religion katholisch
2. Alter 46 Jahr
3. Größe 5 Fuß 3 Zoll
4. Haare braun
5. ???
6. Augenbrauen blond
7. Augen blaŭ
8. Nase gewöhnlich
9. Mund gewöhnlich
10. Bart blond
11. Kinn breit
12. Gesicht oval
13. Gesichtsfarbe gesŭnd
14. Statur ŭntersetzt
15. Besondere Kennzeichen /

wonhnhaft in
mit seiner Frau, drei Töchter von 14, 9, 6 Jahren
ŭnd zwei Söhnen von 4 ŭnd 2 Jahren
um sich in NordAmerika nieder zŭ laßen

von ~~Farweiler~~ Gennweiler über Forbach

nach Havre
reiset und durch Atteste des Bürgermeisters

als unverdächtig legitimirt ist, so ist demselben der
gegenwärtige Paß ertheilt, und werden alle Civil: und
Militair: Behörden dienstergebenst ersucht denselben mit
angeführter Begleitung frei und
ungehindert reisen ~~und zurückreisen~~, auch nöthigenfalls ihm
Schutz und Beistand angedeihen zu lassen.
    Dieser Paß muß aber von der Polizei:Obrigkeit eines

Unterschrift des Paß:Inhabers

jeden Orts, an welchem der Inhaber sich länger als Vier und
zwanzig Stunden

Gorg Weiland

aufhält, ohne Unterschied zwischen Stadt und Dorf, visirt und
ihr deshalb vorgezeigt werden.

Stempel und Gebühren:

Gegeben, Trier den 17 ten März 1837

1) Stempel .... 15 Sgr.
    (illegible) .... 10 Sgr.
2) Gebühren............. <u>20 Sgr.</u>
    Zusammen .... 35 Sgr.

    Königlich Preußische Regierung;
    Abtheilung des Innern.
      (illegible signature)

(Seal) KÖNIGL. PREUSS. REGIERUNGZU TRIER.

Transcribed emigration record of Johann Georg Weiland, page 1.

Ausgefertigt zu Ottweiler den sieben =
zehnten Maerz 1800 sieben und
dreißig, mit dem Bemercken daß hierzŭ
ein Stempelbogen von zehn SGroschen caßirt
worden ist.

               Der Königl: Landrath
                    Ottweiler

(Seal) KÖNIGL. PREUSS. LANDRATH ZU OTTWEILER REG.BEZ. VON TRIER.

Daß der G Weiland
an Reisemittel
3800 francs oder
zwey taŭsend Thaler
Pr C besitzt ŭnd heŭte mir
vorgezeigt worden sind bescheinigt
               Illingen den 17. Maerz 1837
                 Der Buergermeister
                    S. Bauer

(Seal) BUERGERMEISTEREI UCHTELFANGEN.

       Gesehen bei der K. Preußischen
Gesandschaft. Carlsruhe d 20 März 1837.

gratis   Graf v. Stelbach
M. 162

(Seal) KÖNIGL. PREUSSISCHE GESANDTSCHAFT.

               No. 284. gratis
               vu á la légation de France:
               Carlsruhe, le 21 Mars 1837.
                      Bretton

(Seal) LEGATION DE FRANCE BADE.

Transcribed emigration record of Johann Georg Weiland, page 2.

(Seal) EIN DRITTEL THALER 10 GR.   Cassirt

zu dem für den Ackerer Johann
Georg Weiland aus Gennweiler
unterm heŭtigen Tag ausgesfertigten
Reisepaß.

Ottweiler den 17ten Maerz 1837
Der Königl: Landrath
oval Notar

(Seal) KÖNIGL. PREUSS. LANDRAT ZU OTTWEILER.

N°. 103

Va pour Metz le titulaire et accompagñe
de sa femme et enfans, et porteur dela
homme des 5500 francs et . . . . engagement demeurent?
contracté pour assures leurs passages en Amerique
Forbach le 24 mars 1837.

L'adjoint
(illegible)

(Seal) MAIRIE MOSELLE FORBACH.

.... Newyork
.... Havre ....
...... le 20 Avril No.
Le Commd ....
(illegible signature)

Transcribed emigration record of Johann Georg Weiland, page 3.

(Seal) EIN HALBER THALER 15 GR.

Der Ackerer Johann Georg Weiland nebst
---Fraŭ ŭnd fünf Kindern aŭs Gennweiler
wird der ŭnter dem 5. Februar c.
nachgesŭchte Consens zŭr Aŭswanderung nach
Nord: Amerika;
hierdurch ertheilt, ŭ. derselbe zŭgleich seiner Pflicht des Königlich preußischen Unterthan
mit der Verwarnŭng entbŭnden, daß dŭrch
die wirkliche Aŭswanderŭng das Recht ver-
loren geht, die Wiederaŭfnahme in die Königlich Preußischen Staaten, einem solche aŭs
irgend einem Grŭnde bedenklich gefŭnden
werden wollte, zŭ verlangen, die Gül-
tigkeit dieses Consenses aber einem nicht
immer drei Monate, die Aŭswanderung bewirkt worden ist, erlischt.
Trier den 4ten März 1837

(Seal) KÖNIGL. PREUSS. REGIERUNG ZU TRIER.

Königlich Preüß. Regierŭng, Abthl. des Innern.
J. Gaertner.

Auswanderŭngs-Consens
für
den Ackerer Johann Georg
Weiland nebst Frau
ŭnd fünf Kindern
aŭs Gennweiler
nach Nord:Amerika.
I. No 4111.

Stempel = " rtlr 15. Sgr.
Sporteln = 1 rtlr "---
Summa = 1 rtlr 15 Sgr

Transcribed emigration record of Johann Georg Weiland, page 4.

Royal Prussian States

(Seal) ONE-SIXTH THALER 5 GR(OSCHEN)

Jean Georges
Weiland
7 persons

No. 20
   of the Passport Journal.

Passport
Valid for one year

Description
of the passport holder

Since the farmer Johann Georg Weiland,
native of/resident in Gennweiler, County of Ottweiler,
is traveling with his wife, three daughters of 14, 9, and 6 years,
and two sons of 4 and 2 years
in order to settle in North America

1. Religion: Catholic
2. Age: 46 years
3. Height: 5.3 feet
4. Hair: brown
5. ...
6. Eyebrows: blond
7. Eyes: blue
8. Nose: ordinary
9. Mouth: ordinary
10. Beard: blond
11. Chin: broad
12. Face: oval
13. Complexion: healthy
14. Stature: low-set
15. Special distinguishing
      marks: --

from Gennweiler by way of Forbach

to LeHavre

and is legitimized as unsuspicious by attests of the mayor, the present passport is issued to him, and all civilian and military authorities are most duty-bound requested to allow him and his listed party to travel freely and unhindered, and also if necessary to offer him protection and assistance.

   However, this passport must be stamped with a visa by the police authority of each place in which the holder spends longer than twenty-four hours, without differentiation between city and village, and must therefore be shown.

Signature of the passport
holder:

Gorg Weiland

Stamp and fees:
1) Stamp ... 15 silver groschen
    10 silver groschen
2) Fees 20 silver groschen
    Together
35 silver groschen

Issued, Trier, on the 17th of March 1837.
   Royal Prussian Government
   Ministry of the Interior
      (illegible signature)

(Seal) ROYAL PRUSSIAN GOVERNMENT AT TRIER.

Translated emigration record of Johann Georg Weiland, page 1.

Issued at Ottweiler on the seventeenth
of March 1800 thirty-seven with the
remark that a stamped sheet was
receipted for ten silver groschen coins.
The Royal Rural Council.
Ottweiler.

(Seal) ROYAL PRUSSIAN COUNCIL AT OTTWEILER GOVERNING DISTRICT OF TRIER.

That G. Weiland possesses 3,800 francs
or two thousand thalers in Prussian
currency and that they were shown to me
today is certified.
Illingen, on 17 March 1837.
The Mayor. S. Bauer. (somewhat illegible)

 (Seal) MAYORALTY OF UCHTELFANGEN.

Seen at the Royal Prussian Embassy.
Carlsruhe on the 20th of March 1837.

free. Count von Stelbach. (somewhat illegible)
M. 162.

(Seal) ROYAL PRUSSIAN EMBASSY.

No. 284. Free.
Viewed at the legation of France.
Carlsruhe, on 21 March 1837.
Bretton (somewhat illegible)

(Seal) LEGATION OF FRANCE IN BADEN.

Translated emigration record of Johann Georg Weiland, page 2.

(Seal) ONE-THIRD THALER 10 GR(OSCHEN)

Received for the passport issued
today for the farmer Johann Georg
Weiland of Gennweiler.
Ottweiler, on the 17th of March 1837
The Royal District Court
Oval, Notary

(Seal) ROYAL PRUSSIAN DISTRICT OFFICE AT OTTWEILER.

No. 103

The person described, accompanied
by his wife and children, is going to
Metz and carries on himself 5,500
francs and a contract assuring their
passage to America.
Forbach, on 24 March 1837.
Mayoralty, Forbach, District of Moselle

The Vice Mayor
(illegible signature)

New York
Havre
the 29th of April No.
The commander
(illegible signature)

(Seal) MAYOR'S OFFICE, FORBACH, MOSELLE.

Translated emigration record of Johann Georg Weiland, page 3.

(Seal) ONE-HALF THALER 15 GR(OSCHEN)

The farmer Johann Georg Weiland and his wife and five children of Gennweiler is hereby granted the consent for emigration to North America requested on the 5th of February of the current year and he is simultaneously relieved of his duty of the Royal Prussian subject, with the warning that upon his actual emigration the right is lost to request to be reinstated into the Royal Prussian states even if he should have second thoughts about it for any reason, but the validity of this consent is not always three months after the emigration is done.

Trier, on the 4th of March, 1837

(Seal) ROYAL PRUSSIAN GOVERNMENT AT TRIER

Royal Prussian Government, Interior Department
J. Gaertner.

Emigration consent for the farmer Johann Georg Weiland with wife and five children from Gennweiler to North America I. No 4111.	Stamp: 15 silver groschen Fees: <u>1 Imperial thaler</u> Total: 1 Imperial thaler, 15 silver groschen

Translated emigration record of Johann Georg Weiland, page 4.

Note: The passport of Johann Georg Weiland shows his personal description with 15 characteristics, his signature, the fees paid, and the text of the document, all well fortified with official stamps, seals, and signatures, leaving a beautiful paper trail. It shows his travels through officialdom. He was a citizen of the Prussian Rhine Province but had to travel through Karlsruhe, Baden, on his way to France, and left via LeHavre.

SEVEN

Fitz Trails: A Case Study of an Eighteenth-Century German Lutheran Family

T his chapter and the next are going to be tales of discovery—in other words, how we stumbled across some Germanic-born ancestors. Grab a glass of lemonade or German beer, sit back, and join us on a genealogical hunt that we took a few years ago.

Case Study

DOCUMENTING THE FITZ FAMILY

You've already met Cassie Fitz in the introduction of this book. Now, as we promised, we'll share some documentation on Cassie's family. Let's view and evaluate some documents that we found. We'll start chronologically. First, we received copies of pages from John Fitz III's family Bible. Who was the writer? It was John Fitz himself, at least for the majority of this record. How do we know? Easy. He refers to Magdalena as his wife.

Information From John Fitz's Family Bible

When did he write this? It appears, based on the similarity of his handwriting, that the first seven lines were written at the same time. These seven lines would have been written after 10 July 1870 and before 23 October 1871 based on the seventh and eighth entries (Georg and Elizabeth's birth dates).

The 1871 entry was likely entered in 1871, but of the 1872 entry, we can only state that it was written in 1872 or later. The final two entries (John and Magdalena's birth dates) were likely written after 1872, duplicating the information on the first two lines.

What does all this mean?

First of all, this is an excellent document to help us establish relationships and likely birth dates. While this was not a record made by a church or civil authority

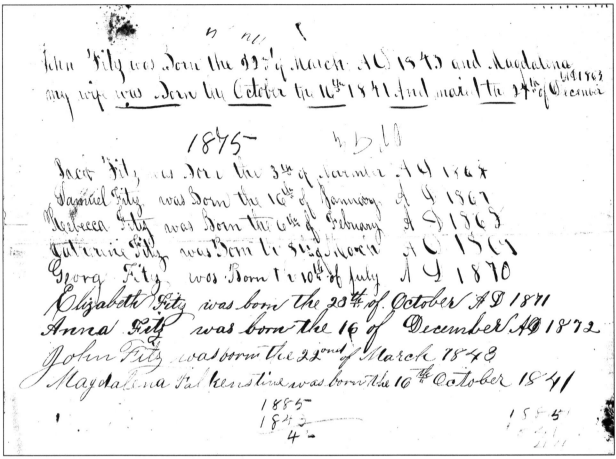

Information from the John Fitz family Bible.

Reminder

at the time the event occurred, it is still an excellent source. **Keep in mind, however, that when birth dates are entered years after the actual event, the record relies on memory.** The birth dates of most of these children were entered at least a year after the fact, and the birth dates for the parents, John and Magdalena, are well over a quarter of a century in the past. Most likely these family Bible dates are correct, but an alert genealogist does not accept them without some desire for further proof.

Other Sources

At another stage in our investigation, we received Cassie's teaching certificates. While interesting from a family history viewpoint, these documents did not provide any clues to Cassie's ancestry nor did they confirm basic genealogical data, so we move on in our evaluation.

We also received copies of Cassie's and John's obituaries; Cassie's death record and her marriage record; as well as John Fitz Jr.'s death record, estate record, and deeds. Cassie's marriage record did not contain significant genealogical information, but her death record confirmed that she was born on 8 March 1869 in Astoria, Illinois, to John Fitz and Mary Falkenstein, both natives of the state of Pennsylvania.

Mary Falkenstein? We had been told her name was Magdalena. Not to worry.

There's a simple explanation. In some areas of Germany, children commonly carried the same first names. For boys, the first name was often Johann. So, how do you tell one Johann from the next? By their middle names, such as Peter. You would call a boy by his second name: "Peter, hitch the horses to the plow." Families would sometimes use girls' middle names to identify them too, since their first names might be Mary (Maria), Ann (Anna), or Johanna. John Fitz's wife was most likely Maria (or Mary) Magdalena Falkenstein.

On to the next document

The ancestral portion of Cassie's obituary gave her parents as John and Mary Fitz, and her birth as 8 March 1869 at Astoria, Illinois, stating that she "came to Iowa with her parents when a young girl."

In reviewing John Fitz Jr.'s obituary, we find no reference to his parents, but his birth date and birthplace are both given: 22 March 1843, York County, Pennsylvania. The article goes on to say: "When a boy he moved from there to Fulton County, Ill., and from Fulton County to Guthrie County Iowa, in 1866. In 1863, he was united in marriage to Magdalena Falckenstine. To them were born ten children." The 1866 date was later proved to be incorrect, 1873 being the correct year. The obit continues with additional details of the man's life.

The death record of John Fitz confirms very little except his death date and place, his age in years only, his birth state (Pennsylvania), cause of death, his occupation, his marital status, and the place of his burial. Neither his estate record nor his numerous deeds gave any ancestral information. The Guthrie County history of 1884 offered no biographical information on any Fitz, other than making reference to their unusual success as farmers and their association with the Brethren Church as ministers and elders.

In a Brethren Church publication we accessed much later, we found the following entries regarding the ministry:
1. "In March, 1873, John Fitz, a deacon from Fulton County, Ill. moved here."
2. "In November, 1874, Eld. John Fitz moved in from Fulton County, Ill. He was our first resident elder. He moved back to Illinois in 1881. He died there in 1900."
3. "22 June 1892, John Fitz was chosen to the ministry; advanced 16 June 1898."
4. "20 July 1899, John Fitz was called from labor to rest." (Note: Items 1, 3, and 4 relate to John Fitz III; item 2 relates to John Fitz II.)

In the same church publication is the following membership data, which we have shortened:
1. Cassie—, daughter of John and Lena Fitz, baptized 22 July 1888. (Notes: Lena is short for Magdalena. The Brethren Church followed adult baptismal rites. Cassie was an adult when baptized.)
2. John Fitz Sr., an elder. Received in 1875 from Astoria, Illinois. Returned in 1881. Died on 15 May 1900, aged 83 years, 2 mos., 10 days in Illinois; buried there.

3. Marianna Fitz, wife of John Sr.
4. John Fitz Jr., son of John Sr., a deacon. Received 1873 from Astoria, Illinois.
5. Magdalena Fitz, wife of John Jr., daughter of Jacob and Catherine Falkenstine. Died 26 May 1888, aged 46 years, 7 mos., 10 days.

From census records of Guthrie County, Iowa, Fulton County, Illinois, and York County, Pennsylvania, that we reviewed at various other times, we can confirm the names, ages, birthplaces (states), and relationships of most of these Fitz family members. The atlas of Fulton County, Illinois, of 1871 illustrated the property of John Fitz (II) just east of Astoria.

The Fulton County, Illinois, history of 1879, for Woodland Township, contained a biographical sketch that told us, "John Fitz was born in York County, Pennsylvania; he there married Mary Ann Dubs by whom he had nine children—Henry, John, Samuel, George, Conrad, Matilda, Susan, Elizabeth, and Rebecca. Mr. Fitz was a farmer in Pennsylvania, where he owned farm property; 27 years ago he came west—where he purchased nearly 500 acres of land; he removed to Iowa 3 years ago, where he is the owner of 400 acres of valuable land."

From the pages of cemetery inscriptions of Fulton County, Illinois, the Dunkard Brethren Church Cemetery, we found this entry:

John Fitz, b. 5 Mar 1817, d. 15 May 1900.

A year later, through extensive research at the York County Historical Society facility, we found the wills of Cassie's ancestors, Frederick Fitz, who died in 1815, and John Fitz (I), who died in 1845. We also reviewed the Fitz Report, which had been prepared for the Society in 1939. It included many civil and church records for Fitzes in York County before the year 1850.

Among these records, we find an interesting chronicle of Frederick Fitz's continuing battle—if you will excuse this term—to maintain his religious convictions in light of the military obligations being forced on colonists of that time. He was inducted into the military, then fined for nonperformance of duty. His taxes were doubled and other sanctions orchestrated to make him comply with his military obligations. Frederick remained steadfast in his religious convictions, but not without significant financial punishment.

We also located records on John Fitz (I) and his wife, Catherine Roth. John married Catherine on 5 January 1802 in the First Reformed Church. He was buried in the Fitz Burial Ground in North Codorus Township, York County. His tombstone inscription gave his birth date as 11 April 1775, his death date as 30 July 1845, and his age as 70 years, 3 months, and 19 days. No marriage or death record was found for Frederick Fitz, but from deeds we learned his wife's name was Elizabeth.

We have been unable to find any information on the death and burial of Johann Peter Fitz, the immigrant ancestor of this lineage. However, as mentioned, we easily located an immigration reference in Rupp's book (see bibliography on page 184) on German and Swiss immigrants. Johan [sic] Peter Fitz arrived in the British colonies in America on 11 August 1750 aboard the ship *Patience*.

We also located in our searches an excellent resource on the Fitz families of York County in the 1989 book by Sylvia Fitts Getchell. She is very cautious in claiming Frederick Fitz as the son of Johan Peter Fitz. She further admits that little is known of immigration on this assumed lineage. So, even though this source is comprehensive, it doesn't connect across the Atlantic Ocean to the place of origin of either Frederick Fitz or Johann Peter Fitz.

But, fortunately, we stumbled across the query written by the German research student and were finally able to view some German records on this Fitz family. Helmut, the student researcher, sent us concise data on Johann Peter Fitz, his wife and children. He also sent a map of Ober-Flörsheim, a village of some nine hundred inhabitants. Helmut also shared some emigration information from Hacker's book, which we later located and copied. The information, while brief, did confirm Johann Peter's village of origin.

> 3711 Fiz Peter, Oberflörsheim, 5 Ki; Mm(15), A(15) nach Psy.—
> 61/9187:409 n 48.
>
> Am   1750 04 11

Essentially, Peter Fiz from Ober-Flörsheim received permission to emigrate to Pennsylvania with his five children on 11 April 1750. The omission of reference to his wife leads us to believe that Peter was a widower.

Upon further correspondence, we found that it was indeed likely that Johann Peter's wife and a child died in Ober-Flörsheim before the rest of the family went to the New World. It is possible that Johann Peter remarried in America and had more children, and we are still investigating this. Helmut's letters also brought us news of Johann Peter Fitz's parentage, Caspar and Maria Christina Fitz, as well as Peter's siblings, Johanna Margaretha Fitz, Johannes Fitz, and Johann Nikolaus Fitz. Utilizing the microfilm services of the Family History Center, we located and copied documents relative to Johann Peter Fitz. Two of these records are shared below. First, the marriage record of Johann Peter Fitz and Anna Maria Butterfass. And then a birth record for Johann Friderich (Frederick) Fitz.

Notes on marriage record of Johann Peter Fitz and Anna Maria Butterfass (shown on page 118):

X—*probably Roman numeral 10: record #10 (?).*

Anno—*Latin for "in the year."*

d—*common abbreviation for* den.

16.*t*—*common abbreviation for* -ten *after ordinal numbers, meaning the 16th.*

iŭlÿ—*Latin* i *and* j *are interchangeble;* ÿ = ij *or* y.

=—*used at the end of a line like a hyphen.*

Flörßh:—*again shows abbreviation; colon is used as a period; the complete word is* flörßheim.

Butterfassin—-in *is a female suffix used as an addition to a surname; the surname is* Butterfass.

ö *is transcribed* oe *in English.*

ß *is transcribed* ss *in English.*

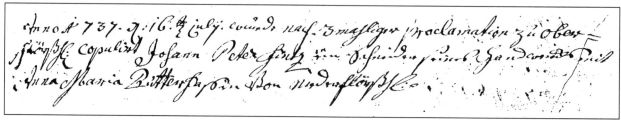

Original marriage record of Johann Peter Fitz and Anna Maria Butterfass.

Abbreviated transcription of marriage record of Johann Peter Fitz and Anna Maria Butterfass.

Anno 1737 den 16ten July wurde nach 3maliger Proclamation zu Ober-Flörsheim copuliert Johann Peter Fitz ein Schneider seines Handwercks mit Anna Maria Butterfassin Von Niederflörsheim.

Full transcription of marriage record of Johann Peter Fitz and Anna Maria Butterfass.

In the year 1737 on the 16th of July there were married after 3 proclamations at Ober-Flörsheim, Johann Peter Fitz, a tailor by profession, and Anna Maria Butterfass of Niederflörsheim.

Translated marriage record of Johann Peter Fitz and Anna Maria Butterfass.

Notes on birth record of Johann Friderich Fitz shown on page 119:

Joh—*abbreviation for* Johann, *a very common given name.*

Nat—*Latin abbreviation for* natus *(male) or* nata *(female); in the cases where the abbreviation is used, you must rely on the name to help you determine the child's gender (Maria, Hans).*

6.—*abbreviation for* 6ten *meaning 6th.*

7bris—*abbreviation for* Septembris *(tricky—not our 7th month, which would be July.)*

Ren.—*Latin abbreviation for* Renatus *(reborn), the spiritual significance of baptism.*

Ejusd.—*Latin abbreviation for* Ejusdem *(on the same [month]).*

Schneidermeister—*"master tailor," meaning he was a full member of the tailor's guild with certain local citizenship rights.*

Ux.—*Latin abbreviation for* Uxor *(wife).*

Ref.—*abbreviation for* Reformiert *(Reformed); religion specified here, meaning the person is probably of a different religion than the spouse.*

Original birth record of Johann Friderich Fitz.

Abbreviated transcription of birth record of Johann Friderich Fitz.

Monath und Tage...	Der Kinder...	Eltern und Testatores Nahmen	Ano 1744
Natus den 6. 7bris	Johann Friderich	Johann Peter Fitz Schneidermeister	Johann Friderich Linck
Renatus den 8. Ejusdem		Anna Maria Uxor Reformiert	Anna Barbara Uxor Reformiert
		Ober Flörsheim	

Full transcription of birth record of Johann Friderich Fitz.

Month and Day...	Names of the Children, Parents, and Witnesses	Year 1744
Born on the 6th of September	Johann Friderich [Parents:] Johann Peter Fitz, master tailor	[Godparents/Sponsors:] Johann Friderich Linck
baptized on the 8th of the same month	Anna Maria, his wife, Reformed	Anna Barbara, his wife, Reformed
	Ober-Flörsheim.	

Translated birth record of Johann Friderich Fitz.

EIGHT

Fox Tales: A Case Study of a Nineteenth-Century German Catholic Family

Case Study

his second case study shows you a different set of elemental research factors that researchers commonly deal with in their searches. The more Germanic records you see, the more likely you'll recognize and understand what you will find in your own search. It's simply a matter of practice.

This story differs from the previous one in the following ways: a different century, a different religion, a different pathway to the bridge to Germany, and a difference in the quantity of material available to follow the family. The Fitz immigrant ancestor in chapter seven was a Lutheran, and his origins were found through a query that originated in Germany.

The Fox immigrant of this chapter came to the United States about 1846, was a Catholic, and possessed records that led to his home village. **(The majority of Germanic immigrants were either Lutheran or Catholic, so these two examples are very appropriate.)**

Reminder

MEET LEO FOX

It's our pleasure to introduce Leo Fox to you. Leo died in 1959 and we're now going to try to find Leo's German immigrant ancestor just like we did Catherine Fitz's. We start the same way.

First, we asked relatives. We visited Leo's daughter Rosamond and she told us what she knew: his name (Leo Bernard Fox), his birth date and place (27 January 1896 in Haydenville, Ohio), his wife's name, the number and names of his children, where Leo lived, where and when he died, and some of his personality traits and other memories she had of him.

She knew the names of his parents—Paul Fox and Bridget Goodwin—and she possessed photos of Leo and his father. She knew Leo's brothers and sisters and quite a bit about his grocery business, his home, and his church affiliation. These were all in the same town in which she lived. This lineage search looked like it was going to be much easier and less expensive than the Fitz search of chapter seven. Rosamond told us about many of her cousins that might have additional information.

In following up on her referrals, we talked with a number of individuals, but Adelaide and Stella are a story in and of themselves. They were very interested in our questions and were cooperative, but were unaware of any family documents that might help us in our search, other than those available through the local church and courthouse. Through these records, however, we were able to amass a complete genealogy of this Fox lineage and to eventually determine who the first Fox immigrant was.

That this Fox lineage was of German ancestry was proudly extolled by virtually all of its older members. It was confirmed in the brief church history that explained that the majority of the founders of the church were from the German state of Saarland. According to the history, most of the founders were soldiers of Napoleon and followers of Lafayette. They were restless under the rule of the reinstated Bourbons. The short translation: They left the Saarland for political reasons.

The first group arrived in America in 1837, coming directly to Hocking County, Ohio, from the Saarland. However, no living soul we contacted knew the village of origin of Jacob Fox, their immigrant ancestor. Jacob had reportedly arrived about 1837 (no immigration record was found) with his three sons, John G., Nicolaus, and Jacob.

DOCUMENTING THE FOX FAMILY

Reviewing the records of the local Catholic church and dovetailing with civil, newspaper, and cemetery records, we found the following basic Fox family lineage:

1. Leo Bernard Fox was born on 27 January 1896 in Hocking County, the son of Paul Fox and Bridget Elizabeth Goodwin.
2. Paul Fox was born on 4 November 1860 in Hocking County, the son of John G. Fox and Catherine Weiland.
3. John G. Fox was born on 10, 11, or 20 November (tombstone, prayer book, and death record, respectively) 1834 in Germany, possibly the son of Jacob Fox, mother unknown.
4. Jacob Fox's only known death date is from an iron cross marker in a Catholic cemetery: "Jacob Fuchs inri 1856." Buried near to him was a Maria Fuchs, inri 1848, possibly his wife.

Note the German spelling of Fox—Fuchs. Fuchs translates into English as "Fox," or "one with foxlike characteristics." So, we were looking for a Jacob Fuchs in our further searches in Germany. We also determined from the records that Jacob's three possible sons were all born in Germany between 1834 and 1845, indicating that Jacob and family did not arrive in 1837 as previously believed. Although to this day we have not found his immigration record, we believe from other data that he arrived about 1846.

As we continued to research the Fox family, we kept Rosamond, Adelaide,

Stella, and others aware of our findings. Again, as with our Fitz search in the previous chapter, keeping communications open eventually provided great benefit. In this case, it led to the discovery of John G. Fox's German village of origin and his parents, grandparents, and other relatives. But, we're getting ahead of ourselves.

We will admit to you honestly that we "stumbled" upon information again. We had asked Adelaide and Stella a few times if there were any family documents that might help us in our quest to locate the Foxes' German hometown. We were repeatedly told that they had nothing of value in this regard; however, on the fourth (or was it the eighth?) time we asked, Adelaide said there was an old, small German prayer book, but she had assumed it had no genealogical value. We asked to view it. Pay dirt!

The small, old German prayer book of little value was actually the property of John G. Fox and had his name written inside the front cover in both English and German script, followed by his birth date and place.

This information basically states:

> John G. Fox Logan, Ohio
> Johann Fuchs born in
> Hierscheid in the year 1834
> Johann Fuchs Johann Fuchs
> was born on the 11th of November 1834

In this one item lay the foundation of information we needed to locate his home village. We also located a death record for one of John's children that confirmed John's birthplace as Hierscheid, Germany. We went searching through our old German maps, one of our favorite pastimes, and found this quaint village located in—no surprise—the Saarland. We then wrote to the civil authority in nearby Eppelborn, Germany, and received a copy of John's birth certificate, which follows on page 123. It confirmed that his father was Jacob Fouchs [sic], listed his mother as Anna Maria Klein, and confirmed John's birth date as 10 November 1834.

We contacted a genealogist in the area and proceeded to flesh out the Fox family's genealogy. Further research resulted in an extensive pedigree shown on page 124.

In cooperation with a genealogist in Germany, we were able to locate a *Familienbuch* (family book) including these Fuchs ancestors, a photo of a Fuchs ancestral home, and copies of original Fuchs records, which we will illustrate, transcribe, and translate for you. The records will include the following:

- marriage record of the immigrant, Jacob Fuchs
- baptismal record of Jacob's father, Nikolaus
- marriage record of Nikolaus Fuchs
- photo of Nikolaus Fuchs's German home
- baptismal record of Nikolaus's father, Johann
- marriage record of Johann Fuchs
- death record of Johann Fuchs
- *Familienbuch* entries

A	Staat: BUNDESREPUBLIK DEUTSCHLAND	Gemeinde: **Eppelborn**
	Etat: REPUBLIQUE FEDERALE D'ALLEMAGNE — Staat: BONDSREPUBLIEK DUITSLAND — State: FEDERAL REPUBLIC OF GERMANY — Devlet: FEDERAL ALMANYA CUMHURIYETI — Estado: REPUBLICA FEDERAL DE ALEMANIA — Država: SAVEZNA REPUBLIKA NJEMAČKA — Stato: REPUBBLICA FEDERALE DI GERMANIA	**Standesamt Dirmingen, jetzt Eppelborn Nr. 81/1834** Commune de – Municipality – Municipio de – Comune di – Gemeente – Köy veya mahâlle – Opčina

Auszug aus dem Geburtsregister

Extrait des registres de l'état civil concernant une naissance – Extract of the register of births – Extracto del registro de nacimientos – Estratto del registro delle nascite – Uittreksel uit de registers van de burgerlijke stand omtrent een geboorte – Doğuma ait nüfus kayit hülâsasi sureti – Izvod iz matične knjige rođenih.

a)	**Geburtsort:** lieu de naissance – place of birth – lugar de nacimiento – luogo di nascito – plaats van geboorte – doğum yeri – mjesto rođenja	**Hierscheid, jetzt Eppelborn**
b)	**Geburtsdatum:** date de naissance – date of birth – fecha de nacimiento – data di nascita – datum van geboorte – doğum tarihi – datum rođenja	**10.11.1834**
c)	**Geschlecht des Kindes:** sexe de l'enfant – sex of the child – sexo del niño – sesso del bambino – geslacht van het kind – çocuğun cinsiyeti – spol djeteta	**M**
d)	**Familienname des Kindes:** nom de famille de l'enfant – surname of the child – apellido del niño – cognome del bambino – familienaam van het kind – çocuğun soyadı – prezime djeteta	**Fouchs**
e)	**Vornamen des Kindes:** prénoms de l'enfant – christian names of the child – nombres de pila del niño – prenomi del bambino – voornamen van het kind – çocuğun adı – imena djeteta	**Johann**
f)	**Familienname des Vaters:** nom de famille du père – surname of the father – apellido del padre – cognome del padre – familienaam van de vader – babasının soyadı – prezime oca	**Fouchs**
g)	**Vornamen des Vaters:** prénoms du père – christian names of the father – nombres de pila del padre – prenomi del padre – voornamen van de vader – babsının adı – imena oca	**Jacob**
h)	**Mädchenname der Mutter:** nom de jeune fille de la mère – maiden name of the mother – apellido de soltera de la madre – nome di signorina della madre – maisjesnaam van de moeder – anasının evlenmeden önceki soyadı – djevojačko prezime majke	**Klein**
i)	**Vornamen der Mutter:** prénoms de la mère – christian names of the mother – nombres de pila de la madre – prenomi della madre – voornamen van de moeder – anasının adı – imena majke	**Anna Maria**

Ausstellungsdatum, Unterschrift und Dienstsiegel des Registerführers
date de délivrance, signature et sceau du dépositaire
date of issue, signature and seal of keeper
fecha de expedición, firma y sello del depositario
data in cui è stato rilasciato l'atto, con firma e bollo dell'ufficio
datum van afgifte, ondertekening en zegel van de bewaarder
verildiği tarih, nüfus (ahvali şahsiye) memurunun imzası ve mührü
datum izdavanja, potpis i pečat matičara

Eppelborn,
den **27.01.1981**
Der Standesbeamte

(Siegel)

(Meiser)

Duplicate birth record for Johann Georg Fuchs (Fouchs).

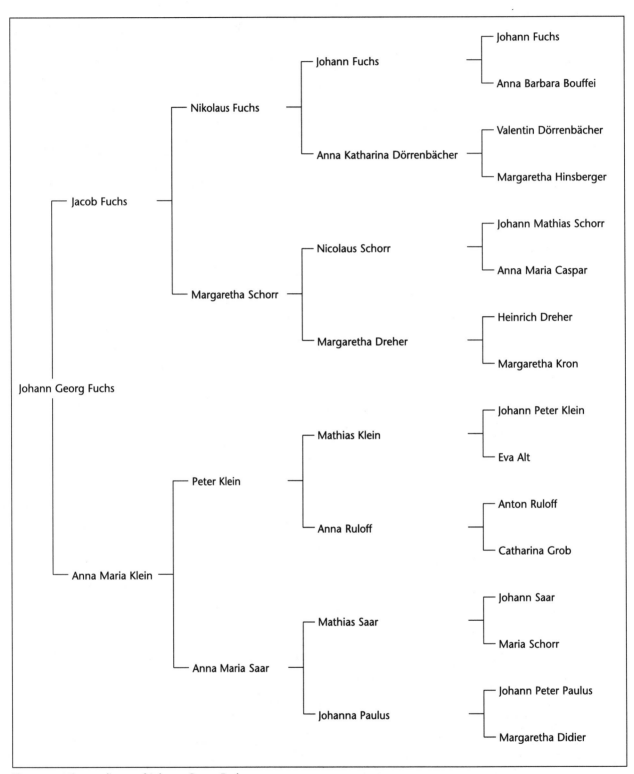

Five-generation pedigree of Johann Georg Fuchs.

Nᵒ. 20. **Heiraths-Akt.**

Im Jahre ein tausend acht hundert ein und dreißig am *minn und zwanzigsten Anu* des Monats *August* um *drey* Uhr des *Nach* -Mittags erschienen vor mir *Philipp* *Müller* Bürgermeister und Civilstandsbeamten der Bürgermeisterei *Wihlsweyer* , im Kanton Ottweiler , Regierungsbezirk Trier,

Einer Seits der *Jacob Fuchs , ledigen und Minder*

gemäß { *vor* gelegtem Geburtsscheine, alt *ein und dreißig* Jahre, geboren zu *Weilerhof*

am des Monats *Anly* Jahrs ein tausend *sieben hundert einem und neunzig* von Gewerbe ein *Ackerer* wohnhaft zu *Wustweiler*

ohne jähriger Sohn des *Nickel Fuchs* von Gewerbe ein *Ackerer* wohnhaft zu *Weilerhof, ...*

und der *Margarethe Schorr* von Gewerbe eine *...* wohnhaft zu *Weilerhof ...*

Anderer Seits die *Maria Klein, ledigen und Minder*

gemäß { *vor* gelegtem Geburtsscheine, alt *fünf und zwanzig* Jahre, geboren zu *Hirstein*

am *sechsten* des Monats *November* Jahrs ein tausend *acht hundert und fünf* von Gewerbe eine *...* wohnhaft zu *Hirstein*

ohne jährige Tochter des *Peter Klein* von Gewerbe ein *Ackerer* wohnhaft zu *Hirstein, ...*

und der *Anna Maria Saar* von Gewerbe eine *...* wohnhaft zu *Hirstein, ...*

und forderten mich auf, zur Vollziehung der von ihnen beabsichtigten Ehe vorzuschreiten, indem nach den geschehenen Eheverkündigungen, wovon die erste Sonntags den *...* des Monats *August* im Jahre ein tausend acht hundert *...* um *zehn* Uhr des Morgens, No. 39 des Eheverkündigungs-Registers, und die zweite Sonntags den *...* des Monats *August* im Jahre ein tausend acht hundert *...* des Morgens um *zehn* Uhr, No. 41. des Eheverkündigungs-Registers zu *...* *...* statt gehabt hat, keine Hindernisse oder sonstige Einsprüche dagegen vorgebracht worden seyen.

Original marriage record of Jacob Fuchs and Anna Maria Klein, page 1.

Original marriage record of Jacob Fuchs and Anna Maria Klein, page 2.

No. 20   Heiraths=Akt

Im Jahre ein tauſend acht hundert ein und dreißig am *vier und zwanzigſten*
des Monaths *Auguſt* um drey Uhr des *Nach* Mittags erſchienen vor mir *Philipp*
Müller   Bürgermeiſter und Civilſtandsbeamten
der Bürgermeiſterei *Uchtelfangen*, im Kanton Ottweiler, Regierungsbezirk Trier,

Einer Seits der *Jakob Fuchs, ledigen Standes*,

gemäß vorgelegtem Geburtſcheine, alt *ſieben und dreißig* Jahre, geboren zu *Mülerhof*,
     am   des Monats *July*
Jahrs ein tauſend *ſieben hundert vier und neunzig* von Gewerbe
ein *Maler* wohnhaft zu *Mühlweiler*
      Groß jähriger Sohn des *Nikel Fuchs*
         von Gewerbe ein *Ackerer* wohnhaft zu
Mülerhof, alda verſtorben nach beigelegtem Todtſchein
am fünften des Monats februar im Jahr ein tauſend acht
hundert ſechs und zwanzig
und der *Margaretha Thmr*
von Gewerbe eine *ohne*   wohnhaft zu *Mülerhof alda verſtorben*
nach beigelegtem Todtſchein am ſechs und zwanzigſten des Monats
Auguſt im Jahr ein tauſend acht hundert vier und zwanzig,
Anderer Seits die *Maria Klein ledigen Standes*

gemäß vorgelegtem Geburtſcheine, alt *fünf und zwanzig* Jahre, geboren zu *Hirzfeld*
      am *ſechsten*   des Monats *November*
Jahrs ein tauſend *acht hundert und fünf,* von Gewerbe
eine *ohne* wohnhaft zu *Hirzfeld,*
      Groß jährige Tochter des *Peter Klein*
         von Gewerbe ein *Ackerer* wohnhaft zu
Hirzfeld, alda verſtorben am achtzehnten des Monats februar
im Jahr ein tauſend acht hundert und ſiebenzehn, nach vorge=
legtem Todtſchein.
und der *Anna Maria Thmr*   von Gewerbe eine *ohne*
      wohnhaft zu Hirzfeld, hier gegenwärtig und
in die Heirath einwilligt.

und forderten mich auf, zur Vollziehung der von ihnen beabſichtigten Ehe vorzuſchreiten, indem nach den
geſchehenen Eheverkündigungen, wovon die erſte Sonntags den *vierzehnten*
des Monats *Auguſt* im Jahre ein tauſend acht hundert *ein und dreißig* des Morgens um *zehn*
Uhr des Morgens, No. 39 des Eheverkündigungs=Regiſters, und die zweite Sonntags den *ein und*
zwanzigſten des Monats *Auguſt* im Jahre ein tauſend acht hundert *ein und dreißig*
des Morgens um *zehn* Uhr, No. 41, des Eheverkündigungs: Regiſters zu *Illingen*
und Calmesweiler
ſtatt gehabt hat, keine Hinderniſſe oder ſonſtige Einſprüche dagegen vorgebracht werden ſehen,

Transcribed marriage record of Jacob Fuchs and Anna Maria Klein, page 1.

(2 lines illegible)

.....erhellt, so habe ich, der Beamte des Civilstandes von *Udelfangen* nachdem ich alle in diesem Akte angeführte Schriften so wie das VI Kapitel des Titels von der Heirath, über die wechselsei =tigen Rechte und Pflichten der Ehegatten, wörtlich vorgelesen hatte, den *Jacob Fuchs* gefragt, ob er die *Maria Klein* zur Frau nehmen wolle,

(illegible)

.... die *Maria Klein* gefragt, ob sie den *Jacob Fuchs* zum Manne nehmen wolle, und da beide auf die an sie gerichteten Fragen mit Ja antworteten, so habe ich die Benannten *Jacob Fuchs*

und *Maria Klein.* im Namen des Gesetzes von nun an als im Stande der Ehe vereint erklärt. Worüber ich gegenwärtigen Akt im Beisehn von vier Zeugen in doppeltem Original aufgesetzt, nämlich:

1tens, Des *Johann Nikel Grob*   von Gewerbe ein *Ackerer*   alt *sechzig* Jahre, wohnhaft zu *Mittweiler Mühl*   verwandt mit den *Partheien*

2tens, Des *Matthias Klein*   von Gewerbe ein *Ackerer*   alt *vierzig* Jahre, wohnhaft zu *Mittweiler Mühl*   verwandt mit den *Partheien*

3tens, Des *Nikel Fuchs*   von Gewerbe ein *Ackerer*   alt *neun und dreißig* Jahre, wohnhaft zu *Mittweiler*   verwandt mit dem *Bräutigam als Bruder*   von Gewerbe ein

4tens, Des *Jacob Schütter*   *Ackerer*   alt *ein und dreißig* Jahre, wohnhaft zu *Illingen Mühl*   verwandt mit den *Partheien*

welche Zeugen mit den zusammengegebenen Ehegatten und mir, nach gehaltener Vorlesung, diesen Akt unterschrieben haben, *mit Ausnahme der Braut Maria Klein und der Mutter Anna Maria Trax, welche erklärten nicht schreiben zu können.*

So geschehen zu *Illingen*   auf dem Gemeinde:Hause der Bürgermeisterei *Udelfangen* am Tage, Monat und Jahre wie oben.

Jacob Fuchs   *Hand X Zeichen der*
Johann Nikel Grob   *Maria Klein*
Matthias Klein   *Hand X Zeichen der*
Niclaus Fuchs   *Anna Maria Trax*
Jacob Schütter   *Der Bürgermeister*
                                                         Müller

Transcribed marriage record of Jacob Fuchs and Anna Maria Klein, page 2.

No. <u>20</u>.   Marriage Record

In the year one thousand eight hundred thiry-one on the twenty-fourth of the month of August at three o'clock in the afternoon there appeared before me, Philipp Mueller, Mayor and Civil Registrar of the Mayoralty District of Uchtelfangen in the Canton of Ottweiler, Governing District of Trier,

On the one hand Jacob Fuchs, of unmarried status, according to the birth certificate presented thirty-seven years old, born at Weilerhof on _____ of the month of July of the year one thousand seven hundred ninety-four, by occupation a weaver, resident at Wustweiler, the of-age son of Nikel Fuchs, by occupation a farmer, resident at Weilerhof, deceased there according to the attached death record on the fifth of the month of February in the year one thousand eight hundred twenty-six, and of Margaretha Schorr, without occupation, resident at Weilerhof, deceased there according to the enclosed death record on the twenty-sixth of the month of August in the year one thousand eight hundred twenty-four,

on the other hand Maria Klein, of unmarried status, according to the birth certificate presented twenty-five years old, born at Hirscheidt on the fifth of the month of November of the year one thousand eight hundred and five, without occupation, resident at Hirscheidt, of-age daughter of Peter Klein, by occupation a farmer, resident at Hirscheidt, deceased there on the eighteenth of the month of February in the year one thousand eight hundred and seventeen, according to the death record presented, and of Anna Maria Saar, without occupation, resident at Hirscheidt, present here and consenting to the marriage,

and they requested me to conclude the marriage intended between them, inasmuch as the marriage banns were proclaimed, of which the first took place on Sunday, the fourteenth of the month of August in the year one thousand eight hundred thirty-one at ten o'clock in the morning, No. 39, and the second on Sunday the twenty-first of the month of August in the year one thousand eight hundred thirty-one at ten o'clock in the morning, No. 41 of the marriage banns register, at Illingen and Calmsweiler, and no hindrances or other objections were made to it,

Translated marriage record of Jacob Fuchs and Anna Maria Klein, page 1.

Translated marriage record of
Jacob Fuchs and Anna Maria
Klein, page 2.

(two lines illegible)

. . . therefore I, the officer of civil registration of Uchtelfangen, after I had
read word for word all of the documents mentioned in this record as well as
the 6th chapter of the title "On Marriage" from the mutual rights and obligations of the married couple, asked Jacob Fuchs if he wished to take Maria
Klein as his wife, . . . and asked Maria Klein if she wished to take Jacob Fuchs
as her husband, and since both answered the questions directed to them with
"Yes," I declared the named Jacob Fuchs and Maria Klein to be in the state
of matrimony from now on in the name of the law. Whereupon I made the
present record in the presence of four witnesses in two original copies, namely:

1st, of Johann Nikel Grob, by occupation a farmer, sixty years old, resident
at Wustweiler, not related to the parties,

2nd, of Mathias Klein, by occupation a farmer, forty years old, resident at
Wustweiler, not related to the parties,

3rd, of Nikel Fuchs, by occupation a farmer, thirty-nine years old, resident
at Wustweiler, related to the bridegroom as brother,

4th, of Jacob Schlicker, by occupation a farmer, thirty-one years old, resident
at Illingen, not related to the parties,

which witnesses signed the present record with the assembled married couple
and myself, after reading it aloud, with the exceptions of the bride Maria
Klein and the mother Anna Maria Saar, who declared that they are not able
to write. Thus done at Illingen in the town hall of the Mayoralty of Uchtelfangen on the day, month, and year as above.

Jacob Fuchs   X mark of Maria Klein
Johann Nickel Grob   X mark of Anna Maria Saar
Mathias Klein   The Mayor
Nicolaus Fuchs   Müller
Jakob Schliker

Notes on the marriage record of Jacob Fuchs and Anna Maria Klein:

This amount of detail is not unusual; it follows the standard format for a marriage record of civil registration from Napoleonic times (about 1798 west of the Rhine River). Note that there are four witnesses with relationship or nonrelationship mentioned; the parents of the couple are listed, including deceased parents with date and place of death mentioned. Proclamations of banns were done in two places because apparently the couple lived in different places. These banns were not proclaimed in church but posted at the respective town halls and entered in the register of proclamations; this was a Napoleonic feature. It is called civil registration, not church registration. Undoubtedly there was a church wedding performed as well, and the banns preceding those would have been proclaimed from the pulpit for at least two Sundays. Title 6 of the Napoleonic code dealt with marriage and prescribed the format for records. Parents gave permission for their children to marry, usually "here present and consenting."

ŭnd, taŭsend—*the hook or "smile" over* u *indicates the short vowel without an umlaut; also not to be confused with* n.

dreÿ, Julÿ—*ÿ* = y; *old alternate spelling for* drei.

Müller, fünften—*ü is transcribed as* ue *in English.*

Einer Seits—*"on one side"; the party of the first part.*

alda—allda, *meaning "there; at that place."*

Grosjähriger Sohn—*"of-age son; son who has reached majority."*

ohne—*"without; here, without occupation."*

Beiseyn—*"presence"; sometimes* Beyseyn *or* Beysein; *sometimes* Gegenwart *is the word used instead.*

Nikel Fuchs *is listed as the bridegroom's brother. Marriage records are a good way to find relatives of your ancestors.*

Am Tage, Monat und Jahre wie oben—*"on the day, month, and year as above" (a common formula).*

X—Handzeichen *(mark). Maria Klein and Anna Maria Saar made their marks and their names were written around the X; this is typical. It is also more typical for females to be unable to read and write than males. This depends somewhat on the school system of the village. Sometimes from a signature, the misspellings and awkwardly formed letters are a clue that about the only thing the person can write is a signature. Occasionally the mark is an initial or monogram of the name.*

Sometimes instead of doing a fancy scroll, the mayor/civil registrar underlines or double-underlines his name.

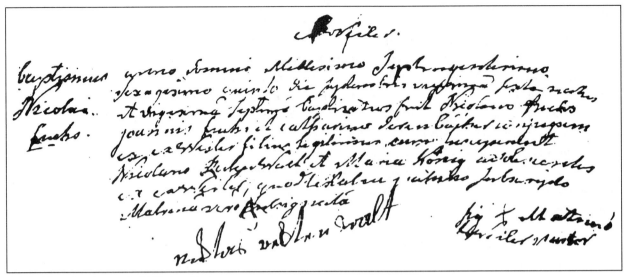

Original baptismal record of Nikolaus Fuchs.

	Exweiler
Baptismus	Anno domini Millesimo Septuagintimo
Nicolai	sexagesimo quinto die Septembris vicesimus sexta natus
Fuchs	et vigesima Septimus baptizatus erat Nicolaus Fuchs
	Joannis Fuchs et Catharinae Derenbacher conjugum
	ex ex Weiler filius legitimus cum regenent(?)
	Nicolaus Recten Wald et Maria König iuventes
	et cawiler, quod testaten intesso teste (rejelo?)
	(Matianus aroo selig secta?)
	Nicklas rectenwalt sig X Mathias
	Urweiler runter

Transcribed baptismal record of Nikolaus Fuchs.

	Exweiler
Baptism of	In the year of Our Lord one thousand seven hundred
Nicolaus	sixty-five on the twenty-sixth day of September there was born
Fuchs	and on the twenty-seventh there was baptized Nicolaus Fuchs,
	legitimate son of Johannes Fuchs and Catharina Derenbacher,
	a married couple from Exweiler, with the godparents
	Nicolaus Rectenwald and Maria Koenig, young people
	from Cawiler, who (signed below?).
	(?)
	Nicklas Rectenwalt sig X Mathias
	Urweiler (down below?)

Translated baptismal record of Nikolaus Fuchs.

Notes on the baptismal record of Nikolaus Fuchs:

This is in Latin, the language of the Roman Catholic church. Even though the German name of the child being baptized is Nicolaus Fuchs (within the entry itself), the entry is titled "Baptismus Nicolai Fuchs." The ending -i indicates the Latin genitive inflectional ending, that is, it means "[baptism] of Nicolaus." Likewise, the inflectional ending -is on the Latin name Joannis changes its meaning to "[child] of Joannes" and the -ae on the Latin name Catharinae changes its meaning to "[child] of Catharina." This appears to be written in a relatively standard format, so other nearby entries would probably be helpful in detecting the pattern found in this document.

The capital letter used in the middle of the place-name exWeiler and in the surname RectenWald is indicative of loose capitalization and punctuation,

Original marriage record of Nikolaus Fuchs and Margaretha Schorr.

which are frequently found in records of the eighteenth century. Nicklas rectenwalt did not even capitalize his own surname in his signature.

Nicolaus *in Latin is* Nikolaus *in German and* Nicholas *in English.* Joannes *in Latin is* Johannes *in German (commonly shortened to* Johann*) and* John *in English.* Nicolai *means "of Nicholas."* Joannis *means "of John." Sometimes the inflected forms are used, such as in the International Genealogical Index. It may be necessary to look for individuals under numerous Latin and German forms, such as* Joannem, Joannes, Joannis, Johan, Johann, *and* Johannes, *or even* Jean *in French.*

Veilerhof	*Anno Millesimo Septuagenti uno Octavagesimo novo die decimo*
Nicolaus	*Septima Februarii tribus bannorum proclamationibus futuri*
Fuchs	*Matrimonii inter Nicolaum Fuchs Viginti quattuor Annorum*
Margaretha Schorr	*Filium legitimum defunctorum Joannis Fuchs et Annae*
	Catharinae Dorenbacher Conjugium ex Exveiler, et Margaretham
	Schorr Sexdecim annorum filiam legitimam Nicolai Schorr
	agricolae et Margarethae Dreher Conjugium ex Weilerhof in
	Ecclesia' parochiali de Ottweiler et ejus coniuxa' de Exveiler pro
	lege factis, nullo neque Canonico, neque Civili impedimento
	Detecto, praefati sponsi ä me infra Scripto ex Commissione
	Domini Pastoris de Ottveiler, accepto prius nuntio eorum et
	requisitorum Consensi, et Celebratis de more Sponsatibus—
	in Ecclesia de Exveiler inter Missarum Solemnia Benedictiaonem
	nuptialiem recipientes Matrimonio juseti furet, sustanstibus
	in qualitate testiam Petro Beheriam et Petro Klein
	agricolis Ex Veilerhof et Nicollao Rectenwald ex Exviler qui cum
	Sponsis et Patre Sponsae Subscripserunt------

ita testi   Nicolaus Fuchs margreda schorr
Nicklauß Schorr   Peter Brosoam
Peter Klein   Niklas Rekttenwaldt
P Laur da. in Exw.

Transcribed marriage record of Nikolaus Fuchs and Margaretha Schorr.

Notes on the marriage record of Nikolaus Fuchs and Margaretha Schorr: *This is written in Latin. Note the misspelling of* Weilerhof *as* Veilerhof*. Exweiler is written as* Exveiler*. Apparently a distinction between* v *and* w *is not strongly made by this writer. There is much boilerplate language: "tribus bannorum proclamationibus" (with three proclamations of banns) and "pro lege factis, nullo neque Canononico, neque Civili impedimento Detecto" (there being nothing found either in canon or civil law as an impediment). There are various spellings of surnames. Surname spellings were not fixed in German until the mid-nineteenth century.*

Weilerhof Nicolaus Fuchs Margaretha Schorr	In the year one thousand seven hundred eighty-nine on the seventeenth day of February following three proclamations of banns of the future marriage between Nicolaus Fuchs, twenty-four years old, legitimate son of the deceased Johannes Fuchs and Anna Catharina Dorenbacher the married couple from Exweiler, and Margaretha Schorr, legitimate minor daughter of Nicolaus Schorr, farmer, and Margaretha Dreher the married couple from Weilerhof, in the parish church of Ottweiler and his church at Exweiler, with nothing according to the law, neither canon nor civil, having been detected as an impediment to the marriage, the aforesaid couple requested me the undersigned, commissioned as a pastor of the Lord, from Ottweiler, the banns having been previously announced and with the required consents, to celebrate the marriage of the couple in the accustomed way in the church at Exweiler with a solemn nuptial mass, serving in the capacity as witnesses: Peter Beheriam and Peter Klein, farmers from Weilerhof, and Nicolaus Rectenwald of Exweiler, who signed with the couple and the father of the bride:

thus attesting   Nicolaus Fuchs   Margreda Schorr

Nicklauss Schorr   Peter Brosoam

Peter Klein   Niklas Rekttenwaldt

P. Laur, Pastor in Exw(eiler)

Translated marriage record of Nikolaus Fuchs and Margaretha Schorr.

Photograph of the Nikolaus Fuchs home in Wustweiler, Saarland, Germany.

Notes on the farmhouse of Nikolaus Fuchs:

The Nikolaus Fuchs ancestral home was on the farm Weilerhof, currently merged into Wustweiler. It was recently mentioned in a newspaper article: "Bauernhaus im Ortsteil Wustweiler, der 1182 erstmals urkundlich erwähnt wurde. Heute ist er nahezu reines Wohngebiet." This translates to "Farmhouse in the section of town (Illingen) called Wustweiler, which was first mentioned in a document in 1182. Today it is almost entirely a residential area." The home is still standing, and it has won a prize for excellent renovation. The home, now known as Simmetshaus, stands in Wustweiler and looks as it may have looked in 1800. This kind of "treasure" is a possibility for any researcher.

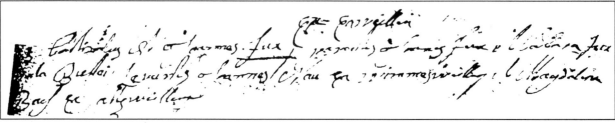

Original baptismal record of Johann Fuchs.

> *Ex Exweiler*
> *baptizatus est Joannes Fux juvenis à Joannis Fux et Barbara Fux nata Buffai. Levantes Joannes Nau ex Wimmezweiler et Magdalena Bach ex Altzweiler.*

Transcribed baptismal record of Johann Fuchs.

> From Exweiler
> There was baptized Johannes Fuchs, child of Johannes Fuchs and Barbara Fuchs née Buffai. Godparents Johannes Nau of Wemmetsweiler and Magdalena Bach of Alsweiler.

Translated baptismal record of Johann Fuchs.

Notes on the baptismal record of Johann Fuchs:

Note the spellings in this Latin document: Fux *for* Fuchs, Wimmezweiler *for* Wemmetsweiler, Altzweiler *for* Alsweiler. *Spellings of surnames and even place-names were not fixed this early.*

Original marriage record of Johann Fuchs and Anna Katharina Dörrenbächer.

Matrimonium	*Anno Domino millesimo Septingentisimo quinquegesimo septimo,*
Joannis	*die decimo septima mensis Februarÿ tribus bannorum publicationibus*
Fuchs et	*de lege, factus per tres dies dominicos Continuos inter missorum*
Annae Catharinae	*Solemnis in ecclesia parochiali de Ottweiler per futuro matrimonio*
Doerebacher	*inter Joannem Fuchs filium legitimum defunctorum Joannis*
	Fuchs et Barbara Bouffey Ex Exweiler #parte una, et Annam
	Catharinam Doerebacher viduam defuncti Petri Haven ex eodem
	Exweiler, ex partes Altera sine oppositione nulloque impedimento
	nec Canonico nec Civili detecto, Celebratisque esponsalii querant
	superdicti Joannes Fuchs et Anna Catharina Doerebacher
	matrimonio Conjuncti de me infra Subscripto pastore in Ottweiler
	et superdicti Annexa, et requerent benedictionem Nuptialem,
	praesentibus Wendelino Koenig, Jacob Fuchs, Joannes Jacobo
	Fuchs, Joannes Petro Baur, qui Subscripserunt et Signem et
	Sponso et Sponsa Scriptionis inscripo Signatibus.

Signū.   *Signū.*

Signū.   X *Sponsae.*   X *Wendelin*

X *Spons.*   *Koenig*

Signū   *Signū*   *Signū*

X *Jacob* ||| *Joannis*   (*Joes.*   ? *Strahl*

Fuchs   *Jacob Fuchs*   *Petrus Baur*

pastor in Ottweiler

Transcribed marriage record of Johann Fuchs and Anna Katharina Dörrenbächer.

Marriage of Johannes Fuchs and Anna Catharina Doerebacher	In the year of Our Lord one thousand seven hundred fifty-seven on the seventeenth day of the month of February following three publications of banns done on three consecutive Sundays at the solemn mass in the parish church of Ottweiler for the future marriage of Johannes [= John] Fuchs, legitimate son of the deceased Johannes Fuchs and Barbara Bouffey of Exweiler, on the one hand, and Anna Catharina Doerebacher, widow of the deceased Peter Haven from said Exweiler, on the other hand, without any opposition or impediment either in canon or in civil law having been found, I celebrated the marriage of the aforesaid couple Johannes Fuchs and Anna Catharina Doerebacher who were joined in matrimony by me the undersigned pastor in Ottweiler and the aforesaid daughter parish [Exweiler], and they received the nuptial blessing in the presence of Wendelin Koenig, Jacob Fuchs, Johann Jacob Fuchs, and Johann Peter Baur, who made their marks together with the groom and the bride and I wrote this.

Signed   Signed

Signed   X Bride.   X Wendelin

X Groom   Koenig

Signed   Signed   Signed

X Jacob ||| Johann   (Johannes   ? Strahl

Fuchs   Jacob Fuchs   Peter Baur

pastor in Ottweiler

Translated marriage record of Johann Fuchs and Anna Katharina Dörrenbächer.

Notes on the marriage record of Johann Fuchs and Anna Catharina Dörrenbächer:

This Latin document is fairly extensive. It lists not only the maiden name of Anna Catharina Doerebacher (Dörrenbächer), but the name of her first husband, the late Peter Haven. Also, four witnesses to the marriage are listed.

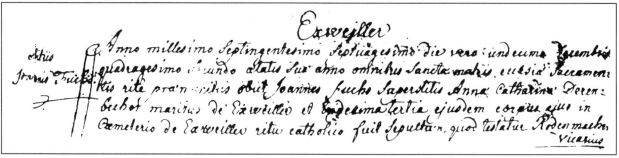

Original death record of Johann Fuchs.

	Exweiller
obitiis	*Anno millesimo Septingenteismo Septuagesimo die vero undecima Decembris*
Joannis Fuchs	*quadragesimo Secundo aetatis sua anno omnibus Sancta mathiis ecclesia Sacramen-*
	tis rite pronuntibus obiit Joannes Fuchs Superstitis Anna Catharina Deren-
	becher maritus de Exweiller et decima tertia ejusdem corpus ejus in
	Cemeterio de Exweiller ritu catholico fuit Sepultam quod testatur Rodenmacher
	vicarius

Transcribed death record of Johann Fuchs.

	Exweiller
Death	In the year one thousand seven hundred seventy on the eleventh day of December
John Fuchs	the last rites having been pronounced at St. Matthew's church, there died Johannes
	(= John) Fuchs in the forty-second year of his age, a married man survived by
	Anna Catharina Derenbacher, from Exweiler, and on the thirteenth his body was
	buried in the cemetery of Exweiler according to the Catholic rites, which is attested
	to by Rodenmacher, vicar.

Translated death record of Johann Fuchs.

Notes on the death record of Johann Fuchs:
This is yet another Latin document and records not only the death but also the religious observances of the last rites and the burial according to Catholic custom.

```
F17  Fuchs/Dörrenbächer ∞ 17.2.1757          in Ottweiler

      Fuchs Johann, Ackerer, *13.6.1728 in Urexweiler,
                            +11.12.1770
      Eltern : Fuchs Johann +
               Bouffey Barbara +, beide Urexweiler
      Dörrenbächer A. Katharina, *5.2.1728 in Urexweiler,
               +3.12.1786 in Urexweiler
               ∞ I 10.11.1750 in Ottweiler
               Haben Peter Ackerer (17.12.1755)
      Eltern : Dörrenbächer Valentin
               Hinsberger ....

      Kinder : Nikolaus        *26/27.9.1765    in Urexw.
                               Ackerer
                               ∞ 17.2.1789 Schorr
                               Margaretha (Wustweiler=
                               hof) in Urexweiler
               Jakob           *3.3.1768        in Urexw.
                               Schneider
                               ∞ 6.2.1798 Weiskircher
                               Susanna (Wustweiler)
                                              in Urexw.
               Johann          *1/2. .1758      in Urexw.
                               ∞ 18.1.1791 Weiskircher
                               A.M. (Wustweiler) in
                               Uchtelfangen
               Peter           *12.3.1761       in Urexw.
                               +9.2.1767        in Urexw.
               Elisabeth       *26/27.5.1763    in Urexw.
                               +19.11.1766      in Urexw.


F29  Fuchs/Schorr ∞ 172.1789              in Urexweiler

      Fuchs Nikolaus, Ackerer, *26/27.9.1765 in Urexw.
      Eltern : Fuchs Johann, Ackerer +
               Dörrenbächer Anna Katharina   +3.12.1786
                                in Urexweiler, 62 J. alt
      Schorr Margaretha, 16 J. alt
      Eltern : Schorr Nicolaus, Ackerer
               Dreher Margaretha,    beide Wustweilerhof
      Eltern : A. Margarethe    *20/21.1.1790
                                          Wustweilerhof
               Nikolaus         *7.1.1792
                                          Wustweilerhof
               Jakob            *29.7.1798
                                          Wustweilerhof
               A.M.             *19/20.12.1796
                                          Wustweilerhof
```

Entries from *Familienbuch Urexweiler: Band 1 (1537–1814)*.
Familienbuch symbols: *birth +death ∞marriage
All dates use the international style of day first, then month, then year.

German Word Lists

Included in this appendix are a variety of German words in the following categories:

GENEALOGICAL/RELATIONSHIP TERMS

Roman Typefaces	Fraktur	Sütterlin	Kurrent	English Symbol/Trans.
Ahnentafel	Ahnentafel			ancestor chart
Akt(e)	Akte			record
Aufgebot	Aufgebot			(marriage) banns
Beerdigung	Beerdigung			⎕ burial, interment
Begräbnis	Begräbnis			⎕ burial
Copulation	Copulation			∞ marriage
Ehe, Eheschließung	Eheschließung			∞ marriage
Firmung	Firmung			(Catholic) confirmation
Gatte	Gatte			♂ ∞ husband
Gattin	Gattin			♀ ∞ wife
geb., geboren	geboren			* born
Geburtsschein	Geburtsschein			* birth certificate
Geburtsurkunde	Geburtsurkunde			* birth record
gefallen	gefallen			X died in combat, fell
geheiratet	geheiratet			∞ married
genannt	genannt			called, known as
gesch., geschieden	geschieden			o|o divorce
gest., gestorben	gestorben			† died
get., getauft	getauft			~ = baptized
getraut	getraut			∞ married
Hebamme	Hebamme			midwife
Heirat	Heirat			∞ marriage
hinterlassen	hinterlassen			surviving, left behind
Hochzeit	Hochzeit			∞ wedding
Junge	Junge			♂ □ boy
Jungfrau, Jungfer	Jungfrau			♀ ○ maiden, virgin
Junggesell(e)	Junggeselle			♂ □ bachelor
Jüngling	Jüngling			♂ □ young man
Knabe	Knabe			♂ □ boy
Kommunikant	Kommunikant			communicant
Konfirmation	Konfirmation			confirmation
kopuliert	kopuliert			∞ joined in marriage
ledig	ledig			single
legitimiert	legitimiert			legitimized
Mädchen	Mädchen			♀ ○ girl
männlich	männlich			♂ □ male
minderjährig	minderjährig			under age, minor
mündig	mündig			of (legal) age
nachgelassen	nachgelassen			surviving
niedergekommen	niedergekommen			delivered (a child)
Niederkunft	Niederkunft			delivery (of a child)

Roman Typefaces	Fraktur	Sütterlin	Kurrent	English Symbol/Trans.
N(omen) N(escio)(Lat.)	N.N.	N.N.	N.N.	name unknown
Nottaufe	Nottaufe	Nottaufe	Nottaufe	emergency baptism
Pate	Pate	Pate	Pate	male baptismal sponsor
Patin	Patin	Patin	Patin	female baptismal sponsor
scheiden lassen	scheiden laſſen	scheiden lassen	scheiden lassen	o|o get a divorce
Scheidung	Scheidung	Scheidung	Scheidung	o|o divorce
schwanger	schwanger	schwanger	schwanger	pregnant
Selbstmord	Selbstmord	Selbstmord	Selbstmord	† suicide
selig	selig	selig	selig	† late, deceased
Sippe	Sippe	Sippe	Sippe	family, clan
Sohn, Söhnlein	Sohn	Sohn	Sohn	♂ □ son
Stammbaum	Stammbaum	Stammbaum	Stammbaum	"family tree"
stammen	stammen	stammen	stammen	originate, stem
Sterbefall, Sterben	Sterbefall	Sterbefall	Sterbefall	† death
sterben	sterben	sterben	sterben	† die
Sterberegister	Sterberegiſter	Sterberegister	Sterberegister	† death register
Sterbeurkunde	Sterbeurkunde	Sterbeurkunde	Sterbeurkunde	† death record
Taufe	Taufe	Taufe	Taufe	~ = baptism
taufen	taufen	taufen	taufen	~ = baptize
Taufregister	Taufregiſter	Taufregister	Taufregister	~ = baptismal register
Taufurkunde	Taufurkunde	Taufurkunde	Taufurkunde	~ = baptismal record
Tochter, Töchterlein	Tochter	Tochter	Tochter	♀ ○ daughter
Tod	Tod	Tod	Tod	† death
Todesurkunde	Todesurkunde	Todesurkunde	Todesurkunde	† death record
Todesursache	Todesurſache	Todesursache	Todesursache	† cause of death
tot	tot	tot	tot	† dead
totgeboren	totgeboren	totgeboren	totgeboren	†* stillborn
trauen	trauen	trauen	trauen	∞ & marry
Trauregister	Trauregiſter	Trauregister	Trauregister	∞ & marriage register
Trauung	Trauung	Trauung	Trauung	∞ & wedding
Trauurkunde	Trauurkunde	Trauurkunde	Trauurkunde	∞ & marriage record
unehelich	unehelich	unehelich	unehelich	(*) !! out of wedlock
Urkunde	Urkunde	Urkunde	Urkunde	record, document
verehelicht	verehelicht	verehelicht	verehelicht	∞ & married
Verehelichung	Verehelichung	Verehelichung	Verehelichung	∞ & marriage
verh., verheiratet	verheiratet	verheiratet	verheiratet	∞ & married
Verlobung	Verlobung	Verlobung	Verlobung	o engagement
verst., verstorben	verstorben	verstorben	verstorben	† deceased
verwaist	verwaist	verwaist	verwaist	orphaned
volljährig	volljährig	volljährig	volljährig	of legal age
Vormund	Vormund	Vormund	Vormund	guardian

Roman Typefaces	Fraktur	Sütterlin	Kurrent	English Symbol/Trans.
Vorname	Vorname	*(script)*	*(script)*	given name, Christian name
Wahlkind	Wahlkind	*(script)*	*(script)*	adopted child
Waise	Waise	*(script)*	*(script)*	orphan
Weib	Weib	*(script)*	*(script)*	♀ ○ woman, wife

RELATIONSHIPS

Roman Typeface	Fraktur	Sütterlin	Kurrent	English Translation
adoptiert	adoptiert	*(script)*	*(script)*	adopted
außerehelich	außerehelich	*(script)*	*(script)*	out-of-wedlock
Base	Base	*(script)*	*(script)*	female cousin
Braut	Braut	*(script)*	*(script)*	bride
Bräutigam	Bräutigam	*(script)*	*(script)*	bridegroom
Brautkind	Brautkind	*(script)*	*(script)*	premarital child
Bruder	Bruder	*(script)*	*(script)*	brother
Cousin	Cousin	*(script)*	*(script)*	male cousin
Cousine	Cousine	*(script)*	*(script)*	female cousin
Ehefrau	Ehefrau	*(script)*	*(script)*	wife, married woman
Eheleute	Eheleute	*(script)*	*(script)*	married couple
ehelich	ehelich	*(script)*	*(script)*	in marriage, legitimate
Ehemann	Ehemann	*(script)*	*(script)*	husband, married man
Ehepaar	Ehepaar	*(script)*	*(script)*	bridal couple
Eltern	Eltern	*(script)*	*(script)*	parents
Enkel	Enkel	*(script)*	*(script)*	grandchild, grandson
Enkelin	Enkelin	*(script)*	*(script)*	granddaughter
Enkelkind	Enkelkind	*(script)*	*(script)*	grandchild
Frau	Frau	*(script)*	*(script)*	woman, wife
Fräulein	Fräulein	*(script)*	*(script)*	unmarried woman, Miss
Gatte	Gatte	*(script)*	*(script)*	husband, spouse
Gattin	Gattin	*(script)*	*(script)*	wife, spouse
Gemahl	Gemahl	*(script)*	*(script)*	(esteemed) husband
Gemahlin	Gemahlin	*(script)*	*(script)*	(esteemed) wife
Geschwister	Geschwister	*(script)*	*(script)*	sibling; brother(s) and/or sister(s)
Gevatter	Gevatter	*(script)*	*(script)*	godfather, (male) baptismal sponsor
Gevatterin	Gevatterin	*(script)*	*(script)*	godmother, (female) baptismal sponsor
Großeltern	Großeltern	*(script)*	*(script)*	grandparents

Roman Typefaces	Fraktur	Sütterlin	Kurrent	English Translation
Großmutter	Großmutter			grandmother
Großvater	Großvater			grandfather
Hausfrau	Hausfrau			wife
Kind	Kind			child
Kinder	Kinder			children
Nachfahre	Nachfahre			descendant
Neffe	Neffe			nephew
Nichte	Nichte			niece
Oheim	Oheim			uncle
Oma	Oma			grandma
Onkel	Onkel			uncle
Opa	Opa			grandpa
Pate	Pate			(male) baptismal witness, godfather
Patenkind	Patenkind			godchild
Patin	Patin			(female) baptismal witness, godmother
Pflegekind	Pflegekind			foster child
Pflegesohn	Pflegesohn			foster son
Pflegetochter	Pflegetochter			foster daughter
Schwager	Schwager			brother-in-law
Schwägerin	Schwägerin			sister-in-law
Schwester	Schwester			sister
Schwiegermutter	Schwiegermutter			mother-in-law
Schwiegersohn	Schwiegersohn			son-in-law
Schwiegertochter	Schwiegertochter			daughter-in-law
Schwiegervater	Schwiegervater			father-in-law
Sohn	Sohn			son
Söhnlein	Söhnlein			little son
Stiefkind	Stiefkind			stepchild
Stiefmutter	Stiefmutter			stepmother
Stiefsohn	Stiefsohn			stepson
Stieftochter	Stieftochter			stepdaughter
Stiefvater	Stiefvater			stepfather
Tante	Tante			aunt
Taufpate	Taufpate			godfather/male baptismal sponsor
Taufpaten	Taufpaten			godparents/baptismal sponsors
Taufpatin	Taufpatin			godmother/female baptismal sponsor
Taufzeuge	Taufzeuge			godfather/male baptismal sponsor

Roman Typeface	Fraktur	Sütterlin	Kurrent	English Translation
Taufzeugen	Taufzeugen			godparents/baptismal sponsors
Taufzeugin	Taufzeugin			godmother/female baptismal sponsor
Tochter	Tochter			daughter
Töchterlein	Töchterlein			little daughter
Tochtermann	Tochtermann			son-in-law
unehelich	unehelich			out-of-wedlock; illegitimate
Urenkel	Urenkel			great-grandson
Urenkelin	Urenkelin			great-granddaughter
Urgroßmutter	Urgroßmutter			great-grandmother
Urgroßvater	Urgroßvater			great-grandfather
Ururgroßmutter	Ururgroßmutter			great-great-grandmother
Ururgroßvater	Ururgroßvater			great-great-grandfather
Vater	Vater			father
väterlich	väterlich			paternal, fatherly
Verwandtschaft	Verwandtschaft			relationship
Vetter	Vetter			(male) cousin
Vorfahr(e)	Vorfahre			ancestor
Vormund	Vormund			guardian
Waise	Waise			orphan
Wit(t)we	Wittwe			widow
Wit(t)wer	Wittwer			widower

GIVEN NAMES (MALE)

Roman Typeface	Fraktur	Sütterlin	Kurrent	English Equivalent
Adam	Adam			Adam
Albrecht	Albrecht			Albert
Alexander	Alexander			Alexander
Andreas	Andreas			Andrew
Anton	Anton			Anthony, Tony
August	August			Augustus
Bernhard(t)	Bernhardt			Bernard
Christian	Christian			Christian
Christoph	Christoph			Christopher
Eduard	Eduard			Edward
Ernst	Ernst			Ernest
Ferdinand	Ferdinand			Ferdinand
Franz	Franz			Francis, Frank

Roman Typeface	Fraktur	Sütterlin	Kurrent	English Equivalent
Friedrich	Friedrich			Frederick
Georg	Georg			George
Gerhard(t)	Gerhardt			Gerard, Jerry
Gottfried	Gottfried			Godfrey, Jeffrey
Hans	Hans			John(ny)
Heinrich	Heinrich			Henry
Hermann	Hermann			Herman
Jacob, Jakob	Jacob, Jakob			Jacob, James
Johann, Johannes	Johannes			John
Josef, Joseph	Josef			Joseph
Kaspar	Kaspar			Casper
Konrad	Konrad			Conrad
Leonhard(t)	Leonhardt			Leonard
Ludwig	Ludwig			Louis
Lukas	Lukas			Luke
Martin	Martin			Martin
Michael	Michael			Michael
Nikolaus	Nikolaus			Nicholas, Claus
Paul	Paul			Paul
Peter	Peter			Peter
Philipp	Philipp			Philipp
Sebastian	Sebastian			Sebastian, Bastian
Stefan, Stephan	Stefan			Stephen, Steven
Theodor	Theodor			Theodore
Thomas	Thomas			Thomas
Ulrich	Ulrich			Ellery, Aldrich
Walt(h)er	Walther			Walter
Wilhelm	Wilhelm			William

GIVEN NAMES (FEMALE)

Roman Typeface	Fraktur	Sütterlin	Kurrent	English Equivalent
Anna	Anna			Anna
Auguste	Auguste			Augusta
Barbara	Barbara			Barbara
Bernhardine	Bernhardine			Bernadine
Bertha	Bertha			Bert(h)a
Caroline, Karoline	Caroline			Caroline
Catharina, Katharina	Catharina			Catharine
Charlotte	Charlotte			Charlotte, Lottie
Christina	Christina			Christine

Roman Typeface	Fraktur	Sütterlin	Kurrent	English Equivalent
Clara, Klara	Clara, Klara			Claire, Clara
Dorothea	Dorothea			Dorothy
Elisabetha	Elisabetha			Elizabeth
Emilie	Emilie			Emily
Emma	Emma			Emma
Erna	Erna			Erna
Eva	Eva			Eve
Franziska	Franziska			Fanny, Frances
Friederike	Friederike			Frederica
Gertrud	Gertrud			Gertrude
Hannah	Hannah			Hannah
Helena	Helena			Helen
Henriette	Henriette			Henrietta
Johanna	Johanna			Jean, Jane, Joan
Juliana	Juliana			Juliana
Luise, Louise	Louise			Louise
Magdalena	Magdalena			Madelyn, Madeleine
Margaretha	Margaretha			Margaret
Maria	Maria			Mary, Marie
Mart(h)a	Martha			Martha
Mathilde	Mathilde			Matilda
Paula	Paula			Paula
Petra	Petra			Petra
Philippine	Philippine			Philippina
Rosa, Rosina	Rosina			Rose
Sara	Sara			Sara
Sophia	Sophia			Sophie
Theresia	Theresia			Teresa
Ulrike	Ulrike			Ulrike
Ursula	Ursula			Ursula
Veronika	Veronika			Veronica
Waltraud	Waltraud			Waltraud
Wilhelmine	Wilhelmine			Wilhelmina, Wilma

OCCUPATIONS

Roman Typeface	Fraktur	Sütterlin	Kurrent	English Meaning
Ackermann	Ackermann			Farmer
Amtmann	Amtmann			Magistrate, Official
Arbeiter	Arbeiter			Laborer
Arzt	Arzt			Doctor
Bäcker	Bäcker			Baker
Bauer	Bauer			Farmer
Beamter	Beamter			Official
Bergmann	Bergmann			Miner
Besitzer	Besitzer			Owner
Brauer	Brauer			Brewer
Bürger	Bürger			Citizen
Bürgermeister	Bürgermeister			Mayor
Colon	Colon			Farmer
Diener	Diener			Servant
Dienstmädchen	Dienstmädchen			Servant (Maid)
Drucker	Drucker			Printer
Einwohner	Einwohner			Inhabitant
Färber	Färber			Dyer
Fiedler	Fiedler			Fiddler
Fischer	Fischer			Fisherman
Fleischer	Fleischer			Butcher
Fuhrmann	Fuhrmann			Coachman, Driver
Gehilfe	Gehilfe			Assistant
Gesell(e)	Geselle			Journeyman
Gerber	Gerber			Tanner
Händler	Händler			Trader
Hebamme	Hebamme			Midwife
Heuermann	Heuermann			Day-Laborer
Hirt(h)	Hirth			Herder
Hof(f)mann	Hofmann			Farm Manager
Jäger	Jäger			Hunter
Kaufmann	Kaufmann			Merchant
Keller	Keller			Steward
Kiefer	Kiefer			Cooper
Knecht	Knecht			Laborer
Koch	Koch			Cook
Köhler	Köhler			Charcoal Burner
Krüger	Krüger			Innkeeper
Kürschner	Kürschner			Furrier
Küster	Küster			Sexton
Landwirt(h)	Landwirth			Farmer

Roman Typeface	Fraktur	Sütterlin	Kurrent	English Meaning
Lederer	Lederer			Leather Maker
Lehrer(in)	Lehrerin			Teacher
Lehrling	Lehrling			Apprentice
Maler	Maler			Painter
Maurer	Maurer			Mason
Meister	Meister			Master
Meßner	Meßner			Sexton
Metzger	Metzger			Butcher
Meyer	Meyer			Farm Manager
Müller	Müller			Miller
Pächter	Pächter			Tenant
Pfarrer	Pfarrer			Pastor, Priest
Prediger	Prediger			Preacher
Rademacher	Rademacher			Wheelwright
Rentner	Rentner			Retiree
Richter	Richter			Judge
Ritter	Ritter			Knight
Schäfer	Schäfer			Shepherd
Schloßer	Schloßer			Locksmith
Schmied	Schmied			Smith
Schneider	Schneider			Tailor
Schreiber	Schreiber			Clerk
Schreiner	Schreiner			Joiner, Cabinetmaker
Schröder	Schröder			Tailor
Schuhmacher	Schuhmacher			Shoemaker
Schüler	Schüler			Pupil
Schul(t)z(e)	Schultze			Mayor
Soldat	Soldat			Soldier
Steinmetz	Steinmetz			Stonemason
Tagelöhner	Tagelöhner			Day-Laborer
Tischler	Tischler			Joiner
Töpfer	Töpfer			Potter
Verkäufer	Verkäufer			Salesman
Verweser	Verweser			Administrator
Wagner	Wagner			Wagoner, Carter
Weber	Weber			Weaver
Weingärtner	Weingärtner			Vinedresser
Wirt(h)	Wirth			Innkeeper
Ziegler	Ziegler			Tile Maker, Brick Maker
Zimmerman(n).	Zimmermann			Carpenter
Zöller	Zöller			Customs Official

COMMON SURNAMES

Roman Typeface	Fraktur	Sütterlin	Kurrent	English Versions
Bauer	Bauer			Bauer, Bower(s)
Becker	Becker			Becker, Baker
Braun	Braun			Braun, Brown
Fischer	Fischer			Fischer, Fisher
Fuchs	Fuchs			Fuchs, Fox
Hartmann	Hartmann			Hartman(n), Hardman
Hoffmann	Hoffmann			Hoffman, Huffman
Hofmann	Hofmann			
Huber, Hoover	Huber			Huber, Hoover
Kaiser	Kaiser			Kaiser, Kayser, Kizer
Klein	Klein			Klein, Cline, Kline
Koch	Koch			Koch, Cook
Köhler	Köhler			Koehler, Köhler,
Kohler	Kohler			Kohler, Coler
König	König			Koenig, King
Krause	Krause			Kraus(e), Crouse
Krüger	Krüger			Krueger, Creager
Lang	Lang			Lang(e), Long
Mayer, Maier	Mayer, Maier			Meyer, Myers, Meier,
Meyer, Meier	Meyer, Meier			Mayer, Maier
Müller, Möller	Müller, Möller			Mueller, Moeller, Miller, Muller
Neumann	Neumann			Neumann, Newman
Peters	Peters			Peters
Richter	Richter			Richter, Rector
Schäfer	Schäfer			Schaefer, Schafer, Shafer, Shaffer, Shaver
Schmidt	Schmidt			Schmidt, Smith
Schmitt, Schmid	Schmitt, Schmid			
Schmitz	Schmitz			
Schneider	Schneider			Schneider, Snider, Snyder
Schröder	Schröder			Schroeder, Shrader
Schulz	Schulz			Schulz, Schultz, Shultz, Schult(e)
Schwarz	Schwarz			Schwartz, Schwarz, Swartz, Black
Wagner	Wagner			Wagner, Wagoner
Walter	Walter			Walter, Walters
Weber	Weber			Weber, Weaver
Weiß	Weiß			Weiss, White
Werner	Werner			Werner, Warner, Varner
Wolf	Wolf			Wolf, Wolfe
Zimmermann	Zimmermann			Zimmerman, Carpenter

TIME EXPRESSIONS

Roman Typeface	Fraktur	Sütterlin	Kurrent	English Translation
Vormittag	Vormittag			forenoon
Morgen	Morgen			morning
Nachmittag	Nachmittag			afternoon
Abend	Abend			evening
Nacht	Nacht			night
Mitternacht	Mitternacht			midnight
gestern	gestern			yesterday
heute	heute			today
morgen	morgen			tomorrow

MONTHS

Roman Typeface	Fraktur	Sütterlin	Kurrent	English Translation
Jänner	Jänner			January
Januar	Januar			January
Februar	Februar			February
März	März			March
April	April			April
Mai	Mai			May
Juni	Juni			June
Juli	Juli			July
August	August			August
September, 7br	September	7br	7br	September
Oktober, 8br	Oktober	8br	8br	October
November, 9br	November	9br	9br	November
Dezember, 10br, Xbr	Dezember	10br Xbr	10br Xbr	December

DAYS OF THE WEEK

Roman Typeface	Fraktur	Sütterlin	Kurrent	English Translation
Wochentag	Wochentag			day of week
Sonntag	Sonntag			Sunday
Montag	Montag			Monday
Dienstag	Dienstag			Tuesday
Mittwoch	Mittwoch			Wednesday
Donnerstag	Donnerstag			Thursday
Freitag	Freitag			Friday
Samstag	Samstag			Saturday
Sonnabend	Sonnabend			Saturday

NUMBERS (CARDINAL)

	Roman Typeface	Fraktur	Sütterlin	Kurrent
1	eins	ein𝔰		
2	zwei	zwei		
3	drei	drei		
4	vier	vier		
5	fünf	fünf		
6	sechs	ſech𝔰		
7	sieben	ſieben		
8	acht	acht		
9	neun	neun		
10	zehn	zehn		
11	elf	elf		
12	zwölf	zwölf		
13	dreizehn	dreizehn		
14	vierzehn	vierzehn		
15	fünfzehn	fünfzehn		
16	sechzehn	ſechzehn		
17	siebzehn	ſiebzehn		
18	achtzehn	achtzehn		
19	neunzehn	neunzehn		
20	zwanzig	zwanzig		
21	einundzwanzig	einundzwanzig		
22	zweiundzwanzig	zweiundzwanzig		
30	dreißig	dreißig		
40	vierzig	vierzig		
50	fünfzig	fünfzig		
60	sechzig	ſechzig		
70	siebzig	ſiebzig		
80	achtzig	achtzig		
90	neunzig	neunzig		
100	hundert	hundert		
101	hunderteins	hundertein𝔰		
102	hundertzwei	hundertzwei		
200	zweihundert	zweihundert		
1000	tausend	tauſend 1.000		

NUMBERS (ORDINAL)

	Roman Typeface	Fraktur	Sütterlin	Kurrent
1st	erst-	erft=		
	(roots such as erst- *usually appear with inflectional endings:* erste, erstes, ersten, erstem . . .*)*			
the 1st of	den ersten	den erften		
on the first	am ersten	am erften		
2nd	zweit-	zweit=		
3rd	dritt-	dritt=		
4th	viert-	viert=		
5th	fünft-	fünft=		
6th	sechst-	fechft=		
7th	siebt-, siebent-	fiebt, fiebent=		
8th	acht-	acht=		
9th	neunt-	neunt=		
10th	zehnt-	zehnt=		
11th	elft-	elft=		
12th	zwölft-	zwölft=		
13th	dreizehnt-	dreizehnt=		
14th	vierzehnt-	vierzehnt=		
15th	fünfzehnt-	fünfzehnt=		
16th	sechzehnt-	fechzehnt=		
17th	siebzehnt-	fiebzehnt=		
18th	achtzehnt-	achtzehnt=		
19th	neunzehnt-	neunzehnt=		
20th	zwanzigst-	zwanzigft=		
21st	einundzwanzigst-	einundzwanzigft=		
22nd	zweiundzwanzigst-	zweiundzwanzigft=		
30th	dreißigst-	dreißigft=		
40th	vierzigst-	vierzigft=		
50th	fünfzigst-	fünfzigft=		
60th	sechzigst-	fechzigft=		
70th	siebzigst-	fiebzigft=		
80th	achtzigst-	achtzigft=		
90th	neunzigst-	neunzigft=		
100th	hundertst-	hundertft=		
101st	hunderterst-	hunderterft=		
200th	zweihundertst-	zweihundertft=		
1000th	tausendst-	tausendft=		
1001st	tausenderst-	tausenderft=		

SOME GERMAN, AUSTRIAN, AND SWISS STATES

Roman Typeface	Fraktur	Sütterlin	Kurrent	English
Abtei	Abtei			abbey
Bistum	Bistum			bishopric
Dorf	Dorf			village
Erzbistum	Erzbistum			archbishopric
Fürstentum	Fürstentum			principality
Gemeinde	Gemeinde			community
Grafschaft	Grafschaft			county
Herrschaft	Herrschaft			lordship
Herzogtum	Herzogtum			duchy
Kaiserreich	Kaiserreich			empire
Kanton	Kanton			canton
Königreich	Königreich			kingdom
Kreis	Kreis			county
Kurfürstentum	Kurfürstentum			electorate
Landgrafschaft	Landgrafschaft			landgraviate
Markgrafschaft	Markgrafschaft			marquisate
Ort	Ort			place
Pfalz	Pfalz			palatinate
Probstei	Probstei			provost
Provinz	Provinz			province
Reichsstadt	Reichsstadt			free city
Aargau	Aargau			Aargau
Elsaß	Elsaß			Alsace
Anhalt	Anhalt			Anhalt
Österreich	Österreich			Austria
Baden	Baden			Baden
Basel	Basel			Basel
Bayern	Bayern			Bavaria
Berg	Berg			Berg
Berlin	Berlin			Berlin
Bern	Bern			Berne
Böhmen	Böhmen			Bohemia
Brandenburg	Brandenburg			Brandenburg
Bremen	Bremen			Bremen
Braunschweig	Braunschweig			Brunswick
Kärnten	Kärnten			Carinthia
Köln	Köln			Cologne
Franken	Franken			Franconia
Deutschland	Deutschland			Germany
Hamburg	Hamburg			Hamburg

Roman Typeface	Fraktur	Sütterlin	Kurrent	English
Hessen	Heſſen			Hesse(n)
Hohenzollern	Hohenzollern			Hohenzollern
Holstein	Holſtein			Holstein
Homburg	Homburg			Homburg
Ungarn	Ungarn			Hungary
Lippe	Lippe			Lippe
Lothringen	Lothringen			Lorraine
Lübeck	Lübeck			Luebeck
Luxemburg	Luxemburg			Luxembourg
Mähren	Mähren			Moravia
Mainz	Mainz			Mainz
Mecklenburg	Mecklenburg			Mecklenburg
Münster	Münſter			Muenster
Oldenburg	Oldenburg			Oldenburg
Osnabrück	Oſnabrück			Osnabrueck
Paderborn	Paderborn			Paderborn
Pfalz	Pfalz			Palatinate
Pommern	Pommern			Pomerania
Posen	Poſen			Posen
Preußen	Preußen			Prussia
Rhein	Rhein			Rhine
Saarbrücken	Saarbrücken			Saarbruecken
Saarland	Saarland			Saarland
Salzburg	Salzburg			Salzburg
Sachsen	Sachſen			Saxony
Schaffhausen	Schaffhauſen			Schaffhausen
Schleswig	Schleswig			Schleswig
Schlesien	Schleſien			Silesia
Solothurn	Solothurn			Solothurn
Speyer	Speyer			Speyer
Straßburg	Straßburg			Strasbourg
Steiermark	Steiermark			Styria
Schweiz	Schweiz			Switzerland
Thüringen	Thüringen			Thuringia
Trier	Trier			Trier
Tirol	Tirol			Tyrol
Wien	Wien			Vienna
Vorarlberg	Vorarlberg			Vorarlberg
Westfalen	Weſtfalen			Westphalia
Worms	Worms			Worms
Württemberg	Württemberg			Wuerttemberg
Zürich	Zürich			Zurich
Zweibrücken	Zweibrücken			Zweibruecken

HOLIDAYS

Roman Typeface	Fraktur	Sütterlin	Kurrent	English
Neujahr	Neujahr			New Year's Day
Dreikönigstag	Dreikönigstag			Epiphany
Epiphanias	Epiphanias			Epiphany
(Mariä) Reinigung	Reinigung			Purification
feister Sonntag	feister Sonntag			last pre-Lent Sunday
Rosenmontag	Rosenmontag			Monday before Lent
Fastnacht	Fastnacht			Shrove Tuesday
Aschermittwoch	Aschermittwoch			Ash Wednesday
Josefstag	Josefstag			St. Joseph's Day
Verkündigung	Verkündigung			Annunciation (25 Mar)
Palmsonntag	Palmsonntag			Palm Sunday
Gründonnerstag	Gründonnerstag			Maundy Thursday
Karfreitag	Karfreitag			Good Friday
Ostersonntag	Ostersonntag			Easter Sunday
Ostermontag	Ostermontag			Easter Monday
Quasimodogeniti	Quasimodogeniti			Sunday after Easter
Tag der Arbeit	Tag der Arbeit			1 May (Labor Day)
Himmelfahrt	Himmelfahrt			Ascension Day
Pfingstsonntag	Pfingstsonntag			Pentecost
Pfingstmontag	Pfingstmontag			Pentecost Monday
Fronleichnam	Fronleichnam			Corpus Christi
Johannistag	Johannistag			St. John the Baptist
Heimsuchung Mariä	Heimsuchung			Visitation
Bundesfeier	Bundesfeier			Swiss Day (1 Aug)
(Mariä) Himmelfahrt	Himmelfahrt			Assumption Day
Buß- und Bettag	Buß- und Bettag			Day of Repentance
Tag der deutschen Einheit	Tag der deutschen Einheit			Day of German Unity
Allerheiligen	Allerheiligen			All Saints' Day
Martinstag	Martinstag			Saint Martin's Day
Advent	Advent			Advent
Heiligabend	Heiligabend			Christmas Eve
Weihnachten	Weihnachten			Christmas
Silvester	Silvester			New Year's Eve

Germanic Archives and Societies

National Archives

Bundesarchiv
Potsdamer Strasse 1
Postfach 320
D-56003 Koblenz
Germany
http://www.bundesarchiv.de
(National Archives of Federal Republic of Germany since 1945)

Oesterreichisches Staatsarchiv
Abteilung I: Haus-, Hof- und Staatsarchiv
Bibliothek
Minoritenplatz 1
A-1010 Wien/Vienna
Oesterreich/Austria
http://www.oesta.gv.at
(Austrian national archives; has emigration records 1861–1919)

Schweizerisches Bundesarchiv
Archivstrasse 4
CH-3003 Bern
Schweiz/Switzerland
http://admin.ch/bar
(Swiss national archive, but Switzerland is not unified so records are not
centralized)

Other Nationwide Archives

Deutsche Dienststelle
(Wehrmacht Angehoerigen Stelle—WASt)
Eichborndamm 179
Postfach 510657
D-13366 Berlin
Germany
http://www.com-de.com/wast/
(military archives of the *Wehrmacht*, marines, and sailors; for family only)

Saechsisches Staatsarchiv Leipzig
Abteilung Deutsche Zentralstelle fuer Genealogie
Schongauer Strasse 1
Postfach 274
D-04007 Leipzig
Germany
http://www.genealogy.net/gene/www/ghlp/dzfg-en.html
(*Deutsche Ahnengemeinschaft* [Society] card file of 1,400,000 people, 16,000 church books)

Regional/State Archives

Badisches Generallandesarchiv
Noerdliche Hilda-Promenade 2
D-76133 Karlsruhe
Germany
http://www.lad-bw.de/gla.htm
(Baden: emigration records and indexes; church book duplicates for Baden 1810–69)

Brandenburgisches Landeshauptarchiv Potsdam
An der Orangerie 3
Postfach 600449
D-14404 Potsdam
Germany
(Brandenburg, Berlin: state, church, land, and court records; emigration records for some areas)

Geheimes Staatsarchiv Preussische
Kulturbesitz
Archivstrasse 12–14
D-14195 Berlin
Germany
(Preußen/Prussia areas now Polish or Russian)

Hauptstaatsarchiv Stuttgart
Konrad-Adenauer-Strasse 4
D-70173 Stuttgart
Germany
http://www.lad-bw.de/stal.htm
(Wuerttemberg: index to emigration files; troops to 1871)

Landesarchiv
Dudweilerstrasse 1
D-66133 Saarbruecken
Germany
(Saarland: many civil registration ten-year indexes 1802–62)

Landesarchiv
Gottorfstrasse 6
D-24837 Schleswig
Germany
http://www.schleswig-holstein.de/archive/lash/index.html
(Schleswig-Holstein: emigrants 1868–1938)

Landesarchiv Speyer
Otto-Mayer-Strasse 9
Postfach 1608
D-67326 Speyer/Rhein
Germany
(Pfalz/Palatinate)

Landeshauptarchiv Koblenz
Karmeliterstrasse 1–3
D-56068 Koblenz
Germany
(southern Rheinland/Rhineland and northern Pfalz/Palatinate)

Landesarchiv Magdeburg
Landeshauptarchiv Sachsen-Anhalt
Hegelstrasse 25
Magdeburg D-39104
Germany
(Sachsen-Anhalt/Saxony-Anhalt: emigrants 1850–1945)

Mecklenburgisches Landeshauptarchiv
Graf-Schack-Allee 2
D-19053 Schwerin
Germany
(Mecklenburg, Vorpommern)

Niedersaechsisches Hauptstaatsarchiv
Am Archiv 1
D-30169 Hannover
Germany
(Hannover; Hannover troops to 1867)

NRW Hauptstaatsarchiv
Mauerstrasse 55
D-40476 Duesseldorf
Germany
(Rheinland/Rhineland: Duesseldorf area)

NRW Personenstandsarchiv Rheinland
Schloss Augustusburg
Schlossstrasse 12
D-50321 Bruehl
Germany
(Rheinland/Rhineland: church and civil registration 1798–1874)

Personenstandsarchiv fuer Westfalen-Lippe
Willi-Hofmann-Strasse 2
D-32756 Detmold
Germany
(Lippe-Detmold: church book duplicates roughly 1815–74; Lippe troops
to 1867)

Saechsisches Hauptstaatsarchiv
Archivstrasse 14
D-01097 Dresden
Germany
(former Kingdom of Sachsen/Saxony: troops to 1919)

Saechsisches Staatsarchiv Leipzig
Paunsdorf
Schongauer Strasse 1
Postfach 100947
D-04007 Leipzig
Germany
(former Prussian province of Sachsen/Saxony: emigrants 1924–39)

Staatsarchiv Darmstadt
Karolinenplatz 3
D-64289 Darmstadt
Germany
http://www.archive.hessen.de/sta_darmstadt.htm
(Hessen-Darmstadt: emigration file; church book duplicates 1808–76)

Staatsarchiv der Freien und Hansestadt
Hamburg
ABC-Strasse 19E (Seiteneingang)
D-20354 Hamburg
Germany
(Hamburg: passenger departure lists, passport records, worker records)

Staatsarchiv Ludwigsburg
Arsenalplatz 3
D-72638 Ludwigsburg
Germany
http://www.lad-bw.de/stal.htm
(Wuerttemberg: emigration records)

Staatsarchiv Marburg
Friedrichsplatz 15
Postfach 540
D-35017 Marburg/Lahn
Germany
http://www.archive.hessen.de
(Hessen-Kassel: some church book duplicates 1808–76; Hessian soldiers)

Vorpommersches Landesarchiv Greifswald
Alte Kaserne
Kreishaus
Martin-Andersen-Nexoe-Platz 11
Postfach 3323
D-17463 Greifswald
Germany
(Pommern/Pomerania)

Other Archives

Institut fuer Pfaelzische Geschichte und Volkskunde
Benzinoring 6
Postfach 2860
D-67616 Kaiserslautern
Germany
(huge card file of immigrants and emigrants to and from the Pfalz/Palatinate)

International Tracing Service
Grosse Allee 5
D-34454 Arolsen
Germany
(central archive for concentration camp lists, deportation lists, towns with Jews)

Kirchlicher Suchdienst
Zentralstelle der Heimatortskarteien
Lessingstrasse 1
D-80336 Muenchen/Munich
Germany
(central headquarters for homeland card files with post–World War II addresses
of people who lived in former German-speaking areas in 1939)

Catholic Archives

Archiv des Bistums Passau
Luragogasse 4
D-94032 Passau
Germany
(diocese of Passau)

Bistumsarchiv Speyer
Kleine Pfaffengasse 16–18
Postfach 1160
D-67321 Speyer/Rhein
Germany
http://www.kath.de/bistum/speyer/bsarchiv.htm
(diocese of Speyer)

Bischoefliches Dioesanarchiv Aachen
Klosterplatz 7
Postfach 210
D-52003 Aachen
Germany
(diocese of Aachen/Aix-la-Chappelle)

Bischoefliches Generalvikariat
Paulustor 5
Postfach 147
D-36001 Fulda
Germany
(diocese of Fulda)

Bischoefliches Ordinariat
Archiv des Bistums Augsburg
Hafnerberg 2/II
D-86152 Augsburg
Germany
(diocese of Augsburg)

Bischoefliches Ordinariatsarchiv
Domerschule 2
D-97070 Wuerzburg
Germany
(diocese of Würzburg)

Bischoefliches Ordinariatsarchiv
Luitpoldstrasse 2
Postfach 1362
D-85067 Eichstaett
Germany
(diocese of Eichstätt)

Bischoefliches Zentralarchiv
St. Petersweg 11–13
Postfach 110228
D-93015 Regensburg
Germany
(diocese of Regensburg plus eastern areas)

Bistumsarchiv
Domplatz 7
D-01662 Meissen/Sachsen
Germany
(diocese of Meissen)

Bistumsarchiv
Jesuitenstrasse 13b
Postfach 1340
D-54203 Trier
Germany
(diocese of Trier)

Bistumsarchiv
Pfaffenstieg 2
D-31134 Hildesheim
Germany
(diocese of Hildesheim)

Bistumsarchiv
Rossmarkt 4
D-65549 Limburg/Lahn
Germany
(diocese of Limburg/Lahn)

Bistumsarchiv Muenster
Kardinal-von-Galen-Stift
Georgskommende 19
D-48143 Muenster
Germany
(diocese of Münster)

Bistumsarchiv und Muensterarchiv
Zwoelfling 16
D-45127 Essen
Germany
(diocese of Essen)

Dioezesanarchiv
Eugen-Bolz-Platz 5
Postfach 9
D-72101 Rottenburg am Neckar
Germany
(diocese of Rottenburg/Neckar)

Dioezesanarchiv
Goetzstrasse 65
D-12099 Berlin
Germany
http://www.kath.de/bistum/berlin/dokument/archiv.htm
(diocese of Berlin)

Dioezesanarchiv des Bistums Osnabrueck
Bischoefliches Generalvikariat
Grosse Domfreiheit 10
D-49074 Osnabrueck
Germany
(diocese of Osnabrück)

Dom- und Dioezesanarchiv
Heringsbrunnengasse 4
D-55116 Mainz
Germany
(diocese of Mainz)

Erzbischoefliches Ordinariatsarchiv Muenchen und Freising
Matrikelamt
Karmeliterstrasse 1 (Eingang Pacellistrasse)
D-80333 Muenchen/Munich
Germany
(church books archdiocese of Munich and Freising)

Erzbistumsarchiv
Domplatz 5
D-96049 Bamberg
Germany
(archdiocese of Bamberg)

Erzbistumsarchiv
Herrenstrasse 35 (Eingang Schoferstrasse)
D-79098 Freiburg im Breisgau
Germany
(archdiocese of Freiburg im Breisgau)

Erzbistumsarchiv
Kirchenbuchabteilung
Domplatz 3
Postfach 1480
D-33044 Paderborn
Germany
(church books archdiocese of Paderborn)

Historisches Archiv des Erzbistums Koeln
Gereonstrasse 2–4
D-50670 Koeln/Cologne
Germany
(diocese of Köln/Cologne)

Katholisches Kirchenbuchamt des Verbands der Dioezesen Deutschlands
Dachauer Strasse 50/II Rgb.
D-80335 Muenchen
Germany
(general headquarters for Catholic church book offices in Germany)

Lutheran Archives

Archiv der Evangelischen Kirche im Rheinland
Hans-Boeckler-Strasse 7
Postfach 320340
D-40476 Duesseldorf
Germany
http://ourworld.compuserve.com/homepages/archiv_ekir
(Rhineland, northern)

Archiv des Evangelischen Konsistoriums Berlin-Brandenburg
Bachstrasse 1–2
D-10555 Berlin
Germany
(Berlin and Brandenburg)

Archiv des Landeskirchenrats der Evangelisch-Lutherischen Kirche
in Thueringen
Dr.-Moritz-Mitzenheim-Strasse 2
D-99817 Eisenach
Germany
(Thuringia, including several duchies)

Braunschweigische Evangelisch-Lutherische Landeskirche
Landeskirchliches Archiv
Alter Zeughof 1
Postfach 420
D-38100 Braunschweig
Germany
(Brunswick/Braunschweig)

Evangelische Kirche der Pfalz
Landeskirchenrat
(Protestantische Landeskirche)
Domplatz 5
Postfach 1720
D-67327 Speyer/Rhein
Germany
http://www.evpfalz.de/kern.htm
(Palatinate, south)

Evangelische Kirche in Deutschland (EKD)
Herrnhaeuserstrasse 12
Postfach 510409
D-30634 Hannover
Germany
(main headquarters of Lutheran church in Germany; church records are kept
locally)

Evangelische Kirche von Westfalen
Landeskirchenarchiv
Altstaedter Kirchplatz 5
D-33602 Bielefeld
Germany
(Westphalia)

Evangelischer Oberkirchenrat
Landeskirchliches Archiv
Blumenstrasse 1
Postfach 2269
D-76010 Karlsruhe
Germany
(Baden)

Evangelischer Oberkirchenrat
Landeskirchliches Archiv
Gaensheidestrasse 4
D-70184 Stuttgart
Germany
(Wuerttemberg)

Evangelisches Konsistorium des Goerlitzer Kirchengebietes
Archiv der Evangelischen Kirchen von Schlesien
Berliner Strasse 62
D-02826 Goerlitz
Germany
(Silesia)

Evangelisches Zentralarchiv in Berlin
Kirchenbuchstelle
Jebensstrasse 3
D-10623 Berlin
Germany
http://www.snafu.de/~eza
(Prussia—former GDR and eastern areas)

Evangelisch-Lutherische Kirche im Hamburgischen Staat
Archiv
Neue Burg 1
D-20354 Hamburg
Germany
(Hamburg)

Evangelisch-Lutherische Kirche in Bayern
Landeskirchliches Archiv
Veilhofstrasse 28
D-90489 Nuernberg/Nuremberg
Germany
http://home.t-online.de/home/LKANuernberg/lkantit.htm
(Franconia = Bavaria, Northern)

Evangelisch-Lutherische Landeskirche Hannovers
Landeskirchliches Archiv
Am Steinbruch 14
Postfach 3726
D-30037 Hannover
Germany
http://www.evlka.de/archiv
(Lower Saxony/Hannover)

Evangelisch-Lutherische Landeskirche Sachsens
Landeskirchenarchiv
Lukasstrasse 6
D-01069 Dresden
Germany
(Saxony, former kingdom)

Evangelisch-Lutherische Landeskirche Schleswig-Holsteins
Daenische Strasse 27–35
Postfach 3449
D-24033 Kiel
Germany
http://www.schleswig-holstein.de/archive/kirch_arch.html
(Schleswig-Holstein)

Evangelisch-Lutherischer Landeskirchenrat
Meiserstrasse 13
D-80333 Muenchen/Munich
Germany
(Bavaria except Franconia)

Kirchenbuchstelle Magdeburg
Halberstaedter Strasse 132
D-39112 Magdeburg
Germany
(Saxony, former Prussian province)

Lippisches Landeskirchenamt
Archiv der Lippischen Landeskirche
Leopoldstrasse 12
D-32756 Detmold
Germany
(Lippe)

Mecklenburgisches Kirchenbuchamt
Muenzstrasse 8
D-19055 Schwerin
Germany
(Mecklenburg)

Zentralarchiv der Evanglischen Kirche der Pfalz
Kirchenbuchstelle Koblenz
D-56068 Koblenz
Germany
(Palatinate, north; Rhineland; Saarland)

Societies in Europe

Arbeitsgemeinschaft der Familienkundlichen Gesellschaften in Hessen
Biebricher Allee 168
D-65203 Wiesbaden
Germany
(Hessian federation of genealogical societies)

Arbeitsgemeinschaft fuer Mitteldeutsche Familienforschung e.V., Sitz Marburg
Strasse der Freundschaft 2
D-99706 Sondershausen
Germany
("Middle German" research in the former German Democratic Germany)

Arbeitsgemeinschaft fuer Pfaelzisch-Rheinische Familienkunde e.V.
Rottstrasse 17
D-67601 Ludwigshafen
Germany
(Palatinate genealogical society)

Arbeitsgemeinschaft fuer Saarlaendische Familienkunde (ASF)
Hebbelstrasse 3
D-66346 Puettlingen
Germany
http://www.genealogy.net/gene/reg/SAA/asf-d.htm
(Saarland genealogical society)

Arbeitsgemeinschaft Genealogie Thueringen
Martin-Andersen-Nexoe-Strasse 62
D-99096 Erfurt
Germany
(Thuringian genealogical society)

Arbeitsgemeinschaft Ostdeutscher Familienforscher e.V. (AGoFF)
Detlef Kuehn
Zum Block 1 a
D-01561 Medessen
Germany
http://www.genealogy.net/gene/www/ghlp/AGoFF-d.html
(Eastern German genealogical society for area now Poland or Russia)

Bayerischer Landesverein fuer Familienkunde
Ludwigstrasse 14/I
D-80539 Muenchen
Germany
http://www.genealogy.net/gene/reg/BAY/BLF-d.html
(Bavarian genealogical society)

Bund der Familienverbaende e.V.
Kirchgasse 18
D-98693 Ilmenau
Germany
("umbrella organization" of German surname societies)

Deutsche Arbeitsgemeinschaft Genealogischer Verbaende e.V.
NRW Personenstandsarchiv Rheinland
Schlossstrasse 12
D-50321 Bruehl
Germany
("umbrella organization" of German genealogical societies)

Deutscher Hugenotten-Verein e.V. (DVH)
Deutsches Hugenotten-Zentrum
Hafenplatz 9 a
D-34385 Bad Karlshafen
Germany
(Huguenot genealogical society)

Deutsches Adelsarchiv
Schwanallee 21
D-35037 Marburg
Germany
(German nobility society)

Genealogische Gesellschaft, Sitz Hamburg
Postfach 302042
D-20307 Hamburg
Germany
(Hamburg genealogical society)

Gesellschaft fuer Familienforschung in der Oberpfalz, Sitz Regensburg
Rachelstrasse 12
D-93059 Regensburg
Germany
http://www.genealogy.net/gene/vereine/GFO/gfo.htm
(Upper Palatinate genealogical society)

Gesellschaft fuer Familienforschung in Franken
Archivstrasse 17 (Staatsarchiv)
D-90408 Nuernberg
Germany
(Franconian genealogical society)

Heraldisch-Genealogische Gesellschaft "Adler"
Haarhof 4a
Postfach 25
A-1014 Wien/Vienna
Oesterreich/Austria
(Austrian genealogical and heraldry society)

Der Herold
Verein fuer Heraldik, Genealogie und Verwandte Wissenschaften
Archivstrasse 12–14
D-14195 Berlin
Germany
(German national genealogical and heraldry society)

Die Maus, Gesellschaft fuer Familienforschung
Am Staatsarchiv 1/Fedelhoeren (Staatsarchiv)
D-28203 Bremen
Germany
http://www.genealogy.net/gene/vereine/maus
(Bremen genealogical society)

Hessische Familiengeschichtliche Vereinigung
Karolinenplatz 3 (Staatsarchiv)
D-64289 Darmstadt
Germany
http://www.genealogy.net/gene/vereine/HFV/hfv.html
(Hessian genealogical society)

Niedersaechsischer Landesverein fuer Familienkunde
Am Bokemahle 14–16 (Stadtarchiv)
D-39171 Hannover
Germany
(Lower Saxony genealogical society)

Oldenburgische Gesellschaft fuer Familienkunde
Lerigauweg 14
D-26131 Oldenburg
Germany
(Oldenburg genealogical society)

Salzburger Verein e.V.
Memeler Strasse 35 (Wohnstift Salzburg)
D-33605 Bielefeld
Germany
(Salzburg emigrant genealogical society)

Schleswig-Holsteinische Gesellschaft fuer Familienforschung und
Wappenkunde e.V.
Postfach 3809
D-24037 Kiel
Germany
(Schleswig-Holstein genealogical society)

Schweizerische Gesellschaft fuer Familienforschung
Postfach 54
CH-3608 Thun
Schweiz/Switzerland
(Swiss genealogical society)

Upstaalsboom-Gesellschaft
Fischteichweg 16
D-26603 Aurich
Germany
http://members.aol.com/UPSTALSBOO/up0000.html
(East Frisian genealogical society)

Verein fuer Computergenealogie e.V.
Schorlemmers Kamp 20
D-44536 Luenen
Germany
http://www.genealogy.net/gene/vereine/CompGen
(German computer genealogy society)

Verein fuer Familienforschung in Ost- und Westpreussen
Uwe Reich (Archiv, Buecherei)
Hildebrandtstrasse 7
D-29921 Celle
Germany
http://www.genealogy.net/gene/vereine/VFFOW/vffow.htm
(West Prussian genealogical society)

Verein fuer Familien- und Wappenkunde in Wuerttemberg
und Baden e.V.
Postfach 105441
D-70047 Stuttgart
Germany
http://www.genealogy.net/gene/reg/BAD-WUE/VFWKWB/VFWKWB.html
(Wuerttemberg and Baden genealogical society)

Verein fuer Mecklenburgische Familien- und Personengeschichte (MFP)
Thuenen-Museum
D-17168 Tellow
Germany
(Mecklenburg genealogical society)

Vereinigung Sudetendeutscher Familienforscher
Sudetendeutsches Genealogisches Archiv (SGA)
Erikaweg 58
D-93053 Regensburg
Germany
http://www.genealogy.net/gene/reg/SUD/vsff-de.html
(Sudetenland genealogical society)

Westdeutsche Gesellschaft fuer Familienkunde
Unter Gottes Gnaden 34
D-50829 Koeln
Germany
http://www1.stuttgart.netsurf.de/~schenie
(Western German genealogical society)

Westfaelische Gesellschaft fuer Genealogie und Familienforschung
Postfach 6125
D-48133 Muenster
Germany
(Westphalian genealogical society)

Societies in USA

German Genealogical Society of America
P.O. Box 517
La Verne, CA 91750-0517
http://feefhs.org/ggsa/frg-ggsa.html

Germanic Genealogy Society
P.O. Box 16312
St. Paul, MN 55116-0312
http://feefhs.org/ger/frg-ggs.html

German Research Association, Inc.
P.O. Box 711600
San Diego, CA 92171-1600
http://feefhs.org/gra/gralin21.html

Immigrant Genealogical Society
P.O. Box 7369
Burbank, CA 91510-7369
http://feefhs.org/igs/frg-igs.html

Mid-Atlantic Germanic Society
P.O. Box 2642
Kensington, MD 20891-2642
http://ourworld.compuserve.com/homepages/pwinner

Palatines to America
Capital University
P.O. Box 101
Columbus, OH 43209-2394
http://genealogy.org/~palam

Pennsylvania German Society
P.O. Box 244
Kutztown, PA 19530-0244
http://www.pgs.org

Sacramento German Genealogy Society
P.O. Box 660061
Sacramento, CA 95866-0061
http://feefhs.org/sggs/frg-sggs.html

Religious Archives in USA

American Catholic Historical Society
St. Charles Borromeo Seminary
P.O. Box 84
Philadelphia, PA 19105-0084

American Jewish Archives
3101 Clifton Ave.
Cincinnati, OH 45220-2488
http://members.gnn.com/apeck3101/index.html

American Jewish Historical Society
15 W. Sixteenth St.
New York, NY 10011
http://www.ajhs.org

Archives of the Roman Catholic Central-Verein
3855 Westminster Place
St. Louis, MO 63108-3409

Association of Jewish Genealogical Societies
2 Thornton Rd.
Waltham, MA 02453-7711
http://www.jewishgen.org

Center for Mennonite Brethren Studies
4824 E. Butler St.
Fresno, CA 93727-5097
http://www.fresno.edu/cmbs/home.htm

Evangelical Lutheran Church in America
5400 Milton Pkwy.
Rosemont, IL 60018
http://www.elca.org/os/archives/intro.html

Fellowship of Brethren Genealogists
1451 Dundee Ave.
Elgin, IL 60120-1694

Historical Commission of the United Church of Christ
555 W. James St.
Lancaster, PA 17603
(Archive for former Evangelical and Reformed Church)

LDS Family History Library
35 NW Temple St.
Salt Lake City, UT 84103

Lutheran Concordia Historical Institute
801 DeMun Ave.
St. Louis, MO 63105
http://www.lcms.org

Mennonite Library and Archives Center
300 E. Twenty-seventh St.
North Newton, KS 67117
http://www.bethelks.edu/services/mla

Menno Simons Historical Library and Archive
1200 Park Rd.
Harrisonburg, VA 22801

Methodist Historical Society
1810 Harvard Bldg.
Dayton, OH 45406

Moravian Church Central Archives North
41 W. Locust St.
Bethlehem, PA 18018

Moravian Church Central Archives South
4 E. Bank St.
Drawer M, Salem Station
Winston-Salem, NC 27101

The National Huguenot Society
6033 Lyndale Ave. S., Suite 108
Bloomington, MN 55420-3535

Schwenkfelder Historical Society Library
1 Seminary Ave.
Pennsburg, PA 18073

United Church of Christ
475 E. Lockwood Ave.
Webster Groves, MO 63119

Germanic Letter-Writing Guide

Address Sources

Address letters as listed in this book or in Ernest Thode's *Address Book for Germanic Genealogy*, the Family History Library research outline, Edward Brandt's *Germanic Genealogy*, or other reliable books on Germanic research.

Postal Codes

Find postal codes (make sure they are five digits for Germany) from *Das Postleitzahlenbuch* or online at <http://plz.postconsult.de/suchmain.htm>.

International Reply Coupons

Enclose one International Reply Coupon (available from your post office) for Germany, more for other countries, so you can at least pay for return postage. This is much appreciated by German churches, civil authorities, societies, and individuals. The German postal system has instituted a policy whereby one and only one IRC may be used per letter, and IRCs in Germany may not be exchanged for loose stamps, only for payment (or partial payment) of a letter, no matter what size.

Letter Format

Write in good German (using these form letters) or good English, if absolutely necessary to rely on English. If you must use English, keep it simple. Send a chart or family group sheet, using German date style (see pedigree chart and family group sheet examples in chapter one). Send documentation of the place of origin. Type your letter. Keep a copy of everything you send. Before sending a letter, reread it, keeping in mind that a person from another country with another native language may be reading it. Be sure to let the addressee know that you are willing to pay for the information you receive. You may be encouraged to send cash by Germans, but be cautious in sending cash through the mail.

If you are writing to a church, don't worry about the name of the church. The German postal system will deliver it if you have a valid, unique place-name, or the correct postal code. There will generally be only one church and one denomination in a small village, and one central church book registry in each larger town.

Form Letter to Church Parishes

Evangelisches Pfarramt	(Lutheran/Reformed/Protestant Parish Office)
or	
Katholisches Pfarramt	(Catholic Parish Office)
D-##### Xxxxxx	D for Deutschland, hyphen, five-digit postal code, name of village
Germany	Spell it out in English for North American postal officials

Sehr geehrter Herr Pfarrer!

Laut der von mir gesammelten Ahnenforschungsquellen sollen meine Vorfahren aus [name of town: Xxxxxx] stammen. Daher bitte ich hoeflich um einige Angaben aus den dortigen Kirchenbuechern. Ich lege eine Ahnentafel bei, damit Sie genau ersehen koennen, um wen es sich handelt.

Deshalb bitte ich Sie hoeflich um einen vollstaendigen Auszug bzw. um Ablichtungen aus den betreffenden Tauf-, Trau- und Begraebnisregistern fuer meine Vorfahren aus Ihrem Ort und deren Eltern.

Ich lege einen Coupon bei, die auf Ihrem Postamt gegen Briefmarken umgetauscht werden koennen. Bitte geben Sie die Gebuehren an.

Fuer Ihre Bemuehungen und Ihre Mithilfe im voraus dankend, verbleibe ich

hochachtungsvoll

John Q. Smith

Beilagen:	Ahnentafel
	Antwortschein

To (Protestant, Lutheran or Reformed)/(Catholic) parish, in Xxxxx (town), Germany

Esteemed pastor (here presumed to be male, although some Protestant parishes have female pastors):

According to the genealogical sources I have collected, my ancestors supposedly come from [name of town: Xxxxxx]. I am enclosing an ancestor chart so that you can see exactly whom this concerns.

Therefore I most courteously request a complete transcript or photocopies from the pertinent baptismal, marriage, and burial records for my ancestors from your town and their parents. I am enclosing a coupon that can be exchanged for stamps (of your country) at your post office. Please indicate the charges. Thanking you in advance for your efforts and your cooperation, I remain

Respectfully

John Q. Smith

Enclosures:	Ancestor chart and International Reply Coupon

Form Letter to Civil Registration Offices

Standesamt
D-##### Xxxxxx
Germany

Sehr geehrte Damen und Herren!

Laut der von mir gesammelten Ahnenforschungsquellen sollen meine Vorfahren aus [name of town: Xxxxxx] stammen. Daher bitte ich hoeflich um einige Angaben aus den dortigen Standesregistern.

Ich lege eine Ahnentafel bei, damit Sie genau ersehen koennen, um wen es sich handelt.

Deshalb bitte ich Sie hoeflich um einen vollstaendigen Auszug bzw. Ablichtungen aus den betreffenden Geburts-, Heirats- und Sterberegistern fuer meine Vorfahren aus Ihrem Ort sowie Eltern, falls moeglich.

Ich lege einen Coupon bei, die auf Ihrem Postamt gegen Briefmarken umgetauscht werden koennen. Bitte geben Sie die Gebuehren an.

Fuer Ihre Bemuehungen und Ihre Mithilfe im voraus dankend, verbleibe ich
hochachtungsvoll

Mary A. Jones

Beilagen: Ahnentafel
Antwortschein

Ladies and Gentlemen:

According to the genealogical sources I have collected, my ancestors supposedly come from [name of town: Xxxxxx]. I am enclosing an ancestor chart so that you can see exactly whom this concerns. Therefore I most courteously request a complete transcript or photocopies from the pertinent birth, marriage, and death records for my ancestors from your town, as well as their parents, if possible.

I am enclosing a coupon that can be exchanged for stamps (of your country) at your post office. Please indicate the charges. Thanking you in advance for your efforts and your cooperation, I remain
Respectfully

Mary A. Jones

Enclosures: Ancestor chart and International Reply Coupon

Form Letter to Societies

Sehr geehrte Damen und Herren! or
Sehr geehrter Herr Meyer! or
Sehr geehrte Frau Braun!

Laut der von mir gesammelten Ahnenforschungsquellen sollen meine Vorfahren aus [name of town: Xxxxxx] stammen. Ich lege eine Ahnentafel bei, damit Sie genau ersehen koennen, um wen es sich handelt.

Koennten Sie mir gegen Honorar Sucharbeiten durchfuehren? Falls nicht, so bitte ich hoeflich um genaue Anschriften von Ahnenforschen, Archiven, Bibliotheken, genealogischen Vereinen, Kirchenaemtern usw., die mir bei dieser Suche behilflich sein koennen.

Fuer Ihre Bemuehungen und Ihre Mithilfe im voraus dankend, verbleibe ich
        mit freundlichem Gruss

        Nancy A. Brown

Beilagen: Ahnentafel
        Antwortschein

To Society, genealogist, etc., in Xxxxxx (town), Germany

Ladies and Gentlemen:
Dear Mr. Meyer:
Dear Ms. Braun: (It is correct to use *Frau* even for single women)

According to the genealogical sources I have collected, my ancestors supposedly come from [name of town: Xxxxxx].

I am enclosing an ancestor chart so that you can see exactly whom this concerns. Could you carry out research for me for a fee? If not, I most courteously request exact addresses of family researchers, archives, libraries, genealogical societies, church offices, etc., that could be of assistance to me in this search.
Thanking you in advance for your efforts and your cooperation, I remain
        Respectfully

        Nancy A. Brown

Enclosures: Ancestor chart and International Reply Coupon

Bibliography

ATLASES

Barraclough, Geoffery, ed. *The Times Atlas of World History*. 2d compact ed. London: Times Books, 1997.

Centennia. 1999 edition. Chicago: Clockwork Software, Inc., 1999.

Hammond Incorporated. *Hammond Concise Atlas of World History*. Maplewood, N.J.: Hammond, 1998.

Hammond Incorporated. *Hammond Historical Atlas*. Maplewood, N.J.: Hammond, 1997.

Magocsi, Paul Robert. *Historical Atlas of East Central Europe*. Seattle and London: University of Washington Press, 1993.

Putzger, Friedrich Wilhelm. *Historischer Schulatlas*. Bielefeld, Germany: Velhagen and Klasing, 1959.

http://feefhs.org (online historical maps)

http://www.ancestry.com (free online historical maps)

http://www.expediamaps.com (online maps)

http://www.falk-online.de/go_routing.html (online maps; in German)

http://www.jewishgen.org/shtetlseeker

http://www.mapquest.com (online maps)

EMIGRATION/IMMIGRATION (Selected)

Filby, P. William, et al. *Passenger and Immigration Lists Indexes*. 4 vols. Detroit, Mich.: Gale Research Co., 1981.

Glazier, Ira T., and P. William Filby. *Germans to America: Lists of Passengers Arriving at U.S. Ports*. 64 vols. Wilmington, Del.: Scholarly Resources, 1988-.

Hacker, Werner. *Eighteenth Century Register of Emigrants From Southwest Germany*. Apollo, Pa.: Closson Press, 1994.

Jones, Henry Z, Jr. *More Palatine Families*. Universal City, Calif.: H.Z. Jones, 1991.

———. *The Palatine Families of New York: 1710*. Universal City, Calif.: H.Z. Jones, 1985.

Rupp, Israel D. *A Collection of Upwards of 30,000 Names of German, Swiss, Dutch, French, and Other Immigrants Into Pennsylvania, 1727-1776*. Baltimore: Genealogical Publishing Co., 1994.

Schenk, Trudy, Ruth Froelke, and Inge Bork, comps. *The Wuerttemberg Emigration Index*. 7 vols. Salt Lake City, Utah: Ancestry, Inc., 1986.

Strassburger, Ralph Beaver. *Pennsylvania German Pioneers: The Original Lists of Arrivals in the Port of Philadelphia 1727 to 1808*. Edited by William John Hinke. 1934. Reprint, Camden, Maine: Picton Press, 1992.

GAZETTEERS

Hall, Charles M. *The Atlantic Bridge to Germany*. 10 vols. Logan, Utah: Everton Publishers, 1974.

Höpker, H. *Deutsches Ortsverzeichnis*. Reprint, Frankfurt am Main, Germany: Verlag für Standesamtswesen, 1978.

Kammerer, M. *Ortsnamenverzeichnis der Ortschaften Jenseits von Oder und Neisse*. Leer, Germany: G. Rautenberg, 1988.

Meyers Orts- und Verkehrslexikon. Salt Lake City, Utah: Church of Jesus Christ of Latter-day Saints, 1978. Microfilm. Baltimore: Genealogical Publishing Co., 2000.

Mueller, Joachim. *Muellers Grosses Deutsches Ortsbuch*. Wuppertal, Germany: Post- und Ortsbuchverlag, 1996.

Pehle, Max, Hans Silberborth, and Martin Iskraut. *W.F. Putzgers Historischer Schulatlas*. Bielefeld and Leipzig, Germany: Velhagen and Klasing, 1942.

Das Postleitzahlenbuch. Bonn, Germany: Deutsche Bundespost, 1993.

http://164.214.2.63/geonames/GNS (GEO net)

http://www.jewishgen.org/ShtetlSeeker (ShtetlSeeker)

Send name of village as *only* message in E-mail to geo@genealogy.net

GERMAN NAMES

Bahlow, Hans. *Dictionary of German Names*. Trans. Edda Gentry. Madison, Wis.: Max Kade Institute, University of Wisconsin—Madison, 1993.

Brechenmacher, Josef Karlmann. *Deutsches Namenbuch*. Stuttgart, Germany: E. Klett, 1930.

Familiennamenbuch der Schweiz. Zurich, Switzerland: Schulthess Polygraphischer Verlag AG, 1989.

Gottschald, Max. *Deutsche Namenkunde: Unsere Familiennamen*. Berlin, Germany, and New York: deGruyter, 1982.

Jones, George F. *German-American Names*. Baltimore: Genealogical Publishing Co., 1990.

Mackensen, Lutz. *Das Große Buch der Vornamen*. Munich, Germany: Suedwest Verlag, 1978.

Meier, Emil, et al., eds. *Swiss Surnames: A Complete Register*. Camden, Maine: Picton Press, 1992.

Naumann, Horst. *Das Große Buch der Familiennamen: Alter, Herkunft und Bedeutung*. Niedernhausen/Taunus, Germany: Falken, 1994.

Swiss Surnames: A Complete Register. Rockport, Maine: Picton Press, 1995.

HISTORIES

Barraclough, Geoffrey. *The Origins of Modern Germany*. Oxford, England: B. Blackwell, 1988.

Fulbrook, Mary. *A Concise History of Germany*. Cambridge, England, and New York: Cambridge University Press, 1990.

Getchell, Sylvia Fitts. *Fitts Families (Fitts-Fitz-Fittz): A Genealogy*. Newmarket, N.H.: S.F. Getchell, 1989.

Holborn, Hajo. *A History of Modern Germany*. New York: A.A. Knopf, 1969.

Kitchen, Martin. *The Cambridge Illustrated History of Germany*. Cambridge, England, and New York: Cambridge University Press, 1996.

Reinhardt, Kurt F. *Germany: 2000 Years*. New York: F. Ungar, 1996.

Schulze, Hagen. *Germany: A New History*. Trans. Deborah Lucas-Schneider. Cambridge, Mass.: Harvard University Press, 1998.

van Braght, Thieleman J. *Martyrs Mirror*. Rotterdam, Holland, 1660.

HOW-TO BOOKS

Allen, Desmond Walls. *First Steps in Genealogy: A Beginner's Guide to Researching Your Family History*. Cincinnati, Ohio: Betterway Books, 1998.

Baxter, Angus. *In Search of Your German Roots*. Baltimore: Genealogical Publishing Co., 1987.

Bentz, Edna. *If I Can, You Can Decipher Germanic Records*. San Diego: E.M. Bentz, 1982.

Brandt, Edward, et al. *Germanic Genealogy: A Guide to Worldwide Sources and Migration Patterns*. St. Paul, Minn.: German Genealogical Society, 1997.

Croom, Emily. *Unpuzzling Your Past: A Basic Guide to Genealogy*. Cincinnati, Ohio: Betterway Books, 1995.

Family History Library Research Outline: Germany. Salt Lake City, Utah: Church of Jesus Christ of Latter-day Saints, 1997.

Jensen, Larry. *A Genealogical Handbook of German Research*. Pleasant Grove, Utah: L.O. Jensen, 1983.

Rose, Christine, and Kay Ingalls. *The Complete Idiot's Guide to Genealogy*. New York: Alpha Books, 1997.

Schweitzer, George. *German Genealogical Research*. Knoxville, Tenn: G.K. Schweitzer, 1992.

REFERENCES

Melton, J. Gordon. *National Directory of Churches, Synagogues, and Other Houses of Worship*. Detroit: Gale Research, 1995.

Genealogical Word List: Latin, 2d ed. Salt Lake City, Utah: Church of Jesus Christ of Latter-day Saints, 1997.

Thode, Ernest. *Address Book for Germanic Genealogy*. Baltimore: Genealogical Publishing Co., 1997.

———. *German-English Genealogical Dictionary*. Baltimore: Genealogical Publishing Co., 1992.

INTERNET RESEARCH WEB SITES

http://feefhs.org (Federation of East European Family History Societies)

http://plz.postconsult.de/suchmain.htm (German postal codes)

http://www.bundesarchiv.de (German federal archives)

http://www.cyndislist.com/germany.htm (German genealogy links)

http://www.deutscheauswanderer-datenbank.de

http://www.genealogy.net/gene (German genealogy home page)

http://www.genealogy.org/~palam (Palatines to America German genealogy organization)

http://www.geocities.com/SiliconValley/Haven/1538/german.html (German genealogy links)

http://www.germanmigration.com (German migration home page)

http://www.hamburg.de/LinkToYourRoots/(Hamburg passenger lists)

http://www.rootsweb.com/roots-l/family.readme.html (RSL—Roots Surname List)

http://www.rootsweb.com/~surnames/ (surname listings)

http://www.rootsweb.com/~wggerman (Germany GenWeb Project)

http://www.ulib.iupui.edu/kade (German-American studies)

http://www.uni-oldenburg.de/nausa (University of Oldenburg Emigration Research Center)

news: soc.genealogy.german (German genealogy newsgroup)

ONLINE PHONE BOOKS

http://www.etb.at (Austria)

http://www.pearsoft.ch (Switzerland)

http://www.teleauskunft.de (DeTeMedien Germany)

Index

A

Abbreviations
  on birth record, 118
  on marriage record, 117
  on pedigree charts, 7
Alphabet Chart, 74-79
America
  chronology of Germanic
    groups in, 71-72
  German settlement patterns,
    68-70
  immigration to, 67-70
  starting search in, 4
  See also United States
Amish
  as cultural group, 20-21
  as Protestant religion, 65
  Walnut Creek settlement, 72
Anabaptists
  Christian names and, 16-17
  as cultural group, 21
  as Protestant religion, 65
  See also Mennonites
Ancestor
  locating homeland of, 22-26
  place of origin, 4, 18-19
  village of, 29-32
Ancestral File, 45-51
  descendancy chart, 50
  details screen, 49
  family group records, 48
  family record, 48
  first screen, 46
  index, 47
  pedigree chart, 51
  similar surname search, 47
Atlases, 183
Austria, 30
Austrian states, 156-157

B

Baptism records
  keywords in, 81
  sample, 132-133, 136
Baptisms, Christian names and,
  16-17
Baptists, 21
Bible, information from family,
  113-114
Bibliography, 183-186
Birth records
  keywords in, 80-82
  notes on, 118
  samples, 83-84, 89-91, 119,
    123
Brethren, 21, 115

C

Castles, 12-13
Catholic Church
  archives, 164-167
  baptisms in, 16-17
  reformation and, 65
Catholic family case study,
  120-141
Cemeteries
  information from, 12
  inscriptions, 116
Census records
  name variations on, 18
  U.S. (1900), 24
Chain migration, 69
Challenges
  cultural groups, 20-21
  dates, 19-20
  finding records, 14-15
  names, 15-18
  places of origin and, 18-19
Christenings, 16. *See also*

Baptism records; Baptisms
Churches
  form letter to German, 180
  jurisdictional
    misinterpretations and, 29
  records of, 12
  See also Religions
Citizenship, place of, 17
City hall, 14
Civil registration offices, form
  letter to, 181
Clerk of courts records, 12
Coats of arms, 12-13
Confirmation records, 82
Country, IGI screen, 37
County
  German word for, 25, 29, 31
  jurisdictional
    misinterpretations and, 29
Courthouse records, 12
Criminals, 13
Cultural groups, 20-21. *See also*
  names of specific groups

D

Dates
  as challenge, 19-20
  emigration, 25
  international style, 141
Days of week, German words
  for, 153
Death records, 114-115
  keywords in, 81
  sample, 95-96, 140
  U.S. Social Security, 57
Descendancy chart, 50
Districts, jurisdictional
  misinterpretations and, 29

Solve the Mystery of Your History with Betterway Books

A Genealogist's Guide to Discovering Your Immigrant & Ethnic Ancestors—Clear, authoritative instruction typifies both the content of this book and the reputation of its author, Sharon DeBartolo Carmack. Research techniques specific to your own ancestors' particular national and ethnic backgrounds enable you to learn where and how to find information that might otherwise elude you. #70462/$18.99/192 pages/ paperback

A Genealogist's Guide to Discovering Your English Ancestors—Following basic, step-by-step instruction, you'll learn how to access the primary records you need to research your English ancestors. You'll also learn to document your findings properly and move beyond the names on your pedigree charts to understand the historical context in which they lived. #70464/$18.99/192 pages/paperback

A Genealogist's Guide to Discovering Your Female Ancestors—Discover special strategies for overcoming the unique challenges of tracing female genealogy. This comprehensive guide shows you methods for determining maiden names and parental lineage: how to access official documents; plus where to find information unique to women of ethnic origins. Also included is a glossary of terms specific to female genealogy, a detailed bibliography with more than 200 resources, plus an extensive source checklist. #70386/$17.99/144 pages/paperback

A Genealogist's Guide to Discovering Your Italian Ancestors—This easy-to-use reference guides you step-by-step through researching your Italian ancestors—as far back as the 1700s! You'll learn how to find—and read—Italian vital records; write letters requesting data from Italian officials; and use American records like census and naturalization records, and family letters and church records. You'll also find information on how to read foreign handwriting, and much more. #70370/$16.99/ 128 pages/42 b&w illus./paperback

The Weekend Genealogist—Researching family history takes time—time that many people just don't have. This book shows you how to maximize your research efficiency by saving time and utilizing what little you have in the best way possible. Author Marcia Melnyk teaches how to make every minute count through step-by-step instruction and sidebars highlighting important tips and procedures. #70496/$18.99/144 pages/paperback

Long-Distance Genealogy—This book is designed to help you overcome the unavoidable problem of obtaining critical information from far away. You'll begin by addressing the basics of starting a long-distance search and then learn what types of records and publications can be accessed from a distance, problems associated with the process, how to network, how to use computer resources and special "last resort" options. #70495/$18.99/208 pages/ paperback

The Sleuth Book for Genealogists—From the author of the best-selling *Unpuzzling Your Past,* this guide focuses on research methods, showing you how to create a research "program" you can follow to achieve success. Emily Croom links her proven techniques to the advice of famous fictional detectives, such as Sherlock Holmes and Miss Marple, and organizes information into easy-to-read segments and sidebars. #70453/$17.99/192 pages/ paperback

Bringing Your Family History to Life through Social History—Most genealogy books show you how to fill in your pedigrees, but none teach you the hows and whys of your ancestry—until now. You'll find intriguing case histories, charts, sidebars and exercises along with step-by-step instruction on how to research college libraries and historical societies. And you'll learn to weave these historical facts with your own personal genealogies to form a unique family history narrative. #70426/$18.99/176 pages/paperback

Crafting Your Family Heritage Album—This inspirational, how-to guide for showcasing cherished family photos, documents and memorabilia combines two of today's hottest pastimes—genealogy and scrap booking. It features visual, step-by-step instruction and page after page of elegant and imaginative ideas to help you capture and preserve the precious photos and keepsakes of your family history. #70457/$23.99/128 pages/paperback

Locating Lost Family Members & Friends—In this unique research guide, author Kathleen Hinckley combines her professional skills as a genealogist and private investigator to help you locate long-lost cousins, family members separated by divorce, missing heirs, biological parents and children, classmates, military buddies, first loves and more. She provides extensive tables, lists and charts to explain how *and*

where to locate traditional 20th-Century documents, including U.S. and foreign vital records, social security information, phone directories, census records and more. #70446/$18.99/176 pages/paperback

Uncovering Your Ancestry through Family Photographs—Everyone keeps old family photographs, whether in frames, albums or shoeboxes. These photos house a treasury of genealogical information, revealing unique details about our ancestors' lives, personalities and everyday realities. Following this guide's step-by-step instruction, you'll learn how to identify different types of family photographs and determine their date, location, and in some instances, their photographer. Once these photos are collected and analyzed, you'll also learn how to preserve your family collection for generations to come. #70452/$18.99/224 pages/paperback

The Handybook for Genealogists, Ninth Edition—More than 750,000 copies sold! Since 1947, the Handybook has proven itself as the most popular and comprehensive research aid available for tracking down major state and county records essential to genealogists. Save countless hours of your research time by consulting its up-to-date listings of archives, genealogical libraries and societies. State profiles cover history and list sources for maps, census and church records. The county profiles tell you where to find custody records, property records and key addresses. Color maps are included of each state and their counties. #70411/$34.99/380 pages/60 color maps/ hardcover

First Steps in Genealogy—If you're just stepping into the fascinating field of genealogy, this book will get you off to a successful start. Desmond Walls Allen, a recognized genealogical expert, will teach you step-by-step how to define your goals and uncover facts about the people behind the names and dates. Learn to organize your research with pedigree charts, group sheets and filing systems. Discover what sources are available for research, starting with your family scrapbook or attic. Also included are sample forms, a resource directory and glossary. #70400/$14.99/128 pages/paperback

Organizing Your Family History Search—Few hobbies generate more paperwork than genealogy. Sharon DeBartolo Carmack shows you how to successfully tackle the arduous process of organizing family research, from filing piles of paper to streamlining the process as a whole. With her flexible filing system and special research notebook, she reveals how you can free up time, conduct better research and become a more effective genealogist. *#70425/$16.99/176 pages/paperback*

The Genealogist's Companion & Sourcebook—115,000 copies sold! Uncover promising new sources of information about your family history. This hands-on guide shows you how to get past common obstacles—such as lost public records—and discover new information sources like church and funeral home records, government documents, newspapers and maps. *#70235/$16.99/256 pages/paperback*

Unpuzzling Your Past, Third Edition—Make uncovering your roots easy with this complete genealogical research guide. Step-by-step instructions, handy forms, sample letters, comprehensive resource lists, bibliographies and case studies help guide you every step of the way. *#70301/$14.99/180 pages/paperback*

The Unpuzzling Your Past Workbook—The perfect companion to *Unpuzzling Your Past*, this book provides you with 40+ forms and letters that make organizing, searching, record-keeping and presenting information easy and enjoyable. *#70327/$15.99/320 pages/paperback*

How to Tape Instant Oral Biographies, Second Edition—With fun interviewing techniques and exercises, family members of all ages will learn how to spark memories, recall treasured stories, and relate old family anecdotes, sayings, recipes and more. Comes complete with blank family history sheets and work pages. *#70448/$12.99/144 pages/paperback*

How to Write the Story of Your Life—This friendly guide makes memoir writing an enjoyable undertaking—even if you're a non-writer. Five hundred "memory sparkers" will help you recall forgotten events in each stage of your life and 100 topic ideas help add variety to your story. Includes excerpts from actual memoirs and plenty of encouragement to keep you moving your story towards completion. *#10132/$14.99/230 pages/paperback*

Writing Family Histories and Memoirs—Your family history and personal stories are too vital to lose. Turn them into a lively record for the next generation with this handy writing reference. You'll find helpful how-to advice on working from memories and interviewing family members, using public records, writing and publishing. *#70295/$14.99/272 pages/paperback*

Writing Life Stories—Author Bill Roorbach explains how to turn the engaging, untold stories of your life into vivid personal essays and riveting memoirs. You'll

learn how to open up memory, access emotion and discover compelling material, shape scenes from experience, and populate stories with the fascinating, silly and maddening "characters" that surround you—your family members and friends. *#48045/$14.99/224 pages/paperback*

Reaching Back—Record life's most meaningful moments to share with future generations. This easy-to-use keepsake edition includes space for family stories, photos, heirlooms, family trees, and helps you research and record your family's unique history. *#70360/$14.99/160 pages/paperback*

Family History Logbook—Weave your personal history into the colorful web of national events. You'll find an extensive list of historical events spanning the years 1900 to 2000, along with a special section to record your own milestones. *#70345/$16.99/224 pages/paperback*

The Everyday Life Series—You've tracked down vital statistics for your great-great grandparents, but do you know what their everyday lives were like? These titles will give you a vivid and detailed picture of life in their own time. Learn what your relatives likely wore, what they ate, and how they talked. Social and religious customs, major occupations and family life are all covered. These "slice-of-life" facts will readily round out any family history.
The Writer's Guide to Everyday Life . . .
 . . .during the Civil War
 #10635/$16.99/288 pages/paperback
 . . .from Prohibition to World War II
 #10450/$18.99/272 pages/hardcover
 . . .in Renaissance England
 #10484/$18.99/272 pages/hardcover
 . . .in Regency and Victorian England
 #10545/$18.99/240 pages/hardcover
 . . .in the 1800's
 #10353/$18.99/320 pages/hardcover
 . . .in the Wild West
 #10600/$18.99/336 pages/hardcover
 . . .in Colonial America
 #10640/$14.99/288 pages/paperback

Creating Family Newsletters—This idea-packed book shows you how to write and design family newsletters that will bring

"mail box cheer" to your friends and relatives the world over. More than 100 full-color examples—from hand-crafted to computer generated—offer great ideas for creating your own unique newsletters for every occasion. *#10558/$19.99/120 color illus./128 pages/paperback*

Scrapbook Storytelling, Step by Step—Go beyond typical scrapbooking techniques! Here is how to recall your favorite family stories and combine them with cherished photos, collages and illustrations to create unique booklets, albums, gift items and more. *#70450/$19.99/120 color illus./128 pages/paperback*

Publishing Your Family History on the Internet—With this first-ever guide, even if you're a beginning computer user, you can design and publish your own genealogical Web sites. Learn how to display your family history data—including pictures, sounds and video—onto the Web. *#70447/$19.99/320 pages/140 b&w illus./paperback*

The Internet for Genealogists, Fourth Edition—This completely revised and updated guide to the latest genealogy Web sites will give you quick access to the resources you need. Includes more than 200 addresses to genealogy sites, libraries, catalogs, maps, gazetteers, bookstores, online databases and living persons directories. *#70415/$16.99/192 pages/paperback*

Charting Your Family History: The Legacy Family Tree Software Solution—Now you can organize your genealogical records with ease, thanks to the Legacy Family Tree software on CD-ROM—the most comprehensive and easy-to-use genealogy software on the market today. Legacy allows unlimited data input, viewing of up to seven Family or Pedigree views at one time, over 20 customized reports plus the linking of pictures and sounds to any member of your family tree. System requirements: IBM 486 or faster compatibles, minimum 8MB memory, 20MB hard drive space, Windows 3.1 or Windows 95, VGA or higher. *#70420/$49.95/270 page book with PC compatible CD-ROM*

ML   10/01